VITAL SIGNS, VIBRANT SOCIETY

DR CRAIG EMERSON is the federal member of parliament for the Queensland seat of Rankin. He was elected to parliament in 1998. He has a PhD in economics from The Australian National University. He has been economic adviser to prime minister Bob Hawke and to finance minister Peter Walsh, senior policy adviser to Queensland premier Wayne Goss, and an economic analyst for the United Nations. He is a former director-general of the Queensland Department of Environment and Heritage, and a former CEO of the South-east Queensland Transit Authority. Dr Emerson has published extensively on mineral economics, ecologically sustainable development and a vision for Australia's future.

To Ben, Tom and Laura – hoping that your Dad can make a difference and make you proud.

VITAL SIGNS, VIBRANT SOCIETY

SECURING AUSTRALIA'S ECONOMIC AND SOCIAL WELLBEING

CRAIG EMERSON

UNSW
PRESS

A UNSW Press book

Published by
University of New South Wales Press Ltd
University of New South Wales
Sydney NSW 2052
AUSTRALIA
www.unswpress.com.au

National Library of Australia
Cataloguing-in-Publication entry
    Emerson, Craig.
    Vital signs, vibrant society: Securing Australia's economic and social wellbeing.

    Includes index.
    ISBN 0 86840 883 2.

    1. Australia - Economic policy. 2. Australia - Social
    policy. I. Title.

    338.994

Design Ruth Pidd
Cover design Di Quick
Print Ligare

CONTENTS

Foreword by Ross Garnaut   x

Acknowledgments   xiv

Chapter 1   *A plan for Australia*   *1*

The challenge   1

Thinking big   4

The five I's   5

A big country, a bright future   8

Policies for a better country   10

Can we afford it?   32

Overall wellbeing   33

Chapter 2   *The economic challenge*   *34*

Structural weaknesses exposed   34

An ageing population   35

Faltering productivity growth   35

Weak exports   36

Consumption today, or investment for tomorrow?   37

The deficit – big, and getting bigger   39

Chapter 3   *The economic revival*   42
              Labor's reform program   42
              The rewards of economic reform   48

Chapter 4   *The dimensions of the challenge*   49
              Oh no, not the three P's!   49
              The first P – population   49
              The second P – participation   55
              The third P – productivity   56
              Overall wellbeing   59

Chapter 5   *A new wave of reform*   61
              Securing the next round of productivity growth   61
              Keeping the door open, and pushing it wider   62
              New sources of productivity growth   69

Chapter 6   *Beyond public versus private in*
                health and aged care   75
              Health and aged care in a fair society   75
              Australia's mixed system   76
              Rationing health and aged care   78
              The need for reform   80
              Reforming the health-care system   82
              Reforming the aged-care system   90
              The pharmaceutical benefits scheme   94
              Health and aged-care accounts?   95

Chapter 7   *Beyond public versus private in*
                education and training   96
              Our children are our future   96
              The Australian experience with
                skills development   97
              Educational disadvantage in Australia   101
              Why we need school education reforms   102

A new school funding model 104

Literacy and numeracy support 107

A preschool education for all Australian
children 109

Full-service schools 112

Attracting – and retaining – the best teachers 114

University funding 115

Vocational education funding 125

Chapter 8 *Encouraging Australian ideas* 127

Australia's research and development effort 127

Overseas experience 129

Reforming Australia's R&D incentives 129

Use it or lose it 131

Australia as a free-rider? 132

Chapter 9 *Rewarding Australian initiative* 134

A reward for effort and risk-taking 134

The workforce participation rate 134

Increasing workforce participation 135

Women at work, and fertility 141

Chapter 10 *Populating Australia's regions* 143

Australia's settlement pattern 143

A population policy? 144

Immigration 144

Settling in Australia's dynamic regions 146

Attracting migrants to regional centres 148

Attracting Australians to regional centres 151

Slowing emigration 153

Chapter 11 *Modern infrastructure for Australia's regions* 155

Is Australia's infrastructure failing? 155

Infrastructure funding 156

Regulation of infrastructure   158
A national infrastructure plan   158
Freight   161
Energy   162
What about water?   164

Chapter 12 *Keeping Australia open for business*   166
The tyranny of proximity – too close
    for comfort?   166
The folly of preferential trade deals   167
Opening up Australia's preferential trade deals 173
An Australia–China trade deal?   175
An Australian–ASEAN–New Zealand free
    trade area?   176
Foreign investment liberalisation   176

Chapter 13 *Tax reform*   178
Why we need tax reform   178
But we've just had tax reform!   180
Towards an efficient, fair tax system   180
Abolishing the top rate?   182
A genuine reform proposal   184
A tax reform downpayment in 2006–07   186
Taxing education and training   190
Business tax reform   191

Chapter 14 *Financing the plan*   194
Public investment in the five I's   194
A renewed commitment to superannuation   196

Chapter 15 *Low inflation, low unemployment*   198
Ending the Great Australian Inflation –
    but at what cost?   198
Maintaining low inflation   201

The plan for Australia needs low inflation   204

Notes   205
References   216
Index   227

FOREWORD

Through 2004 into the early months of 2005, I was drawing attention to 'the Great Complacency that descended on Australia in the early twenty-first century'. Australia was then (and is still) enjoying the longest economic expansion in its history since Federation. Inflation and interest rates were (and are) close to the lowest in the living memory of most Australians. Employment and incomes were (and are, although now less exuberantly) increasing, apparently inexorably.

The prosperity emerged from what at the time had been politically contentious and temporarily painful reforms over thirteen years of Labor and four years of Coalition governments. The reforms had been guided by the unprecedented (for Australia) application of economic analysis to policy development – the phenomenon that came to be known pejoratively in Australia (and only in Australia) as 'economic rationalism'. Policy measures to raise productivity and growth were accompanied during the most active reform periods by an expansion of social security and service provision to lower-income Australians – to an extent that the living standards of poorer people held up better, in both absolute and relative terms, than they did in other developed countries through these years.

But by the early twenty-first century, the origins of this prosperity had been lost in time. Prosperity was being taken for granted. Accumulating evidence that sustaining prosperity would require new and different productivity-raising reform, involving difficult structural change and choices among policy objectives, was being ignored. Community discussion of economic policy focused on the government's handing out of the fruits of economic reform, rather than on cultivating the policy orchard. And the distribution of the fruits had become far less discriminating among priorities than at the high tide of reform. The populist discussion of economic policy during the 2004 federal election campaign underlined the weaknesses in the understanding of the consequences of policy choice, both among political elites and in the community.

The Australian policy discussion became more realistic during 2005. The Reserve Bank of Australia and the Treasury contributed to some questioning of the Great Complacency during that year, with discussion of the need for reforms to overcome barriers to continued strong economic growth. The federal and a couple of state governments placed significant reform proposals on the active policy agenda. Several individual members of parliament have made detailed and carefully considered proposals for productivity-raising reform of taxation, social security, infrastructure and other areas of policy.

In the conservative Australian polity, extensive public discussion and comprehension of policy reform is a precondition for success. So the current stirrings can be seen as a necessary – although, in themselves, insufficient – condition for renewed momentum in reform.

Craig Emerson's book will turn out to be the most important single contribution this year by an individual political figure to the improvement in the quality of discussion of economic reform in Australia. It is the most wide-ranging and detailed blueprint for Australian economic reform written by an individual Australian parliamentarian.

Emerson's contribution is remarkable among the published work of politicians who are still practising the art professionally, for being grounded consistently in economic analysis. It is also strongly grounded in social democratic concern for the distributional outcomes of economic policies. This dual intellectual parentage of the work – economic rationalism and social democracy – takes recommended policies beyond the comfort zone of contemporary Australian policy discussion, including within Emerson's own party.

The book's wholesome concern for ends rather than means and instruments frees it from some constraining and damaging shibboleths of Australian politics. I presume that this will get the author into trouble in some places. I hope that support from others is strong enough for Emerson's contemporaries in parliamentary and other active politics to be encouraged into similarly ambitious and thoughtful contributions to the policy debate.

The book is marked by fresh perspectives on old issues, as well as by the introduction of new issues to the policy agenda.

The innovations are, sometimes, extensions and elaborations of the acknowledged work of others; sometimes they are the product of personal innovation by the author. One innovation that deserves a lot of attention – and adoption into the policies of the major parties – is Emerson's proposal for a universal payment to mothers of children under the age of three, in place of current income-tested payments. This is advocated as a cost-effective start on the crucially important task of reducing effective marginal tax rates on the earned incomes of Australians who are recipients of family-related social security payments.

My high opinion of Emerson's efforts in this book should not be read as a blanket endorsement of his policy suggestions. For example, the book's argument that the minimum wage is unimportant to employment levels in a relatively tight labour market such as that experienced today in Australia, and the associated dismissal of tax and social security reforms as alternatives to increasing minimum wages as a means of raising the incomes of unskilled workers, fails to take account of the variation in skills and capacities among 'unskilled' workers. When such variations are given due consideration, a combination of minimum wage restraint and tax–social security reform can be seen to deliver substantially better employment outcomes without damaging the take-home incomes of low-income Australians.

It is unusual for a person with a high level of formal educational achievement in economics to choose an active political life, as Craig Emerson has done. It is more unusual for a political figure with this background to chance his arm with policy innovation based on economic analysis over such a broad area. The Australian policy discussion is the richer for Emerson having decided to take a chance.

Ross Garnaut, Professor of Economics
The Australian National University, Canberra

ACKNOWLEDGMENTS

Many people helped create this book.

My gratitude goes to Bob Hawke, Greg Combet, Ross Garnaut, Geoff Walsh, Blanche D'Alpuget, Paul Keating, Steve Bracks and John Connolly for encouraging me to undertake and persist with such an ambitious project.

When the manuscript was still in a raw and very incomplete form, John Elliot of UNSW Press saw enough potential in it to offer publication. John remained actively interested and provided helpful suggestions throughout.

My journey through the myriad policy issues was guided by discussions with Saul Eslake, Ross Garnaut, Chris Fry, Nicholas Gruen, Greg Combet, Vince Fitzgerald, Ross Gittins, Ric Simes, Peter McDonald, Ann Harding, Glenn Withers, Bruce Chapman, Michael Keating, Steve Dowrick, Glyn Davis, Ross Homel, Grant Belchamber, Nixon Apple, Ken Rowe, Guyonne Kalb and Dean Parham.

Staff of the Parliamentary Library were always helpful, cooperative and surprisingly cheerful. I thank in particular anchorman Dave Richardson, the mystical Indra Kuruppu who can track down any document ever written, Richard Webb, Guy Woods, Stephen Barber, Tony Kryger, Kim Jackson, Dale Daniels, Coral

Dow, Malcolm Park, Marilyn Harrington, Bernard Pulle, Greg McIntosh, Bill McCormick, Barbara Harris, Leo Terpstra, Les Nielson, Peter Yeend, Andrew Kopras and Marilyn Stretton.

Blanche D'Alpuget and Rosemary Barry breathed life into the text with expert editing.

Jennilyn Mann from my office provided enormous support with layout, arranging innumerable meetings and recovering electronic copies of the manuscript when, all too frequently, I lost them or saved them in obscure places somewhere in the upper stratosphere.

CHAPTER 1

A PLAN FOR AUSTRALIA

THE CHALLENGE

Australia has a golden opportunity to enter a new era of prosperity for all its people. It can be an era of prosperity fairly shared, of a cohesive society, of environmental repair, of community wellbeing.

But this golden opportunity is being squandered. Australia is living for today – who is looking after tomorrow?

While our economy has been growing fast, its foundations are weakening. A neglectful federal government has allowed cracks to appear and widen, too busy blowing away the proceeds of growth to pay attention to necessary repair and prevention work. Worse, the government, lacking in imagination and vision, has failed to lay the foundations for a new era of prosperity and opportunity for all Australians.

Australia's export performance is the worst since World War II. The current account deficit has crashed through the mid-1980s barrier that at the time prompted Paul Keating to warn of Australia becoming a banana republic. Foreign debt has reached a staggering $450 billion, more than doubling since the election in 1996 of a Coalition government that promised to bring it down.

Much of this foreign debt has funded consumer spending on imports; and, overwhelmingly, household borrowings have been responsible for Australia's current account deficit. Encouraged by a federal government spending spree, Australia has developed a lustful appetite for consuming today while ignoring investment for tomorrow.

Australia's population is ageing, presenting huge new challenges for the nation. How will we pay for the four million additional Australians over the age of 65 in the next forty years? In this ageing Australia, much less than half of Australia's population will be working – earning the income and paying the taxes to support those too old or too young to work.

And where do we find the resources to remedy the social exclusion that is denying thousands of disadvantaged young Australians the life chances their better-off peers take as a birthright?

The answer is: through productivity growth. Today's productivity growth is tomorrow's prosperity. An economy is performing well if it can produce more and more valuable goods and services for each hour worked. That's productivity growth, and that's why we strive for it. Employees who can produce more for each hour they work are well positioned to command pay rises. And productivity growth can produce the taxation revenue needed for achieving our social goals even at lower tax rates.

In an advanced country like Australia, productivity growth should come from working smarter, not ever harder. But Australia's productivity growth has gone into reverse after a record-breaking decade built on the reforms started by the previous Labor government.

Australia desperately needs another round of productivity growth to sustain prosperity and provide opportunity for all in an ageing population. Our country needs a reform program that not only repairs the economy's foundations, but builds new foundations as a firm footing for economically and ecologically sustainable growth.

Any modern reform program must recognise the tectonic shifts occurring in the global centres of economic activity. China is now the world's second largest economy in purchasing-power parity terms, and India is the sixth largest. In just ten years' time China is expected to surpass the United States as the biggest economy in the world, and India is likely to rank third. China and India will soon resume their dominance of the global economy, a place they occupied for most of human history until the eighteenth century.

For its first two hundred years of European settlement, Australia suffered the tyranny of distance from European and American markets. Now, in the twenty-first century, Australia needs to rise to the challenge and seize the opportunities of proximity to an Asian centre of global economic activity whose five biggest economies together will soon be the same size as the nine biggest economies of Europe and North America.

China's economy is broadly complementary with the present structure of the Australian economy, but India's is not. China's industrialisation has made it hungry for Australian raw materials. India has a huge English-speaking population and a strong IT sector, and is churning out millions of tertiary graduates a year – many of them proficient in English. In this, the Asian century, India will be going head-to-head with Australia's expanding service industries.

Confronted with these challenges and opportunities, Australia cannot afford to be content simply with improving coal export handling facilities, as important as these are. Much more than this, Australia needs to produce many more creative people in our universities, since creative talent will be the dominant source of the wealth of nations in the twenty-first century.

But where is the Coalition government's economic reform agenda beyond the 1980s throwback of more and more labour market deregulation?

History will judge the present government a resounding success in governing for electoral cycles. But at no time since 1996 has the Coalition – or Labor for that matter – presented to the Australian people a long-term plan for our nation.

In modern public policy you only get what you can measure (and not always that). If it's hard to measure it's under-valued and under-supplied. Environmental amenity, the happiness deriving from spending more time with family, the wellbeing associated with a cohesive society – these are all too easily neglected in public policy-making.

And so it is with public goods that offer wider benefits for society. The Coalition government has refused to invest properly in education, research and development, and infrastructure – all of which offer wider benefits vital to Australia's future.

At present Australia is turning a profit – the return from the reforms begun by Labor in the early 1980s. But instead of rein-vesting some of the profit, the Coalition government is squan-dering it. This is the time to commit to the greatest investment of all – the talents of our people.

THINKING BIG

Think of our country in twenty years' time, a country with a bigger population boosted by migrants settling in our dynamic regions, taking the pressure off our sprawling cities.

Think of an Australia in which every child has an equal chance of a fulfilling life, the gift of a quality education.

Imagine an Australia where indigenous and non-indigenous people are reconciled, living in harmony in healthy and tolerant communities.

Let us strive for a society that affords its citizens the dignity of a decent quality of life in their later years.

Cherish a creative Australia, where new thinking, new ideas and new works lift the human spirit.

Take pride in an Australia engaged constructively with our neighbours, joined in the world's struggle against poverty and ignorance.

And picture ours, the oldest continent, with its natural heritage restored, its rivers running again and its land returned to good health.

Is this a vision splendid or a flight of fancy?

Australia could be such a great country. But we must start the journey now, taking the hard decisions and making sacrifices along the way. My plan for Australia invests in the four I's of *intellect*, *ideas*, *initiative* and *infrastructure*, and encourages a fifth I, *immigration* – especially to our regions.

By combining the five I's Australia can enter a virtuous upward spiral, each component of the plan reinforcing the others for growing prosperity in a fair, tolerant and compassionate Australia. Investing in the five I's can assure Australians of continued high living standards, of paying for an ageing population and of preserving our ancient and fragile environment.

The plan put forward in this book embraces and strengthens the open, competitive economy created by the Hawke and Keating Labor governments. It is financially responsible, and it meets Australia's economic, social and environmental challenges head-on. It is a nation-building plan that respects the power of the market and harnesses market forces to shape our country's development. It advances a philosophy of engaging nationalism – a pride in an Australian nation engaged in the global community, a pride engendered out of prosperity, excellence, creativity and a fair go for all.

THE FIVE I'S

This book presents a plan to improve not just the incomes but the overall wellbeing of Australians as we confront the ageing of our population, social disadvantage, overcrowding in our major cities and degradation of our natural environment.

Our children are our future; and this has never been truer than it is today. For their sake and Australia's, we must invest heavily in the *intellect* of all Australian children, helping them to develop their skills and talents to their fullest potential. Young people who choose a trade career need to apply their intellect to the task, using tools such as numbers, computer skills and graphic design to solve problems. But Australia also needs to take big strides forward in the number and quality of the university graduates we turn out each year. The creative talent cultivated by a university education will be the greatest influence on Australia's prosperity in the twenty-first century. Yet the Coalition government is predicting a *reduction* in the annual numbers of Australian university graduates within ten years.

Australia, too, must invest heavily in the development and application of new *ideas* in an innovative culture. We need to develop and attract creative talent in the information age. Education and ideas reinforce each other. Together they can place our nation on a permanently higher growth path, and advance Australia as a tolerant and compassionate society.

Australia must become not a weightless economy but a smart economy, applying intellect and ideas in the development of natural resources and manufacturing enterprises. We can and should have a strong, growing manufacturing sector in the Asian century by embodying skills and ideas in our manufactured products. It is essential that we do so.

We need to reward *initiative*, liberating the Australian entrepreneurial spirit and encouraging the pursuit of excellence. Our tax system is holding Australia back. It is holding back poor Australians wanting to move from welfare to work, middle Australians wanting to get ahead and even honest Australians earning high incomes. Many wealthy Australians are avoiding paying their fair share of tax by taking advantage of the tax breaks created for them by the Coalition government.

Barriers to moving from welfare to work need to be reduced, and working Australians need genuine reward for effort. Small-business owners are obliged to spend too much of their valuable time filling out the paperwork required to comply with an ever more complex tax system. They should be liberated from this burden, freed to spend more time growing their businesses and being with their families.

Over the next forty years Australia will need many more men and women of working age to sustain prosperity, pay for an ageing population and generate the resources needed to provide opportunities for young people. Three-quarters of a million Australians are working overseas at any time. Though Australia can benefit from our best and brightest gaining experience overseas, we cannot afford to stand idly by while many of them leave our shores permanently. We should encourage as many of our professional and creative people as possible to return to our shores, and more of them to stay in Australia, by supporting innovation and initiative at home.

Australia needs to replenish its *infrastructure,* moving away from reactive infrastructure investment to a nation-building infrastructure plan that leads to more dispersed settlement patterns. If they are to attract managers, professionals and creative people, Australia's strongly growing regional centres will need to be equipped with world-class transport, communications and energy supplies as well as top quality schools, university campuses and hospitals.

And Australia needs the fifth I – a new wave of *immigrants* to help build our nation again. Where possible, we should attract skilled migrants to regional Australia through regional migration incentives and a national infrastructure plan that boosts the global competitiveness of our emerging regions, and makes them attractive places in which to live.

Population ageing across the developed world will create a global shortage of skilled migrants in the coming decades, and Australia will need to compete for them in the new world of skilled labour shortages. Community attitudes will need to shift in favour of a bigger immigration program – a program of Australia's choosing.

A BIG COUNTRY, A BRIGHT FUTURE

The centrepiece of the plan is education, the world's most powerful source of modern productivity growth. Education is the torch that brightens Labor's light on the hill, our greatest Labor value – opportunity for all in a fair Australia. Education is the key that unlocks two doors – one leading to prosperity, the other to a fairer Australia.

Giving young Australians a quality education would not only boost productivity growth, it would lift the share of the population participating in the workforce, so paying for the increasing number of Australians who will be too old to work. And it would improve the health and wellbeing of Australians, reducing anti-social behaviour and helping to remedy social disadvantage and exclusion.

If we get education right, much of the rest will follow. But to get education right we must break out of the stifling debate over whether education should be publicly or privately provided, and create new ways to harness private and public resources for the common good. If Australia is to prosper in this, the Asian century, we must take a great stride towards mass participation in higher education and training to unlock the potential of all young Australians – the band of gold within the generations upon whom so much of Australia's future prosperity will depend.

Moving beyond the private versus public debate is essential, too, in health and aged care. Australians don't much care who provides these services, so long as they are affordable and of decent quality. As Australia's population ages, and as marvellous – but expensive – breakthroughs are made in medical technology, health and aged care will make ever greater demands on taxpayers. Medicare should be supplemented by private funding of extra services beyond a quality core Medicare package. And aged-care services of extra quality should be funded by those with a capacity to pay, with some of the proceeds being used to provide decent aged-care services for the less well-off.

If we follow the plan set out in this book, Australia will become a bigger country. Instead of giving up on the bush as the Coalition government has done, the plan would boost regional Australia, from east to west, north to south. Australia's population would be more than thirty million in 2050, a consequence not of setting a population target but of natural increase and net overseas migration of around 125 000 a year – which would be only a modest increase on the rate of 117 600 achieved in 2003–04.

The additional net migration would come mainly from young, skilled migrants, mostly settled outside the Sydney basin, and fewer young professional and creative Australians leaving to live permanently overseas.

In this big country of the mid twenty-first century, many more Australians would be living in a band of gold running from tropical far north Queensland to the cool climes of Warrnambool in Victoria's western district. The band of prosperity – a new engine of Australian growth – would include regional hubs like Townsville, Mackay, Rockhampton, Emerald, Gladstone, Toowoomba, Armidale, Orange, Dubbo, Parkes, Forbes, Cowra, Young, Griffith, Wagga Wagga, Canberra, Albury–Wodonga, Shepparton, Bendigo and Ballarat (see figure 1.1). It would also include the smaller capital cities of Adelaide, Perth, Hobart and Darwin, and nearby areas like Mandurah south of Perth.

Country towns would service these regional hubs in a revival of rural Australia.

Australia has enough water to support this plan. But instead of wasting it we would be conserving it for its highest value uses, including environmental repair. Our rivers and land would be restored to health and we would be living off the environmental interest, not running down the environmental capital.

The plan for Australia would engender a renewed sense of national purpose not seen since the early post-war years, building a prosperous, fair, tolerant and compassionate Australia.

FIGURE 1.1 REGIONAL CENTRES –
A NEW ENGINE OF AUSTRALIAN GROWTH

POLICIES FOR A BETTER COUNTRY

Australia's modern prosperity has been made possible by the creation of Australia as an open, competitive economy. We cannot open the same door twice. We must keep it open and, where possible, push it wider. The next round of productivity growth will come from investing in intellect, ideas, initiative and infrastructure in a bigger population.

AFFORDABLE HEALTH AND AGED CARE

Population ageing and the cost of new medical technologies demand an innovative approach to funding health and aged care. Australians want affordable access to quality health and aged care, but are not especially fussed about who provides it. Australia's universal public health system will need to be supplemented by private funding to ensure quality, affordable health and aged care for all Australians.

General practice (GP) corporate groups have grown up under Medicare. They offer the prospect of combining the best that the private and public sectors have to offer – a high quality, publicly funded health and aged-care system supplemented by private-sector arrangements for those willing and able to pay for extra services.

GP corporate groups should be encouraged to provide a core of high quality, publicly funded services: GP services, pathology, radiology, pharmacy, hospital care and aged care. This core package would be supplemented by privately funded extra services such as physiotherapy, occupational therapy, dental services and core services of higher quality than those provided in the standard package.

Medicare would underwrite the standard package. Extra services would be privately funded. Competition would occur among providers of these integrated services, on both the quality and timeliness of services offered and the range of extra services.

A GP corporate service would offer the attraction of an integrated health and aged-care system. Patients would not have to make inquiries and decisions at each stage and for each type of health care. Once they signed up they would receive coordinated health care in a system in which there was a strong private incentive to achieve both quality care and cost control.

The present system of funding high-care residential aged care (previously known as nursing homes) is unsustainable in an ageing population. Accommodation deposits – or bonds – can be used for low-care places but are prohibited for high-care places. Already 65 per cent of all aged-care residents are in high care. As the population continues to age and new, life-sustaining medical technologies are introduced and extended, the proportion of older Australians in high-care accommodation will grow.

But under the present system families who want to buy top quality high-care accommodation are prohibited by law from doing so. They might be lucky enough to get a so-called extra-service place, where accommodation deposits are legal, but these are limited to 15 per cent of all places.

Why should Big Brother set an upper limit on the quality of aged-care accommodation that families can buy? Imagine the furore if a government passed a law against hotels offering five-star accommodation to guests. Yet that is exactly what the Commonwealth has done for high-care accommodation.

More private funding will be needed if Australia is to provide quality care for the growing number of older Australians who will need high-care accommodation. Accommodation deposits and higher daily care fees should be allowed for those with the capacity to pay, with some of the proceeds being used to subsidise care for the poor. All residents at a facility would benefit from better kitchens, shared living spaces and grounds, and from extra nursing staff.

Accommodation deposits would not apply where a spouse, relative or other carer lives in the resident's former home.

Families who are asset-rich but have heavy mortgage and other financial commitments should be allowed and encouraged to enter into voluntary deals with residential aged-care providers to pay fees, with interest, out of the parents' estate when the parents have passed on. That way the parents can receive high quality aged care and the adult children are able to continue paying off their own homes and meet other family living expenses.

INVESTING IN AUSTRALIA'S CHILDREN

Contrary to the experience of most other rich countries, the contribution of skills development to Australia's productivity growth has slackened off in recent years. In Australia the formation of skills has slowed from the fast pace of the 1980s and early 1990s. In other countries it has accelerated. By applying a brake on the development of skills the Coalition government has allowed acute skill shortages to emerge, and this, in turn, has shifted Australian productivity growth into reverse gear. For example, a proposed redevelopment of a gold mine in Western Australia has been abandoned in the face of skill shortages, and planned expansions in the iron-ore and natural gas industries in the state's north-west are being compromised by shortages of skilled workers. Operators of drilling rigs for mineral exploration were in such short supply in 2005 that exploration programs of small explorers in Western Australia were delayed for up to a year. The federal government has officially listed national shortages of childcare workers, nurses, pharmacists, physiotherapists and radiographers, and building, metal, electrical and mechanical tradespeople. Australia even officially has a shortage of hairdressers.

Productivity growth and future prosperity are not the only things to suffer from the neglect of skills formation. Disadvantage is becoming more entrenched, owing to indifference to the plight of poor children in poor (mostly government) schools. In a shocking indictment of our education system, one in five Australians is functionally illiterate, and there has been no improvement in literacy among children in the last quarter of a century.

In a fundamental reform of Australia's schooling system, funding distinctions between government and private schools must be abandoned. Instead funding should be based on the needs of the child. Schools with larger numbers of disadvantaged children – whether government or private – should receive more funding.

Extra funds should be used on remedial literacy and numeracy support, professional development of teachers and schemes to attract the best teachers and principals to the most disadvantaged schools. Teacher salary structures need reforming to allow the best principals and the best teachers to be offered higher pay.

School principals have a profound influence on the quality of schooling. Their salaries should be boosted over time by an average of at least 25 per cent, with pay variations according to the quality of the principal.

A full range of services should be provided in schools in disadvantaged communities to help address the main underlying cause of poor student performance – dysfunctional family life. Services would include nurses, counselling, a visiting GP, law enforcement and career guidance. A full-service school is being established in the suburb of Marsden in Logan City south of Brisbane. The full-service model should be extended to other disadvantaged communities around Australia.

A Commonwealth scholarship scheme should be introduced for disadvantaged students in years 8 through 12. The value of these scholarships would not be large; their main purpose would be to recognise and encourage high-achieving students in disadvantaged communities, although of course they would also make a welcome practical difference to low-income families.

In acknowledging that the life chances of young people are determined in the early years, Australia should implement a nationally consistent system of compulsory preschool education. Its aim would be to have every child ready to learn from the first day of school. All Australian children would receive a basic preschool education – preferably at a formal preschool but, if necessary, through an accredited program at a child-care centre – designed to give them the social skills and basic learning capabilities needed to participate fully in school learning and school life.

To support full participation in preschool education, family payments to parents of four-year-olds could be made conditional on the children attending formal preschool or its equivalent in a child-care centre. Attendance at preschool would need to be free of charge, at least for the children of disadvantaged families. Mutual obligation of this sort is already practised by requiring the immunisation of children as a condition of receiving child-care benefits. Extending mutual obligation to the attainment of a preschool education could largely alleviate early childhood disadvantage in Australia – a huge investment in the future of these children and of the nation.

Recognising that childhood disadvantage often originates in dysfunctional homes, nationally consistent parenting and early intervention programs should be implemented in all states and territories, based on successful programs already underway such as the Pathways to Prevention Program at Inala in Brisbane's southwest. While these programs might appear expensive, the benefits to the child and the savings to society from well designed early intervention programs have been shown to be massive, their returns potentially exceeding 700 per cent. These savings come from reduced delinquency, domestic violence, drug abuse and crime.

In the twenty-first century, when ideas and creativity are the dominant sources of international competitiveness and prosperity, Australia cannot settle for mostly turning out school leavers who lack tertiary qualifications. At present less than 30 per cent of young people go to university, and around 160 000 obtain university degrees each year. Compare that with China's and India's annual output of more than 2.5 million university graduates each. Absolute numbers are not everything; but Australia needs its own increasing pool of creative talent. The competition out there is tough. Yet for only the second time in half a century, Australia's university enrolments have fallen. As we go backwards in higher education, India and China are flashing past us. So too are Korea and many other countries in our region. In this, the Asian century, Australia will be left wallowing behind in the race to the top unless we get serious about higher education.

In a great stride forward in higher education, public funding of universities should be increased to lift the number and quality of university graduates and to relieve the unrelenting pressure on universities to increase their fees. Although the introduction by Labor in 1989 of the higher education contribution scheme (HECS) has not altered the socioeconomic *composition* of university entrants, subsequent increases in HECS by the Coalition government have lowered the *expected returns* from a university education.

Those expected returns were further (sharply) reduced from

2005 when the government allowed universities to increase their HECS fees by up to 25 per cent – which most of them did. And by allowing universities from 2005 to offer up to 35 per cent of their places to full-fee paying Australian students, the government has driven cash-starved universities to select full-fee paying Australian students over HECS students who achieve better marks at high school.

Before these changes, Australia was already the fifth most expensive place in the world to study for a higher education. The 2005 changes have made the situation in Australia much worse.

Applying prohibitively high fees that exclude talented high-school leavers from gaining access to a university education is appallingly bad public policy. It is making access to a university education much harder for students from less privileged back-grounds, as places are increasingly rationed out to those with a capacity to pay full fees. Students fortunate enough to obtain a subsidised HECS place are confronted with the prospect of massive HECS debts. Many are deciding that a university educa-tion is just not worth it.

The Coalition government is fully aware that its higher educa-tion policies are deterring enrolment by high-school leavers. The government has described Labor as being 'obsessed' with higher education, and is relaxed about forecasting fewer university places for Australian students. Yet Australia desperately needs many more university places, not fewer.

Although public investment in higher education offers good returns for the nation, there are always limits on taxpayer-funded resources. If Australia is to achieve mass participation in higher education, more private resources will be needed to complement extra public funding. These realities call for a new vehicle to mobilise private funding for the public good.

HECS is a form of *debt* financing of higher education. Could private *equity* financing of higher education also be introduced in Australia? Under an equity financing scheme, superannuation funds and other financial institutions could offer to fund a student's university fees and living expenses in return for an agreed share of income earned over a specified period following graduation. Such *Australian student equities* would effectively allow young people to gain access to their own future earnings during their student days. As with HECS, repayments would occur only if the graduate earned specified minimum levels of income. But unlike HECS, if future earnings were large, the return on equity funds invested in the student would be large – making it a potentially attractive proposition for private financiers.

For easier administration and greater public acceptability, legislation should specify a maximum percentage of income that could be collected from each participating student, and it could set a maximum time period over which repayments could occur. Students and their parents could then shop around in a competitive market for the student equity fund that offered to invest the most in them, and/or that sought from them the smallest share of income earned.

By including funding of living expenses, Australian student equities would allow undergraduates to spend more of their time on university studies and participation without the need to work long hours in casual jobs.

Australian student equity funds could enter into financial arrangements directly with universities of their choice to expand the number of student places in preferred courses. This would provide more competition in the university sector, and allow good lecturers to be paid more.

Banks and superannuation funds tend to allocate a share of their capital to ethical investments. There could be no more ethical investment than investing in the talents of Australia's young people.

A combination of HECS, Australian student equities and public funding for universities could provide the financial resources for Australia to take the step up to mass participation in higher education that is essential for achieving prosperity and fairness in the twenty-first century.

Vocational education should remain an option for high-school leavers. But Australia must reject the Coalition government's doctrine that many working-class children are not cut out for a university education. This doctrine perpetuates social stratification. All children deserve a genuine choice. We need to ensure a vocational education is available to those who choose it.

Fees for vocational education are also up-front and rising, and a deterrent to disadvantaged young people gaining trade qualifications. HECS and student equities should be extended to vocational education. And the Commonwealth should develop a legal instrument that sanctions contracts between employers and apprentices whereby the employer pays, say, the minimum adult wage, plus the apprentice's vocational education fees, in return for an agreed share of income earned following the gaining of a trade qualification. In recognition of the value to the employer of the trained employee remaining with the business, the agreed share of income earned could be discounted for each year of subsequent employment in the business.

ENCOURAGING AUSTRALIAN IDEAS

In the information age, when ideas are huge contributors to national prosperity, Australia has fallen badly behind other rich countries in the share of national income devoted to research and development (R&D). Broader measures of innovation also rank Australia well behind many other OECD countries.

Australia's system of encouraging R&D needs a total overhaul. Reductions in the R&D tax concession in 1997 and, later, in the company tax rate have slashed the value of the standard R&D tax concession to a point where it is eliciting little or no extra private R&D. That is not to say that there is no private R&D in Australia; but it is to say that the R&D tax concession, costing $400 million a year, is mostly a gift from taxpayers to companies that would have undertaken the R&D anyway.

The tax concession could be cashed out to create a pool of public funds for encouraging private sector R&D. A cashed-out tax concession could be combined with other, smaller R&D grant programs to create a large *Australian innovation fund* of up to $3 billion.

A portion of the R&D fund could be made available as loans, with repayment contingent on the private innovator achieving a minimum return on investment. If the minimum return was not achieved the loan would not be repaid, but if it was achieved the loan would be repayable over time, with interest. Such a system of loans, modelled on HECS for university fees, would ensure the replenishment of the Australian innovation fund while encouraging the commercialisation of Australian ideas and inventions. To illustrate, a small start-up biomedical company that received a cash injection from the fund would repay the grant with interest if its subsequent profits exceeded a rate of return agreed in advance by the parties.

In determining the merit of applications for funding, Australia's prospective research strengths should be considered. Australia's biological diversity is unique, and the richest of all the continents. Biotechnology might therefore be an area of competitive advantage. So, too, might medical research, including research into cures for sun-induced melanoma. R&D grants should target smaller firms engaged in collaborative research with Australian universities and other publicly funded research institutions.

REWARDING AUSTRALIAN INITIATIVE – TAX AND WELFARE REFORM

Australia is built on the entrepreneurial spirit and initiative of its people. But for many Australians initiative is being stifled by an incentive-crushing tax and social security system. The tax and social security systems are holding back Australia; they are holding back Australians trying to get ahead. And entrepreneur-ship is being repressed by a massively complex *Income Tax Act*, and heavy regulation.

Australia's tax system is consciously designed to encourage speculative property investment financed by debt. Worse, it *reduces* the rewards from investing in education, and from hard work, initiative and entrepreneurship. If you wanted to design a tax system that encourages property speculation financed by debt and discourages hard work and investment in human capital, you need look no further than Australia's income tax system.[1]

Confronted with an ageing population, Australia needs to encourage people of working age to participate in the workforce. Yet the social security and income tax systems impose harsh penalties on the unemployed and on sole parents seeking to move from welfare to work. And it penalises mothers seeking to return to work after having a baby.

Typically these Australians lose more than 60 cents in the dollar from taking on part-time work – and that does not include the cost of child-care, travel or work clothes. Under the govern-ment's so-called welfare reforms introduced in 2005, single mothers are expected to work for just $2 an hour after losing welfare benefits and rent assistance, paying tax and covering the cost of travel and work clothes.

Rewarding work requires an understanding of the critical decision-points for mothers making work and family decisions. The big decisions about returning to work are typically made when the child is under the age of three.

Disincentives for mothers with young children to combine part-time work with family life could be all but removed by elim-inating means-testing of family payments for children up to the age of three. While the cost of raising teenagers is greater than the cost of raising infants, family incomes are typically smaller in the early years as parents are in the early stages of their careers. When couples are having children, one parent – usually the mother –

reduces hours of work to care for young children, or leaves the workforce altogether.

If family payments for children under three were not withdrawn, mothers returning to work would keep an extra 20 cents of every extra dollar they earn. That's a lot of extra incentive.

The cost of moving to a universal family payments system for children under three would be fairly modest, since changes over the last few years have brought nine out of ten families with children into the family payments system.

Mothers of children aged three and older have typically already made their critical work and family decisions. Their work decisions are therefore less likely to be influenced by the withdrawal of government benefits as they earn extra income. Rather than taxing better-off families and returning the money to them as family payments, it would be more sensible and efficient to tax them less in the first place. This can be achieved by a 10 per cent tightening in the means-testing of family tax benefits for children over three. The savings achieved would be sufficient to fund the universal payment for children under three.

Providing a universal family payment for children under three could form a stepping-stone to the staged introduction of a so-called *negative income tax system* that improves work incentives for all income earners. A scheme of this nature could lift workforce participation to world's best practice levels.

Child-care costs can be a strong deterrent for mothers wishing to re-enter the workforce – especially poorer mothers. OECD research indicates that Australia could expect large returns from increased child-care support for lower income families. Although the child-care benefit introduced in 2000 is progressive, subsidising a larger proportion of the child-care costs of low income earners than of the wealthy, the child-care rebate announced in 2004 goes in the opposite direction. It covers 30 per cent of the out-of-pocket expenses remaining after taking account of the child-care benefit. Since child-care costs are a bigger deterrent to working for low-income mothers, the child-care benefit should be increased for poor working families.

Paul Keating remarked in the early 1990s that every parrot in the pet shop was squawking microeconomic reform. Now every parrot is squawking tax reform. But unless the chorus of squawking is accompanied by verses about where spending should be cut, the call for tax reform will never be more than a meaningless cacophony.

Australia's system of payments to families costs $27 billion a year, absorbing almost one quarter of personal income-tax revenue. Although the system of family payments performs the valuable role of redistributing income to the less well-off, the government has extended it through middle Australia and onto the wealthy.

Over a ten-year period when real private incomes have grown by 15 per cent and unemployment has fallen to its lowest level in three decades – greatly reducing the need for welfare payments – the Coalition government has increased real social security spending by one half. Social security payments by the Coalition government are more than 14 per cent of household disposable income – much bigger than the 9 per cent at the end of the Hawke government or the 6 per cent of the Whitlam era. Much of this extra welfare spending has been on middle Australia, and the wealthy. The government now provides cash payments to families earning up to $145 000 a year, and to millionaire couples as long as the mother agrees to stay at home.

The government's manipulation of tax and spending programs for electoral purposes is resulting in income tax being collected from single people and couples who are planning children but have not yet had them, and given to parents, including parents on very high incomes. Its giant recycling machine is taxing these families as well, then returning much of the revenue to them as family payments. Put baldly, the welfare state is out of control. The Coalition government has taken over more and more of the responsibility of running the daily lives of Australians, taxing them only to give the money back as cash payments and in services that they could have arranged for themselves. Armies of bureaucrats are employed to collect the taxes and dispense the proceeds, often to the same people either immediately or later.

Up to $85 billion is spent in this recycling exercise, enough almost to eliminate personal income tax altogether. Another $85 billion is spent on genuine redistribution to those unable to earn sufficient private income for a reasonable standard of living. These funds are put to a valuable social purpose, and should be quarantined from cuts.

But recycling people's money in an ever expanding middle-class welfare state is very costly. In addition to the cost of the army of bureaucrats who have to be paid to collect taxes and administer payments, and the opposing army of accountants and lawyers engaged in the battle against the bureaucrats, the welfare state is destroying incentives to work, save, invest and take risks. The costs are estimated at more than 20 cents in the dollar, which works out at more than $20 billion of Australia's national income squandered every year.

Australia might have been able to afford a bloated welfare state during the most recent period of economic growth, but it has come at the cost of a chaotic income tax system that punishes effort and initiative. And it has come at the expense of sound investments in the nation's future. It's time to trim down for the journey ahead.

Reducing welfare for the wealthy would free up funds to help finance reductions in the higher marginal income tax rates. A government that did this would be handing back responsibility to better-off households for managing their own affairs, cutting their taxes and allowing them to buy services in competitive private markets.

But this would not complete the tax-reform process. Labor in government repaired holes in the income tax base, but the Coalition

government has set about opening up new holes for favoured constituencies. A sound argument exists on both efficiency and equity
grounds for repairing the income tax base to finance reductions in
the higher income tax rates. But there is no consensus on the base-
broadening measures that should be adopted.

If they are to be credible, those advocating a cut in the top
tax rate must nominate the base-repairing measures that would
be adopted to finance reductions in high-income tax rates.
Economists, and Liberal MP Malcolm Turnbull, have nominated
numerous base-repairing measures, including limiting or elimi-
nating deductions for work-related expenses, modifying the
concessionary capital gains tax rate, removing the favoured tax
treatment of some lump-sum payments and removing the concessionary element in the fringe benefits taxation of motor
vehicles.

If serious work were done on repairing the income tax base, and
welfare for the wealthy were pared back, the income tax system
could be fundamentally reformed to restore incentive and give
reward for effort and initiative. First, the 42-cent rate could be
obliterated. Second, the income range over which the 15-cent rate
applies could be extended from $21 600 to $27 000 a year. Third,
a tax-free threshold of $10 000 could be given to all taxpayers
earning less than $70 000 a year. Fourth, the top marginal income
tax rate could be reduced from 47 cents to 39 cents as various base-
repairing measures were implemented.

Under this plan, people earning between $6000 and $27 000
a year would face a marginal tax rate of only 15 cents in the
dollar. Those earning between $27 000 and $125 000 a year
would be on a marginal rate of only 30 cents in the dollar.
Increasing the tax-free threshold from $6000 to $10 000 for
everyone earning less than $70 000 a year would improve incen-
tives to move from welfare to work. Increasing the upper
threshold for the 15 cent rate to $27 000 would increase take-
home pay for Australians earning the minimum wage.

Coalition government promises to simplify the tax system have not been fulfilled. When the present government came to office on a promise of simplifying the income tax system, the *Income Tax Act* ran to around 3600 pages. By 2005 it was 9600 pages. Today Australia's 1.6 million small-business entrepreneurs are burdened with the time and financial cost of complying with the GST, as well as with a massively more complex income tax system.

A highly simplified method of calculating GST obligations, known as the ratio method, should be offered as an option to small businesses. The tax office would, on request, offer a small business a ratio of net GST to sales, calculated using historical data. The small business would be able to apply that ratio to actual sales for the tax period, and remit the resulting amount.

A similar method could be investigated for income tax assessments for small businesses. At the request of a small business, recent historical data on income tax paid by the business, or category of businesses, could be used to calculate for it a ratio of income tax to turnover. Small businesses opting for the ratio method would simply apply the ratio issued by the tax office to turnover for the tax period, and remit that amount.

Under the ratio method, adjustments for extraordinary expenses would be allowed. But no end-of-year reconciliations would be required, and there would be no audits except in cases of suspected fraud. The tax office would retain the right to reassess ratios for future tax periods.

Small-business owners wishing to continue with current arrangements would be free to do so. Those availing themselves of the ratio method would be able to complete their tax returns in minutes, leaving them more time to grow their businesses and be with their families.

Treasury is likely to object strongly to these streamlining proposals, just as it objected strongly to the Hawke government's decision in 1986 to streamline car-logbook-keeping requirements for fringe benefits tax purposes. But those arrangements have stood the test of time, greatly reducing compliance costs while neither over-taxing businesses nor causing significant revenue leakage.

A BUSTLING BUSH

When Australians visualise our country we picture bustling cities and a desolate outback. Too often we overlook the inland regional centres located between surf and solitude. Many of these places have been given a new lease of life by the creation of Australia's open, competitive economy. Regional employment and incomes are growing strongly as these centres produce for national and global markets. Land prices in major cities are forcing commercial activities requiring a lot of land to move out to less expensive locations in regional Australia. Population is now drifting from rural areas and small country towns not to the capital cities, as it did decades ago, but to stronger regional centres.

Other country towns have been losing population without losing their viability. A smaller population is being sustained by diversification into modern, service-based activities quite different from those associated with the agricultural production techniques of a bygone era. These towns could service dynamic regional hubs.

Australia can sustain a larger population settled in the regions. But the rail-freight system in eastern Australia running from south to north is in poor shape, and has suffered massive losses in market share to road freight. And road freight is over-burdening highways and congesting urban transport routes. Broadband rollout has been slow in regional Australia. These are just some of the consequences of infrastructure investment that is too reactive, following population movements rather than seeking to lead them.

Australia's thriving regional centres offer attractive lifestyles to people fed up with congestion and pollution in the big cities. But a lack of modern infrastructure is hindering their competitiveness in a super-competitive Asian region.

A wonderful opportunity exists to shape the pattern of

Australia's settlement towards our stronger regions. If governments take conscious decisions to provide these regional centres
with world-class infrastructure, new settlement patterns can be
consolidated, and, in time, population can be attracted from congested cities to the regions. This is happening already in sea-
change and inland communities in Victoria.

Making these regions globally competitive would require the
installation of efficient, modern transport, communications and
energy-supply systems. But it would also require excellent medical
services, schools and university campuses, all needed to attract
management, skilled staff and creative people to regional areas.

The proposed inland rail system between Melbourne and Brisbane
would enable the timely delivery of the products of inland regions to
national and export markets. In assessing its national worth, account
should be taken of the avoided costs of road transportation and the
easing of congestion in the east-coast capitals. If the analysis stacks up,
a portion of the proceeds from the inevitable sale by the Coalition of
the rest of Telstra should be used to support the inland rail project,
converting one public asset of value to the bush into another.

A national gas grid should be established, connecting eastern
Australia to a major gas supply, most probably Papua New Guinea
and, later, north-western Australia. Gas is a more greenhouse-
friendly energy source than coal. It should be used not to replace
coal but to complement it. Though the supply of gas from Papua
New Guinea and later from the north-west should be led by the
private sector, a case can be made for some public-sector contribution through finance and risk-sharing. Government support for a
major new gas supply would not be unprecedented, and should be
considered if proper analysis shows it to be justified.

More generally, a national infrastructure plan should be developed by a national infrastructure advisory council. The plan
would not only respond to existing infrastructure bottlenecks, it
would anticipate future needs and identify future opportunities,
especially in, but not limited to, regional Australia. An independent

research body like the Productivity Commission would rigorously evaluate infrastructure proposals for their prospective national net benefits, including wider benefits for the nation not accounted for in commercial project evaluations.

Infrastructure proposals that complied with the plan could be subject to favourable financing, risk-sharing and approval conditions. Non-complying infrastructure could still proceed with state and local government approval, but would not be eligible for Commonwealth financial support.

CAN THE ENVIRONMENT SUSTAIN A BUSTLING BUSH?

A population and infrastructure plan for Australia would need to be ecologically sustainable. Water has rightly been identified as a constraint on Australia's future population growth. Yet around two-thirds of Australia's water is used for agriculture, and 90 per cent of that is used for irrigated crops – uses unrelated to population density. Why does Australia produce rice from its scarce water resources when rain in abundance irrigates the paddy fields of Asia? And who takes account of the ecological impact of the chemicals and water used in the production of thirsty cotton crops?

Crops like rice can be imported cheaply, allowing Australia's water resources to be put to better uses such as ecological repair, the production of premium grapes for Australia's export wine industry and consumption by a larger Australian population. Pricing water at its true cost would ensure that it was allocated to its highest uses. A proper system of permanent water-trading would allow farmers producing lower value crops to sell their water entitlements for these higher uses.

MIGRANTS HELPING TO BUILD AUSTRALIA'S REGIONS

Since World War II half the increase in Australia's population has come from migrants and their children. Further strong immigration will be needed just to stop Australia's population from declining from around the middle of the 2030s. But Australians need to recognise that the international market for skilled migrants will become increasingly competitive in the coming decades, and we will not be able to dictate all the terms to prospective migrants in seeking to attract them to our country.

Setting a population target for Australia is pointless; there is no uniquely optimal population. But Australia would benefit from a growing population so long as the social and environmental impacts can be managed.

Government population policy should be directed at the dispersal of the population rather than at absolute numbers. The national infrastructure plan should be integrated with strengthened regional migration incentives.

Regional migration incentives were improved in 2004, based around a Labor proposal of granting permanent residency to migrants who stay in regional Australia for a specified period of time. But concerns linger that migrants settling in regional Australia will move to the big cities when they reach the qualifying period for permanent residency. Further incentives to retain migrants in regional areas should be considered. Migrants usually place a high value on family reunion. If migrants remained in regional Australia for a specified period beyond the permanent-residency qualifying period, applications for family reunion should be given favourable consideration. Family members eligible for reunion should not necessarily be restricted to skilled relatives, as at present. And governments need to provide high-quality resettlement services, including English language training, for migrants moving to regional Australia.

The families of foreign students studying at regional universities should be encouraged to join them during the course of their studies. And they should be allowed to apply for permanent residency while in Australia.

In respect of the regional migration component of the overall immigration program, Canberra's practice of setting annual immigration planning numbers should be abandoned. In its place

should be a bottom-up approach – regional areas and state governments determining their desired intakes in consultation with the
Commonwealth, but without a veto from Canberra. Of course, the
Commonwealth would retain all its responsibilities and capacities
for assessing applicants, including health and security checks.

For the purposes of regional migration incentives, regional
areas should be defined by state and local governments such that
if a state government wanted all the state outside the capital city's
boundaries to be given regional status then the Commonwealth
would not stand in the way. The smaller capitals – Adelaide,
Perth, Hobart and Darwin – should be granted regional status if
the state or territory government requested it.

A bigger humanitarian program should be manageable if the
increase were directed to regional Australia. Refugees are typically
good migrants – young, and highly motivated. Country towns and
cities wanting to boost their local economies should be encouraged
to take more refugees, subject to existing Commonwealth health
and security checks. Regional migration incentives should be
applied to an expanded humanitarian program, with regional
communities and state governments being empowered to sponsor
refugees if they wish.

Victoria is adopting this approach. Other states should consider following Victoria's lead.

KEEPING AUSTRALIA OPEN FOR BUSINESS

Australia's future prosperity will depend fundamentally on our
global competitiveness and our openness to trade. For the 13
years to 2004, Australia's economic growth compared with other
rich countries was its best ever. It was based on the strongest
export expansion in our history. But from 2000, Australia's
export performance deteriorated to its worst result in decades.

The federal government cannot influence export prices, but it
can influence export volumes. As a measure of the failure of trade
policy, Australia has put in its worst export volume performance

in fifty years, despite enjoying its best export prices in thirty years. Not even the fabulous good fortune of some of the highest mineral prices in half a century has been able to compensate for weakening volumes of primary and manufactured goods and services exports.

As the government blames terrorism, SARS, bird flu virus and slow world growth – which would influence most countries' exports – it cannot explain why Australia's *share* of world exports slumped to its lowest level since World War II. Nor can it explain why Australia's diversification into exports of sophisticated manufactured goods and services, so successful in the 1980s and early 1990s, went into reverse from the turn of the century.

Clearly Australia's trade policy has gone awry. A preoccupation with negotiating preferential trade deals with some countries that discriminate against others has marked a fundamental departure from the successful trade policies of the previous Labor government.

The Coalition government, having already negotiated trade deals with the United States, Singapore and Thailand that discriminate against our other trading partners, is busily negotiating new trade deals with some of those other partners to repair the damage. But in the process, it will discriminate further against those remaining trading partners with which we do not have a deal. Each deal will have its carve-outs, exemptions, specific tariff reduction programs and rules for determining the origin of products traded between the two countries. The lunacy of negotiating free-trade agreements that are anything but free trade is creating a paperwork nightmare for exporting and importing businesses.

In government, Labor's trade policies were unilateral and non-discriminatory; Labor did not wait for others in deciding to lower Australia's trade barriers, and did not seek preferential access to foreign markets – just a chance to compete.

Australia now has a once-in-a-generation opportunity to convert bad trade policy into good. Trade policy should revert to the principle of non-discrimination that formed the cornerstone of the world trading system before the rise of preferential deals.

Reductions in Australian protection granted in preferential trade deals with the United States, Singapore and Thailand should be extended to other countries – if necessary, on condition that they extend to us the best trade concessions they have given to other countries.

The relaxation of Australia's foreign investment rules for American investors – by far the largest source of national benefit claimed for the US–Australia free trade agreement – should immediately be extended to investors from other countries.

Manufactured imports from China will not be troubled by Australia's low and falling tariff walls, regardless of whether a preferential trade deal is negotiated with China. It's a bit like a giant stubbing a toe stepping over a brick – a nuisance, but hardly a deterrent. Australian consumers value these inexpensive Chinese manufactured goods.

Producers of Australian manufactured goods will succeed against Chinese imports and on export markets not by competing on the basis of labour costs in a race to the bottom, but on skills and ideas embodied in sophisticated manufactured goods in a race to the top. Labor in government succeeded in revitalising the Australian manufacturing sector through export-oriented industry plans. A modern-day equivalent must be developed and implemented without delay, for in its absence Australian manufacturing will succumb to the giant factory that is modern China.

CAN WE AFFORD IT?

Income tax rates will need to rise sharply in the coming decades if Australia does not successfully meet the challenge of an ageing population. Confronted with very high tax rates, working-age Australians will be discouraged from earning the extra income and paying the taxes needed to support those too old and too young to work. And older Australians will increasingly be required to work beyond their preferred retirement age.

Wise early investment in education, R&D and infrastructure

could avert the need for tax increases and 'work till you drop' schemes. Australia must improve work incentives and lift its national savings effort now. This can be done by reducing high tax rates – funded by cutting back on welfare for the wealthy and repairing the income tax base – and a renewed commitment to superannuation. Generating higher retirement incomes is fundamental to meeting the challenge of an ageing population.

The plan for investing in the five I's can be financed from existing budgetary resources and from announced asset sales without the need for increased taxes. Now is the time to make those investments. It's time to stop governing for electoral cycles and to start investing for the future. The challenges of population ageing and faltering productivity growth leave us with little choice.

OVERALL WELLBEING

International and Australian research finds that, above a level of income that provides for the basics in life, overall personal wellbeing is only weakly linked with further increases in income. Humans are social animals who value relationships and security. We are very conscious of where we are, and where others see us, in the social pecking order. We like striving for a goal, but tend to be happy for only a short time after having achieved it. We are envious of the success of others with whom we like to compare ourselves.

Australians have high levels of measured wellbeing by international standards. The findings of Australian surveys point us in particular directions. People value job security highly, which has implications for so-called labour market reforms designed to weaken job security. And Australians living in accessible regional centres have higher levels of wellbeing than those living in capital cities and remote areas – an encouraging pointer to the idea of boosting our stronger regional centres, especially those located in the band of gold from north Queensland through NSW and on to western Victoria.

CHAPTER 2

THE ECONOMIC CHALLENGE

STRUCTURAL WEAKNESSES EXPOSED

Australia faces serious economic challenges that, until early 2005, were masked by more than a decade of strong growth. A dramatic unmasking occurred in March 2005 when the Reserve Bank lifted interest rates in response to inflationary pressures built up by strong domestic spending colliding with capacity constraints.

If Australia's economic challenges are not addressed, by 2010 Australia could experience a cut of almost one-third in the economic growth rate per person enjoyed in the 1990s. This would be the slowest rate of economic growth per person since the decade of the Great Depression.[1]

How do we know? The Commonwealth Treasury tells us so. Treasury's *Intergenerational Report*, released in 2002, projects this dramatic slump in growth in measured living standards from 2010 onwards.[2] And it is likely to get worse: by the mid-2020s Australia's rate of economic growth per person is projected to slow to half the rate achieved in the early 2000s.[3]

These alarming official projections are the product of two insidious forces at work in the Australian economy: an ageing population, and faltering productivity growth.

AN AGEING POPULATION

More than half the increase in Australia's population to the mid-2040s will be among Australians over 65. By then the proportion of the Australian population over 65 is projected to almost double.[4]

Australia's working-age population typically grows by around 166 000 a year, but trends already in place mean that the working-age population will grow at only one-tenth of this rate during the 2020s. That will leave only a little more than 40 per cent of our population in work to support those too old or too young to work.[5]

Population ageing could be happening faster than the official forecasts lead us to expect. The official projections assume a slowing in the rate of increase in life expectancy in the coming decades compared with the experience of the last few decades. But official projections have systematically underestimated increases in life expectancy. Realistically faster increases in life expectancy would greatly accelerate population ageing.

FALTERING PRODUCTIVITY GROWTH

Australia needs to maintain strong productivity growth to combat the negative economic consequences of population ageing. But the *Intergenerational Report* projects that the strong productivity growth Australia achieved during the 1990s will slip back to its mediocre 30-year average from 2005 onwards.[6]

The OECD warns that Australian productivity growth might be faltering:

> During the four years ending in the financial year 2002–03, capital deepening maintained its trend, but market sector MFP [multifactor productivity growth] slowed down to an average rate of 0.5 per cent. This could indicate the end of its strong trend increase in the 1990s.[7]

In fact, productivity growth turned negative in 2004, and remained negative through 2005. This might be partly due to one-off factors, but any country should be worried about putting in more than a full year of negative productivity growth.

Some of us were warning about an imminent slowdown in productivity growth before the *Intergenerational Report* was released.[8] But those warnings have gone unheeded.

WEAK EXPORTS

Australia's emerging economic problems are being aggravated by a sharp deterioration in our export performance. Since the early 2000s, Australia has been nowhere near paying its way in the world.

Box 2.1 explains some of the terms used in describing our trade with the rest of the world.

BOX 2.1 EXPORT TERMINOLOGY

Merchandise exports are the total value of goods (tangible things we produce, like coal, wheat and manufactured products) we sell abroad. *Merchandise imports* are the total value of goods we buy from overseas.

Total exports are merchandise exports plus the services we sell abroad (like engineering and construction services, the spending of foreign tourists in Australia and the spending of foreign students studying at our universities). *Total imports* are merchandise imports plus the services we buy from abroad (like shipping and insurance).

Export volumes are the quantities of our exports. To get the *value* of exports, we just multiply the quantities of exports by the prices we receive for them.

Terms of trade are the prices of our exports compared with the prices of our imports. An improvement in our terms of trade means we are able to buy more imports from the same volume of exports.

The *trade deficit* is found by subtracting total imports from total exports. When exports are less than imports we are in deficit.

The *current account deficit* is the trade deficit plus income (interest, rent, royalties and dividends) and transfers (aid and pensions) payable abroad, minus income and transfers receivable from abroad.

Net foreign debt is the amount the private and public sectors owe to foreign residents, minus the amount we are owed by foreign residents.

Australia's export competitiveness has deteriorated alarmingly, causing a collapse in the growth of *export volumes*. Between 1986 and 2000 the volume of Australian manufactured exports increased by 12 per cent a year, while the volume of services exported increased by 8 per cent a year, and the volume of primary commodities exported increased by 6 per cent a year. But between 2000 and 2004 the volume of manufactured exports grew by just 4 per cent a year, while services and primary commodity volumes did not grow at all. Net exports detracted from growth for an unprecedented four successive years – Australia's worst export performance since World War II.

Australia's poor export performance has occurred despite our best export prices compared with import prices (*terms of trade*) in 30 years. Australia is again relying heavily on high commodity prices, hoping our luck will not run out as it did in the mid-1980s when primary commodity prices collapsed. And we are obtaining exceptionally cheap manufactured goods from China, the emerging global factory.

When mineral prices fall, as they probably will, Australia's trade deficits can be expected to widen (see figure 2.1). Australia's record run of monthly trade deficits is set to continue well into the future.

CONSUMPTION TODAY, OR INVESTMENT FOR TOMORROW?

Federal government policy has deliberately encouraged consumer spending over investment. From March 2000 to March 2005 around three-quarters of total domestic spending was consumption spending, with only just over one-quarter being investment.

Australians have been spending more than they are earning, financing the shortfall from borrowings against the rising value of their homes and other properties. The housing bubble, inflated by federal government policies, has been very costly, diverting national income into consumption and away from productive investment. Treasury has pointed out that household borrowings have been overwhelmingly responsible for Australia's current account deficit.[9]

Mining investment is responding to high world mineral prices, which is good, but we are not getting the investment in high-value manufacturing and services needed to rebalance growth onto a more sustainable trajectory.

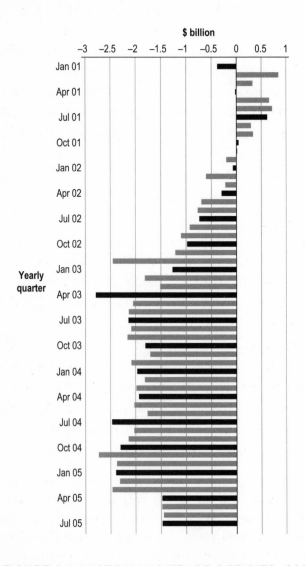

FIGURE 2.1 AUSTRALIA'S TRADE DEFICITS, 2000–05

THE DEFICIT – BIG,
AND GETTING BIGGER

A long series of big current account deficits has contributed to a massive accumulation of foreign debt. When the Coalition rolled out its debt truck in 1995, promising to bring down foreign debt, Australia's net foreign debt was $180 billion. By late 2005 it had reached a staggering $450 billion, or almost $350 billion in 1995 dollars – a real increase of more than 90 per cent.

From the May 2004 Budget through to the end of the 2004 federal election campaign the Coalition embarked on a $66 billion spending spree – of which $60 billion was consumption spending and $6 billion was investment for the future. Following the 2005 Budget the spending spree had reached $103 billion. Constraints on Australia's capacity to supply the extra demand for goods and services have caused that spending to spill over into imports, worsening the trade deficit, the current account deficit and foreign debt.

Australian policy thinking has been dominated for a decade by the view that current account deficits don't matter as long as the foreign money that funds them is used for investment in income-producing assets. In Australia this is known as the Pitchford thesis;[10] internationally it has been labelled the Lawson doctrine.[11]

But more recently experts have become worried about whether Australia's prolonged, large current account deficits can be managed without traumatic disruptions to the economy. The experts include the International Monetary Fund (IMF), Standard and Poor's rating agency and prominent economists, including Professor Ross Garnaut.[12] The IMF advises caution:

> Often called the 'Lawson Doctrine', this view ... has come into question owing to a number of currency crises and sharp current account reversals that have occurred in emerging market and industrial countries in recent years. This issue is of particular relevance to Australia in the current conjecture with the current account deficit around 6 per cent of GDP ...

Since that caution was issued Australia's current account deficit has deteriorated further, passing 7 per cent of GDP. While it is true that a market economy will inevitably adjust to these deficits, it is the adjustment process itself that causes human pain. Slow growth, or contraction, in incomes and jobs causes bankruptcies and unemployment. The burden of adjustment falls most heavily on the most vulnerable – small businesses and workers with low skills.

Whether an economy can successfully reduce large current account deficits without a serious economic slowdown depends on the conditions prevailing at the time. Adjustments can hurt growth where the current account deficit is a symptom of too much domestic spending – that is, where the economy is overheating.[13] These have been the conditions of the Australian economy.

Indeed, a comparison of the economic conditions prevailing immediately before the recession of the early 1990s and those prevailing in the first half of the present decade shows that the imbalances in the latter period have been at least as bad.[14]

Strong economic growth has generated complacency in the Coalition government about the Australian economy's weakening foundations and the fundamental economic challenges confronting Australia. It is hard to identify any coherent economic reform program at any time during the period of the present government.

Formalising the independence of the Reserve Bank in setting interest rate policy targeted at inflation, which continued the practice of the preceding government immediately before the change of government, was a welcome move. Some of the reforms in Australia's international tax regime might have been mildly beneficial to economic growth. Moving the budget into surplus has helped to sustain non-inflationary economic growth.

But this government is now the highest taxing, highest spending government in Australia's history. And the spending cuts of its early years centred not on consumption spending but on superannuation and training programs. Australia will pay a high price for these cuts to training and superannuation. Earlier changes in labour market regulation removed some artificial restrictions on work practices, but most of these were on the way out anyway, thanks to the introduction of enterprise bargaining by the previous Labor government.

The government's so-called Great Tax Adventure produced a $36 billion complex new tax and an explosion in the size and complexity of the *Income Tax Act*. The greatest claim for the GST, that it would boost the competitiveness of our exports, has failed to materialise in any meaningful way. The other main rationale for the GST – a significant shift in the tax mix from income to consumption – has not been achieved either.[15] The Coalition government has continued competition policy reforms initiated by the Keating government, though it has made political concessions to various groups and has increased subsidies for the private health insurance and sugar industries.

But where is the new reform agenda designed to sustain prosperity in the face of an ageing population? Australia desperately needs a modern reform program. The following chapters set out such a program. The policies advocated are not exhaustive, but they constitute the main reforms that need to be implemented over the next decade.

CHAPTER 3

THE ECONOMIC REVIVAL

LABOR'S REFORM PROGRAM

At the beginning of the twentieth century Australia had the highest standard of living in the world. Almost a century later Australia had slipped to around nineteenth in the world.[1]

By the early 1970s our country had shifted from an open, competitive economy to a Fortress Australia. Our markets for goods and services, finance and labour had become heavily regulated, and Australian manufacturing was protected by high import barriers. Protected from competition at home and abroad, Australian manufacturing became inefficient.

But even at these levels of protection, Australian manufacturing was suffering massive job losses. And mining, agricultural and service industries were being punished by the high cost of the manufactured goods they used in their own production processes. The policy response was ever-increasing import barriers for manufacturing, imposing further costs on primary industries and services.

By 1983 the Australian steel industry was on the verge of collapse, and car manufacturing was in deep trouble. Australia was relying heavily for its export income on primary commodities, which contributed almost two-thirds of Australia's exports of goods and services.

The Fraser government's economic policy atrophy has been recognised by former Liberal MP and leading economic dry, John Hyde:

> Fraser's policies were a grab bag of popular measures including some that were inconsistent with the core undertakings to restore the economy to health, return the budget to responsible balance and reduce unemployment. He failed to cut stifling regulations, tariffs and licenses that favoured the few at the expense of the many ... But from 1983 onwards, the Hawke government embarked on a period of genuine radical leadership, to an unusual degree taking the public into its confidence.[2]

The incoming Hawke Labor government was well aware of the weaknesses in the foundations of the Australian economy. They were showing up in poor productivity growth, and an acute vulnerability to any downturn in primary commodity prices.

It has been estimated that as much as 80 per cent of Australia's below-average economic performance was the consequence of our failure to match tariff reductions and accompanying economic reforms in other OECD countries between 1965 and 1984.[3]

From 1983 Labor recognised that today's productivity growth is tomorrow's prosperity.

Productivity is the value of output per hour worked (see box 3.1). An economy is performing well if it can achieve more and more production of valuable goods and services for each hour worked. Employees who can produce more and more for each hour they work are likely to be able to command higher wages.

But as Professor Michael E Porter points out, productivity is more than just the source of higher wages; productivity:

> allows citizens the option of choosing more leisure instead of working longer hours. It also creates the national income that is taxed to pay for public services which again boosts the standard of living [and it] allows a nation's firms to meet stringent social standards which improve the standard of living, such as in health and safety, equal opportunity and environmental impact.[4]

BOX 3.1　WHAT IS PRODUCTIVITY GROWTH?

Labour productivity is simply output per hour worked. *Average labour productivity* for the whole economy is total output divided by total number of hours worked.

Labour productivity growth is increase in output minus increase in hours worked.

Labour productivity growth can be achieved by working harder each hour – for example, by taking fewer breaks, using more physical exertion and concentrating more.

Labour productivity can also be boosted by working smarter. Three broad categories of working smarter can be identified.

The first is using more and better equipment – for example, better tools, automated equipment and faster computers. This is called *capital deepening*.

The second is using better quality labour – for example, a better educated workforce or more experienced staff. This is called *improving human capital*.

The third is the efficiency with which all inputs are used. It is the benefit derived from technological change and from allocating resources to their most productive uses, including the aggregation of all those modest improvements that build up in well-run workplaces. This is called *multifactor productivity growth*. It is the difference between growth in output and growth in all inputs.

Productivity is not simply about the mighty dollar. It is the key to achieving prosperity, a fair and decent society and a clean environment. As eminent contemporary American economist Paul Krugman concludes: 'Productivity isn't everything, but in the long run it's nearly everything'.[5]

With all the inefficiencies in the Australian economy in 1983, there was ample scope for the incoming Labor government to boost productivity. The new government embarked on an economic reform program designed to lift productivity growth while diversifying Australia's export base by engaging with Asia and promoting non-commodity exports.

Labor floated the dollar and deregulated financial and goods and services markets. It developed industry plans in cooperation with the trade union movement and the business community. These plans gradually lowered import barriers while providing adjustment assistance to those adversely affected by industry restructuring. They changed the focus of industry policy from protectionism to productivity enhancement.

The tripartite industry plans – involving government, business and unions – were designed to make industries more viable in open, competitive markets through productivity agreements that involved investment and training commitments. Productivity in industries such as steel-making and the automotive industry rose astonishingly under them. Retaining residual protection was conditional on achieving productivity targets and moving protected Australian industries away from simply competing against imports at home to competing on global markets.

More generally, the Labor government promoted investment in and exports of sophisticated manufactured goods and services to reduce Australia's vulnerability to downswings in world primary-commodity prices. While creating an open, competitive economy, the Hawke and Keating governments vigorously pursued the opening-up of other countries' markets through trade agreements.

Labor's trade policy was not to wait for other countries to open up their markets as a precondition for opening up Australia's markets. The government recognised that opening up the Australian economy to competition from abroad was beneficial in its own right. It did not seek preferential access to other countries' markets, just an opportunity to compete.

The opening-up of Australia's markets for goods and services has resulted in one of the least regulated product markets in the OECD, including having the lowest barriers to trade and investment of any OECD country.[6]

The economic reform program of the 1980s and early 1990s

was designed, in part, to rectify an imbalance between wages and profits that had too much of the nation's income going to wages and not enough to profits. This imbalance was created in the mid-1970s and was worsened by the Fraser government's mishandling of industrial relations in the early 1980s, when nominal wages grew by 14 per cent a year. High wage costs were damaging Australia's international competitiveness, and retarding job-creating investment.

In the early years of the Hawke government a more centralised wage-fixing system was needed to break the Fraser–Howard government's debilitating, inflationary wage–price spiral, and this was established through various incarnations of the accord with the trade union movement.

But, crucially, in exchange for restraint in money wages, the Labor government provided seven rounds of tax cuts in 13 years, returning all of bracket creep and more. It later introduced compulsory superannuation for working Australians – an enduring Keating legacy. And it increased the social wage for working people through targeted increases in family payments, Medicare, child-care subsidies and more affordable access to education.

These improvements in the social wage were paid for by the community through the tax system, relieving employers of extra wage costs and allowing them to improve their competitiveness. The improved competitiveness of Australian business, combined with an active export promotion program, triggered strong growth in Australian exports of manufactured goods and services. Labor's industry plans reoriented manufacturing industries to the export market, giving them a stronger future in an open, competitive economy.

The cooperation of the trade union movement was fundamental to the success of Labor's economic reform program. As the deregulation of financial and product markets proceeded, the government and the union movement gradually moved from centralised wage-fixing towards a decentralised wage-fixing system based on productivity improvements. The government and the unions ushered in a system of enterprise bargaining, with unions voluntarily easing restrictions on work practices in exchange for productivity-based pay rises and the establishment of skill-based career paths.

Under Labor the profit share of gross domestic product (GDP) rebounded strongly. It has continued to grow under the Coalition (see figure 3.1), and according to the 2005–06 Budget Papers is expected to keep growing until at least 2008. The graph shows a historic shift in the profit share from around 18 per cent of GDP to more than 26 per cent. Yet there seems to be no limit to the profit share to which some business groups aspire.

FIGURE 3.1 PROFIT AS A PERCENTAGE OF GDP IN THE AUSTRALIAN ECONOMY, 1959–2004

THE REWARDS OF ECONOMIC REFORM

The Labor government's transformation of Australia to an open, competitive economy unleashed more than a decade of record productivity growth and economic growth. The rewards of this economic reform program took, frustratingly, longer to materialise than had been hoped. It can take at least four years for such reforms to yield any significant benefits, and up to twenty years for the full benefits to be realised.[7]

During the 1990s Australia's productivity growth surpassed that of every country in the western world except Ireland and Finland, but including the United States.[8] In less than a decade Australia had surged through the international field from productivity straggler to the front of the pack. Australia's strong productivity performance during the 1990s is estimated to have boosted average household incomes by around $7000.[9]

But how much of this impressive performance was a result of the economic reform program, and how much came from other sources? Studies on the sources of Australia's productivity revival suggest that about 50 per cent has been from opening up the Australian economy, 30 per cent from local R&D activity and 20 per cent from Australian innovation based on imported information and communications technology (ICT).[10] Opening up the economy has given the latter two sources of increased productivity fertile ground in which to take hold, so that these estimates probably understate the importance of the creation of an open, competitive economy.

Indeed, there is now a general consensus that the economic reform program embarked upon by Labor and extended by the Coalition has been overwhelmingly responsible for Australia's strong productivity growth and the prosperity it has created.[11]

CHAPTER 4

THE DIMENSIONS OF THE CHALLENGE

OH NO, NOT THE THREE P'S!

Australia's economic challenge can be summarised by the three P's: *population, participation* and *productivity*.[1] In principle, the adverse economic effects of the ageing of the population can be offset by a combination of immigration to boost its numbers and rejuvenate its age profile; an increase in labour force participation; and strong growth in productivity.

How is Australia faring on the three P's?

THE FIRST P – POPULATION

A STAGNATING POPULATION

For only the second time in more than two hundred years of European settlement, Australia is facing the prospect of population decline. The first time was in the early post-war period, when a declining population by 2000 was projected.

Australia's great post-war immigration program, and the baby boom, changed all that. But now official projections are for Australia to experience a natural decline in its population some time in the 2030s.[2] Net overseas migration will be needed just to prevent our overall population from falling. Under realistic assumptions of net migration of 100 000 per year – around its recent average level – Australia's population could be expected to plateau at just over 26 million during the 2040s, remaining fairly constant for the rest of the century.[3]

There is no compelling notion of an optimal population for Australia. Some – usually environmentalists – want it much smaller than it is today; others would like to see it much larger. Arguing about some target population level seems futile. While there are clear economic advantages in a larger and growing population, few (except deep greens) would argue the economic merits of a small and stagnating population.

Wealth creation can be easier to achieve in a growing population. Economies of scale can be achieved from larger production runs for a larger population. Population size is very important to the efficient supply of non-traded goods such as long-haul transport, including very fast trains. It also bears heavily on the viability of 'national' goods such as newspapers, magazines, local television production and the arts. However, if the economy is well integrated into the global economy, larger production runs can be used to produce tradable goods for the export market, without having to rely for sales on a big domestic market.

Productivity-enhancing technical improvements can be easier to achieve in larger, growing and skilled populations that have a good supply of younger workers able to create and absorb new technologies:

> The knowledge spillover from population size is that more production generates more ideas about improving production, including through 'learning by doing'. This may be no more than the accumulation of lots of small improvements and can embrace all steps in the value chain from factory to client service. But it is increasingly recognised that this is where so much value creation originates.[4]

A second benefit from a larger population is that of 'thick markets' – from specialising in production and skills to meet demands in niche markets within large overall markets. Thin domestic markets are less likely to offer these niche opportunities.

It would be easy to conclude that the ICT revolution has brought Australia closer to the rest of the world. But, disturbingly, the evidence seems to be that distance is *more* of a problem in the information age.[5] Physical proximity of researchers and creative people to each other and to commercial facilities is becoming more important in determining the competitiveness of a region or country in producing sophisticated goods and services.[6] In this new world, competition is among global cities, not among countries.

Partly offsetting the disadvantages of distance are Australia's fluency in the English language, which is rapidly becoming universal, and our renowned speed in absorbing new technologies invented overseas. But these are not enough in themselves to overcome the disadvantages of distance from global centres of learning and innovation.

Arguments that countries with small populations perform well economically miss the essential point that proximity *does* matter. Small, prosperous European countries like Norway, Denmark, Sweden and Austria are close to and part of the huge European and North American markets. Australia's small population in a large continent remote from many major markets presents challenges for our global competitiveness in the production of sophisticated goods and services.[7]

But now all this is beginning to change. By around 2015, the combined size of the five largest economies in Asia – China, India, Japan, Korea and Indonesia – is likely to be roughly equal to that of the nine largest economies of Europe and North America.[8] The twenty-first century is truly shaping as the Asian century, and Australia is geographically well positioned to take advantage of it.

A larger, and growing, Australian population can be expected to present environmental challenges. Any population increases must be ecologically and socially sustainable. Using up Australia's environmental capital and overcrowding the Sydney basin and the eastern seaboard would be ecologically and socially damaging.

But the challenges should be kept in perspective. A 1994 Commonwealth parliamentary inquiry, testing the proposition that Australia's soils do not have the population-carrying capacity of those of other countries, found that the soil types of the Northern Territory's coastal plains replicate those of southern China, which has a massively denser population. Australia has many types of soil. No-one expects our vast desert areas to support a significant population. But soil quality is unlikely to be a constraint on realistic population increases in the regional areas considered in the plan for Australia.

Water has rightly been identified as a major constraint on Australia's future population growth. Yet two-thirds of Australia's water is used for agriculture, a use not closely related to population density.[9] In fact, more than 60 per cent of the continent's water is used in the production of irrigated crops, like rice,[10] that can be imported cheaply. Importing these products would allow our water to be put to higher uses, such as ecological repair and consumption by a larger Australian population.

Chapter 10 considers a population policy for Australia, and the role that immigration should play in boosting Australia's population.

AN AGEING POPULATION

Of the expected 4.3 million additional Australians over the age of 65 by the mid-2040s, almost 60 per cent will be over the age of 75.[11] The ageing of the population is the dominant cause of the expected slowing in economic growth per person over the next 40 years.[12] Australia's ageing population is the product of two forces: fewer babies, and longer lives.

WE'RE HAVING FEWER BABIES

On average, each Australian woman in the early 2000s is having 1.8 children, down from 2.8 in the early 1970s and 3.5 at the baby-boom peak of the early 1960s (see figure 4.1). Australia's fertility rate fell below the replacement rate in the mid-1970s, and continued to slide until 2001 when it bottomed out at 1.73. It picked up slightly to 1.76 in 2003 and 2004.

A further small rise in fertility probably occurred in 2005. Women in their thirties may be deciding that they do not want to miss out on having a family, and a mini baby boom among women in this age group is now in prospect. Fertility appears to have risen to 1.8, and this might continue for a decade or so.[13] However, fertility among women under 30 is still falling, so it is difficult to envisage the overall fertility rate in Australia rising much above 1.8 in the next two decades.[14]

The Australian experience of declining fertility is shared by other developed countries. Most other OECD countries have lower fertility rates than Australia.

Even immediate increases in fertility could not offset the adverse economic impacts of population ageing for almost two decades when today's newborns begin entering the workforce. Until then budgetary pressures would actually worsen as extra government spending on child-care and education was unmatched

FIGURE 4.1 AUSTRALIA'S TOTAL FERTILITY RATE, 1921–2003

by additional taxation revenue. Plausible increases in the fertility rate above the assumed rate of 1.8 babies could slow the ageing of the population by the 2040s, but not by very much.[15] Lifting fertility rates is in Australia's long term interests, but in the next forty years it would increase rather than reduce the proportion of the population dependent on people of working age.[16]

Nevertheless, if we are serious about dealing with the long-term consequences of an ageing population we must consider policies now to halt the decline in fertility. Productive young workers would begin entering the workforce within twenty years of any increase in fertility and the benefits of a lift in fertility would be well and truly felt forty years out. Chapter 9 addresses these issues.

AND WE'RE LIVING LONGER

At a time when Australians are having fewer babies, we are also living longer. Over the last hundred years male life expectancy has increased from about 55 to 77 years, and female life expectancy has risen from around 59 to 82 years.[17] The *Intergenerational Report* assumes that life expectancy will increase by another five years in the coming four decades. During that period ageing baby boomers born in the 1950s and 1960s will replace the small numbers of older Australians born in the 1930s and 1940s.

The *Intergenerational Report* and the ABS population projections assume a slowing in the rate of increase in life expectancy over the next forty years compared with the last hundred. Yet past ABS projections have systematically *underestimated* increases in life expectancy. Plausibly faster increases in life expectancy would strongly increase the rate at which the population is ageing. Under a high life expectancy scenario Australia would have an extra 700 000 people aged 90 and above by the 2040s, on top of the additional 600 000 envisaged in a mid-range scenario.[18] The ageing of the population could turn out to be even more pronounced than the official projections suggest.

THE SECOND P – PARTICIPATION

The smaller the proportion of the population in the workforce, the greater the burden on them to produce the income and the taxation revenue to pay for those who are dependent on them. In 2004 the participation rate in Australia – the proportion of the population that was in the workforce, either in a job or actively looking for one – was slightly above the OECD average, but there is scope to lift it to the levels of Scandinavian countries.[19] But as people get older they participate less in the workforce. The ageing of Australia's population will reduce the overall participation rate.

The major contributor to declining fertility in Australia is vastly improved educational attainment for young women.[20] The good news is that this better educated group of working-age women will participate far more extensively in the workforce than their predecessors, partly offsetting the ageing impacts. If it were not for these well-educated women continuing to enter and move through the workforce, Australia's participation rate would be even lower.

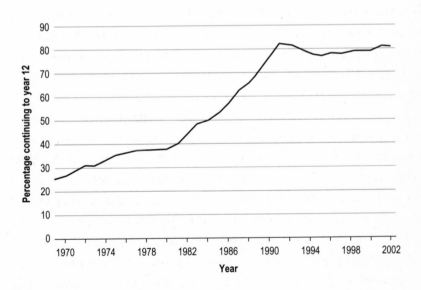

FIGURE 4.2 YEAR 12 RETENTION RATES FOR AUSTRALIAN FEMALES, 1970–2002

The sharp improvement in the high-school education levels of Australian women occurred during the 1980s through to the early 1990s, but then reached a plateau (see figure 4.2).

From now on, even large increases in age-specific participation rates can have only modest impacts on the overall participation rate in the next forty years and therefore on economic growth.[21] Since the most important determinant of the aggregate participation rate over the next forty years will be the ageing of the population, the Productivity Commission considers that plausible increases in participation rates 'do not greatly alter the picture that emerges'.[22] If Australia were to achieve close to world's best practice in overall participation rates – resembling the Scandinavian experience – the aggregate participation rate would still be less than 60 per cent by the mid-2040s, mitigating the effects of ageing by around half.[23]

Though policies to lift workforce participation cannot be the dominant feature of any plan to cushion the economic impacts of population ageing, they can nevertheless play a valuable role. Chapter 9 discusses these policies.

THE THIRD P – PRODUCTIVITY

Much of the heavy lifting in sustaining and increasing Australia's future prosperity will need to be done by productivity growth. Yet the slump in Australia's productivity growth from 2005 assumed in the *Intergenerational Report* would cause cumulative real GDP over the coming forty years to be $4200 *billion* less than it would have been if Australia had been able to maintain the 'miracle' annual productivity growth achieved during the 1990s.[24]

Imagine what a productivity bonus of $4200 billion could do in ensuring that every young Australian had access to an excellent education, and that all Australians could afford quality health care. Imagine the crime that could be prevented by giving disadvantaged young people a flying start in life through early intervention programs. Imagine the boost we could give to the health and life chances of indigenous children. Imagine the dignity and respect we could show to older Australians by guaranteeing a quality life experience in their later years. Imagine the repair work we could do on the Australian environment, and the further damage we could prevent.

The Australian people will accept the creation of better opportunities for the disadvantaged out of economic growth, but not out of stagnation. And economic reforms are much more easily achieved out of a growing economy than out of one that is stagnant. Any viable economic reform program must be unashamedly pro-growth, while being socially and ecologically sustainable.

Australian governments must do everything possible to prevent productivity growth from slipping back from the high rates achieved during the 1990s.

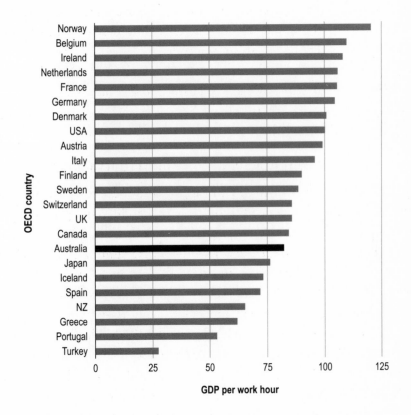

FIGURE 4.3
SOURCE Productivity Commission (2004b, p.151); GGDC (2004).

But how realistic is it to expect Australia to maintain strong productivity growth? Part of the answer lies in a comparison of Australia's *level* of productivity with those of other advanced countries. Although Australia's productivity *growth rate* since the early 1990s has been impressive by international standards, we have not attained the levels of many other countries.

Figure 4.3 shows that Australia ranks below 15 OECD countries in the productivity stakes. If Australia were to achieve, say, US productivity levels, which are still below those of seven other countries, average Australian household income would rise by around 20 per cent.[25]

Can Australia achieve US productivity levels? Most of the gap between Australian and US productivity levels can be explained by Australia's lower level of educational attainment and by its remoteness from world centres of economic activity.[26] Almost two-fifths of the gap can be explained by our remoteness.[27] Figure 4.3 points to the problems of distance in the information age. The countries with higher productivity levels than Australia are geographically much closer to each other than Australia is to them. A major study has found that the spillover benefits of technology decline with distance, and estimates that the distance at which they are halved is about 1200 kilometres.[28]

These difficulties highlight the challenge facing Australia in overcoming the handicap of its geographic isolation by investing in its own innovative ideas. Openness to trade can help offset isolation, and it is in Australia's interests for us to be an open trading nation. And as the development of China and India progresses through the twenty-first century, Australia will be better placed geographically than it was in the twentieth century. China is projected to surpass the United States as the world's largest economy by around 2015, and India is likely to become the world's third largest economy at around the same time, resuming a position of dominance of the world economy that they occupied for the period of recorded human history until the early eighteenth century.[29] The emergence of

China, India and other big Asian economies presents both challenges and opportunities for Australia. Chapters 7 and 12 discuss some of them.

OVERALL WELLBEING

No one believes GDP per person is a perfect measure of people's happiness. Some say money isn't everything – it's the only thing. But most people value relationships, a sense of belonging, security and a clean environment. A growing body of international research is revealing some surprising influences on human happiness. People seem to enjoy striving for a goal, but are not especially happy once they achieve it. One of the seven deadly sins – envy – is deeply entrenched in our psyche: when a colleague moves up the pecking order we tend to be unhappy about it. Keeping up with the Joneses is very important to us.

Australian research confirms overseas findings that the links between life satisfaction and income and wealth are quite weak.[30] Of course, the links are strong at very low income levels; but once a country's income per person exceeds about $US15 000 a year, the satisfaction derived from extra income falls away quite sharply.[31] In the United States, in a period when GDP per person has trebled, measured satisfaction has not changed. Similar results have been found in other developed countries.[32]

Before committing to a plan for Australia to increase GDP per person, we need to ask why higher levels of income do not necessarily make us happier:

> Why is it that the acquisition of income does so little to increase our satisfaction? ... We get a promotion, move into a better house or buy a new car and, for a while, we really feel better off. But all too soon we adapt to our new circumstances and absorb them into the status quo ... The second part of the explanation is rivalry ... we are highly social animals, obsessed by what those around us think of us and what we think of them. Remember Gore Vidal's remark: when I see a friend succeed a little part of me dies.[33]

By international standards Australians have high levels of measured wellbeing, recording an average score of 77 on a 1–100 scale.[34] People value job security highly. Worry about losing a job is more damaging to personal wellbeing than worry about balancing work and family life.[35] The plan to boost regional Australia seems to be on the right track. The highest levels of personal wellbeing are experienced in rural towns, greater than in the capital cities and in remote areas. And yet average incomes in these regional areas are lower than in the big cities and in remote areas.[36]

A Wellbeing Manifesto has been put together by the Australia Institute. It seeks to capture the non-monetary benefits that go into making us happier.[37] The Manifesto calls on us to provide fulfilling work, reclaim our time, protect the environment, rethink education, invest in early childhood, discourage materialism and promote responsible advertising, build communities and relationships, promote a fairer society, and measure what matters, not just GDP. The plan for Australia set out in this book is designed to improve not just GDP per person but overall wellbeing, including many of the attributes identified in the Wellbeing Manifesto.

CHAPTER 5

A NEW WAVE OF REFORM

SECURING THE NEXT ROUND OF PRODUCTIVITY GROWTH

How can Australia maintain the 'miracle' productivity growth of the 1990s so essential in combating the effects of population ageing?

Productivity cannot grow in an economy marked by episodes of high inflation, high unemployment and big, persistent deficits with the rest of the world. A stable economic environment is necessary for nurturing productivity growth. Chapter 15 sets out the elements of a sound macroeconomic policy for Australia. But having a stable economic environment does not of itself guarantee productivity growth. We cannot rely again on the main sources of Australia's record-breaking decade of productivity growth. Having opened the door to global and local competition, we cannot open the same door again. The economic reform program of the 1980s and early 1990s got rid of most of the inefficiencies in the economy. It's pretty lean now. A major OECD study finds that there are diminishing catch-up possibilities as countries continue along the economic development path.[1] A country at the early stages of development can gain a lot from using the technologies of more developed countries and from implementing economic reforms that make the economy more efficient. At some point, however, the catch-up possibilities begin to diminish, and the country needs to look at new sources of productivity growth. This is the present Australian story.

Keeping the door open is essential to Australia's future productivity growth, and it should be pushed wider where possible. But the biggest potential gains in productivity must come from new sources of productivity growth: intellect, ideas and infrastructure.

KEEPING THE DOOR OPEN, AND PUSHING IT WIDER

FOREIGN TRADE LIBERALISATION

Australia now has one of the most open economies in the world, thanks mainly to the trade-liberalising policies of the Hawke and Keating governments. Most of our tariff protection has been dismantled, and the few remaining tariffs are being phased out. Quantitative restrictions have been removed.

As a result, the *trade intensity* of the Australian economy – defined as exports plus imports as a proportion of GDP – increased sharply from around 27 per cent in the mid-1980s to 44 per cent in the early 2000s. But by 2005 trade intensity had slipped back to just over 40 per cent, at a time when high mineral prices should have driven it higher. This is a terrible indictment of Australia's export performance in the early years of the twenty-first century.

Trade liberalisation is estimated to have lifted Australia's annual economic growth per person by three-quarters of a percentage point.[2] In the context of annual growth per person of around two percentage points in the early 2000s, this is a very big contribution.

Government policy can influence export *volumes*, but it cannot normally set export *prices*, since these are determined globally. Australia's performance in export volume terms in the 2000s has been so poor that the current account deficit is the worst in fifty years, despite some of the best export prices in thirty years.

The previous government consciously sought to diversify Australia's exports to reduce the country's reliance on primary commodity exports. That policy, involving support for industry to refocus from the small domestic market to global export markets, the promotion of services exports, and international trade diplomacy into the rapidly growing East Asian market, succeeded in sharply lifting Australia's exports of sophisticated manufactured goods and services (see figure 5.1). But policy complacency has contributed to a sharp deterioration in the growth of these exports since 2000.

The government has blamed external circumstances such as international terrorism, a global economic slowdown, SARS and bird flu virus in seeking to excuse Australia's poor export performance in the 2000s. But these factors should not adversely affect Australia's market *share* in various trading regions. Yet since 1996 Australia has lost market share in East Asia (including China), Europe and the world as a whole. Australia contributes

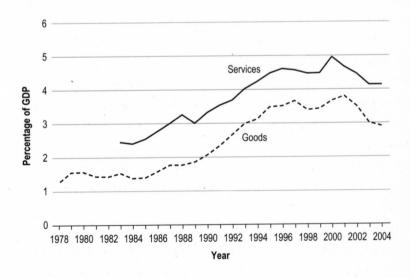

FIGURE 5.1 AUSTRALIA'S EXPORTS OF SOPHISTICATED GOODS AND SERVICES, 1978–2004

less than 1 per cent of world exports, our lowest market share in more than half a century. Australia's declining share of world export markets indicates a failure of trade policy. Chapter 12 sets out a new trade and foreign investment policy for Australia.

FURTHER REFORM OF GOODS AND SERVICES MARKETS

Although most parts of the Australian economy now run efficiently, there is plenty of room for improvement in the delivery of health and aged-care services, education, and training and infrastructure.[3] Chapter 6 considers health and aged-care policy, chapter 7 examines education and training policies, and chapter 11 looks at infrastructure issues.

FURTHER LABOUR MARKET DEREGULATION

The Coalition government claims that the key to future productivity growth is further labour market deregulation.[4] It has legislated for the virtual dismantling of the Australian Industrial Relations Commission, the establishment of a new body to set the minimum wage, the promotion of individual contracts in preference to collective agreements and the effective removal of unfair dismissal laws. Over time, just five minimum conditions of work will replace the system of awards.

These changes will result in one of the most deregulated labour markets in the developed world. But who says an almost completely deregulated labour market is the best for the country? Surely not all regulation is bad. For example, in product markets there is not much point in buying and selling goods and services if you can steal them. So regulations are put in place through legislation to establish property rights. These regulations are needed for the efficient functioning of markets. And to encourage innovation, intellectual property is protected for specified periods so that others cannot simply copy the invention or breakthrough.

In the labour market, most of the productivity-stifling restrictive work practices of the 1970s and 1980s were removed through enterprise bargaining and award modernisation initiated by the Labor government and continued under the Coalition. Those who argue that further labour market deregulation is the key to the next round of productivity growth should identify the restrictive work practices that are retarding this growth.

Highly skilled professionals will not be affected by the government's deregulatory agenda, since they have never relied on this sort of regulation. They establish their pay and working conditions individually, comfortably relying for their bargaining power on the market value of the skills they have to offer.

But low paid workers rely variously on the minimum wage, awards and the enhanced bargaining power of collective bargaining. The government's deregulatory agenda is directed at them – at the setting of the minimum wage, the award system and collective bargaining.

Since 1996 employees have not been able to choose their representative in negotiations; the employer has a right of veto over collective bargaining and representation by unions. A right that can be vetoed is no right at all. Imagine how a business would react if employees were legally able to veto its chosen representative in enterprise bargaining. The inability of working Australians to choose collective bargaining sets us apart from most countries of the western world, many of them with much higher productivity levels than Australia – including Finland, Sweden, Belgium and Austria.

No one has been able to demonstrate beyond mere assertion that abolishing unfair dismissal laws or expanding the use of Australian workplace agreements (AWAs) will unleash big productivity gains.

The Treasurer refers to an OECD survey about the possible employment impacts of unfair dismissal laws in Australia and asserts that it shows that the abolition of unfair dismissal laws for small business would create 77 000 jobs.[5] In truth, the OECD finds that Australia's system of protection against unfair dismissal is one of the least strict of all OECD countries.[6]

An OECD analysis of employment protection legislation concludes that 'a reasonable degree of employment protection legislation could be welfare-improving'.[7] The OECD advocates reasonable employment protection legislation in combination with a modest system of redundancy payments and effective re-employment services, arguing that this policy combination contributes to an efficient labour market.[8] And since the OECD finds that Australia's employment protection system is one of the least strict among OECD countries, and concludes that there are net economic and social benefits from moderate employment protection legislation, the government cannot be said to have established a credible case for abolishing unfair dismissal laws.

Rather, there is a case for streamlining the unfair dismissal procedures for small business (including by removing unscrupulous ambulance-chasers from the system). In the absence of a streamlined system operating like a small claims court, disgruntled employees will seek remedies through the much more protracted unlawful dismissal and anti-discrimination procedures, at potentially much greater cost to employers.

As for the spreading of AWAs throughout the workforce, there is already a market for competing contractual arrangements covering workplace relations in Australia. More than 75 per cent have chosen collective agreements and common law contracts. Another 20 per cent have engaged in employment under the award system, leaving only three or four per cent on AWAs.

If contemporary awards were as rigid and outmoded as the government asserts, many more employers and employees would be opting for AWAs to boost workplace productivity and take-home pay. Long-time advocates of labour market deregulation, like Professor Mark Wooden, have concluded that the government's agenda goes too far:

But what if AWAs are not desired by workers? Currently, there do not appear to be measures that ensure that workers have the ability to choose between individual contracts and collective agreements. If the aim is to provide employees with real choices, then I am on Greg Combet's side – the right to bargain collectively needs to be protected. Further, the government should have a vested interest in ensuring collective bargaining continues to flourish if it believes, as it has stated so often in the past, that enterprise bargaining has been fundamental to the productivity gains of the 1990s.[9]

In pursuing further labour market reform there will always be some scope for ongoing modernisation and simplification of awards. But if awards are to reflect the realities of modern workplaces, this is best done by the relevant parties rather than by prescriptive government legislation. Further modernisation and simplification of awards could be a productive exercise all round, and is well worth pursuing.

As Saul Eslake points out, there is no obvious correlation between the degree of centralisation of wage-setting arrangements and employment growth in OECD countries over the past decade.[10] If sensible proposals for labour market reform are advanced they should be assessed rigorously for their productivity-raising potential. But further labour market deregulation is being used as a diversion from the more challenging task of identifying and supporting new sources of productivity growth.

Sustained productivity growth is best generated in harmonious workplaces. It is created by combining work, initiative, ideas, technology, physical capital and risk-taking. Increases in real wages over the last decade or so have, fundamentally, been caused by the record productivity growth unleashed by the economic reform program of the Hawke and Keating governments in a moderately regulated labour market.

The view that more and more labour market deregulation is good for Australia is grounded in an employer-based ideology and an orthodox economic theory that precedes the rise of behavioural economics pioneered by Nobel Prize winner Daniel Kahneman. One of the policy implications of behavioural economics is that:

> governments and employers could do a lot to raise subjective well-being if they put more emphasis on the enrichment of jobs – increasing job satisfaction by giving workers more personal control, opportunity to use their skills, variety in tasks, respect and status, and contact with others. Taken literally, the economists' model assumes that all work is unpleasant – a disutility – and is undertaken purely to gain the money to buy the things that bring utility. Like the rest of us, economists know that, in reality, work carries much intrinsic satisfaction ... various ways in which labour can be used more efficiently make life unpleasant and even unhealthy for the workers involved: ever changing casual hours, rolling shift work, split shifts and firms continually moving their staff to different cities. When we pursue efficiency at the expense of people, economists have got things around the wrong way, trashing ends so as to advance means.[11]

For more than a century working Australians have taken their rewards from increased labour productivity partly in the form of improved working conditions. There is nothing wrong with this. The purpose of lifting productivity is to improve wellbeing, and much of that improvement comes in the quality of work. The government's deregulatory agenda is not designed to remove (unspecified) artificial obstacles to working people improving their wellbeing; it is to give employers greater freedom and flexibility in the way they deal with their workforce.

It is hard to sustain an argument that real wages need to fall at the bottom end. Seeking to cut real wages is precisely the wrong policy response in a tightening labour market with acute skill shortages emerging in many areas. This is no temporary situation: working-age Australians will continue to be in short supply as our population ages over the coming decades.

In arguing for the effective complete deregulation of the

labour market for low-skilled Australians, some business organisations want any pursuit of fairness to be undertaken through the
government's income-support system. They refuse to recognise or
acknowledge that lower real wages supplemented by taxpayer-
funded income-support payments must involve ever increasing
taxes. Since taxes are a form of regulation that has deterrent
effects on work, savings and investment decisions, a generous
interpretation of their policy position is that they want to substi-
tute one form of regulation for another.

The disincentive effects (deadweight losses) associated with
income tax are estimated at 20 to 30 cents for every dollar of tax
collected[12] – a costly form of regulation indeed. Lowering the real
minimum wage and supplementing it with government cash benefits is an argument for a continued expansion of the welfare state.
This is hardly desirable from the perspective of private incentive.
An ever expanding welfare state to fund income-support payments
for low-paid workers is a costly race to the bottom, seeking to
compete with the countries of Asia on the basis of low skills and
low wages.[13] In the twenty-first century Australia should instead be
engaged in a race to the top, competing on the basis of embodying
high levels of intellect and ideas in its products and services.

NEW SOURCES OF PRODUCTIVITY GROWTH

Extensive international research has been conducted into the
modern sources of productivity growth. The most influential work
has been done by the OECD, which identifies skills formation and
R&D effort as huge contributors to productivity growth.[14]

SKILLS DEVELOPMENT

Skills are developed through school education, higher education,
training and lifelong learning. The international evidence is that
skills development is easily the most powerful source of ongoing
productivity growth.

Orthodox economic growth theories make a nation's income dependent on its endowments of capital and labour. Both capital and labour are assumed to display what is called *diminishing returns*. This means that as more and more capital and labour are applied in production processes, beyond a certain point the extra output they yield declines. It follows from the law of diminishing returns that extra amounts of capital or labour can achieve a permanent lift in economic output over time, but not ongoing growth in output.

New growth theory, pioneered by Romer,[15] suggests that knowledge has special characteristics that mean the constraints of diminishing returns may not apply. Two types of knowledge are identified: *embodied* and *disembodied* knowledge.

Embodied knowledge is the acquisition of *skills*, which are embodied in particular people and die with them. Disembodied knowledge is the development of *ideas*, which can exist forever.

Disembodied knowledge – ideas – has three properties that make it especially valuable. First, one person's use of ideas does not detract from another's use. This is called *non-rivalry*. It differs from physical capital, where one person's use of a piece of equipment prevents another person from using it at the same time.

The second attribute of ideas is that their originator cannot fully prevent others from using them. This is called *non-excludability*. It differs from physical capital, where the owner of a piece of equipment has property rights that can prevent another person from using it.

The third attribute of ideas is that they are not subject to the law of diminishing returns. There is no limit to the number of potentially productive ideas. Indeed, as the total amount of public knowledge grows, researchers have an ever broader field in which to make new discoveries. This *positive feedback* on the level of knowledge from new ideas is what Isaac Newton was referring to when he said: 'If I have seen farther than others it is because I was standing on the shoulders of giants'.

A defining characteristic of modern science is this attribute of building on the achievements of others.[16] A modern version of Newton's view is provided by former US Federal Reserve Board Chairman Alan Greenspan:

> Over the past half century, the increase in the value of raw materials has accounted for only a fraction of the overall growth of US gross domestic product. The rest of that growth reflects the embodiment of ideas in products and services that consumers value. This shift of emphasis from physical material to ideas as the core of value creation appears to have accelerated in recent decades ... Ideas are the centre of productivity growth.[17]

The first and third attributes of ideas – non-rivalry and non-diminishing returns – give them the capacity to contribute to economic growth on an ongoing basis. Not only can investment in new ideas raise economic output to a new *level*, it can keep *growth* going indefinitely. That is, investing in new ideas can have both a *level effect* and a *growth effect*. In contrast, investment in skills has only a *level effect*.

This doesn't mean that investing in skills is less desirable than investing in ideas. Investing in skills favourably affects the rate at which new ideas are generated, and the ability of a country to absorb and adapt new technologies. It also favourably affects the rate at which new ideas are successfully introduced into workplaces:

> the human capital created through education is not only a productive input which directly raises productivity, it also plays a crucial role in the development and adoption of new technologies that drive long run growth.[18]

International research done by Deutsche Bank 'supports the view that human capital is the most important factor of production in today's economies'.[19]

And a new body of research, pioneered by Richard Florida,[20] points to creativity as *the* decisive source of regional competitive advantage. The research finds that places that succeed in attracting creative people prosper, while those that fail to do so languish. Chapter 7 advocates policies for developing the creative talents of Australians, and chapter 10 sets out policies for attracting creative people to Australia.

INVESTING IN TALENT IN SCHOOLS

Research into the experience of OECD countries suggests that a one year increase in the average level of schooling would, over time, increase the *level* of a country's GDP by 6 per cent.[21] For Australia, the estimate is an 8 per cent increase in GDP.[22] It would take forty years for the full 8 per cent increase in GDP to be achieved (as better educated young people enter the workforce between the ages of 16 and 20, and leave it at the age of 60). This implies an average increase in GDP of 0.2 per cent per annum over the forty-year period. And an increase of one year in the average level of schooling would permanently boost GDP growth by an estimated 0.5 percentage points per annum.[23] These are very powerful effects – the best investment Australia could make.

RESEARCH AND DEVELOPMENT

Should investment in ideas be public or private investment? And should Australia be a global free-rider, utilising the technologies developed out of R&D performed abroad without having to make the massive and risky investments needed to develop them? Fortunately there are answers to both these important questions.

The second feature of ideas – non-excludability – means that a business investing in R&D cannot capture for itself the full benefits of that investment. Other businesses, and parts of the community, gain some of the benefits that spill over to them. The reason is that the system of property rights does not, and is not designed to, forever protect one hundred per cent of the intellectual property generated by an R&D investment. Patents do not last forever, copies are made, and adaptations are made to the original breakthrough.

This characteristic of R&D causes the private sector to under-provide it. There is a role for governments to support R&D to remedy this market failure. Economy-wide studies of the social returns to investment in R&D consistently find returns above 50 per cent; usually in the 50 to 60 per cent range.[24] For smaller countries like Australia, the social returns to R&D are found to be even greater, in the order of 85 per cent.

These studies do not distinguish between private and public R&D. Authors of some earlier studies suggested that publicly funded R&D might crowd out private R&D; for example, by drawing scientists and engineers away from private research facilities. But more recent investigations across 17 OECD countries suggest that government funding stimulates private R&D where the publicly funded research is contracted to the private sector, but partially crowds out private R&D when it is carried out in government laboratories. University research is found *not* to crowd out private R&D.[25]

Less aggregated studies identify important spillover benefits from publicly funded research to smaller firms that locate close to public research institutions.[26] These location benefits are weaker for larger firms that have their own research facilities.

The conclusion from these international studies is that public sector R&D contributes significantly to productivity growth, though less strongly than private sector R&D.[27]

INVESTMENT IN INFRASTRUCTURE

The *non-excludability* of ideas that causes the private sector to under-invest in R&D can also apply to particular types of infrastructure. Just as the originator of a new idea cannot fully prevent others from using it, a private investor in a piece of infrastructure might not feasibly be able fully to prevent others from using it. Full enforcement of the investor's property rights might be prohibitively costly, or physically impossible. For example, it would be impractical for the private sector to build and own all suburban roads; charging users and excluding non-payers would not be feasible.

Some forms of infrastructure share a second feature with ideas – *non-rivalry*. For example, the use of radio waves by one receiver does not restrict access by others.

These two attributes of infrastructure provide an economic justification for public investment in particular types of infrastructure. Like skills and ideas, infrastructure is capable of producing benefits that cannot be fully captured by a private provider. From society's viewpoint the private sector, left to its own profit-maximising devices, will under-provide infrastructure that yields these positive spillover benefits.

International empirical evidence attests to the large economy-wide returns from public investment in infrastructure. National rates of return on infrastructure investment in the order of 60 per cent are common, and Australian empirical evidence is consistent with the international evidence.[28] The evidence confirms significant positive spillovers in the core infrastructure areas of roads and water where excludability is difficult to achieve, making them approximate the features of public goods. The spillover effects from electricity supply are much weaker, since excludability is more feasible, making it approximate the features of private goods.[29]

The trouble in Australia is that it is precisely in the areas of transport and water – where the spillover effects are greatest – that public investment has been allowed to decline:

> These areas of the core infrastructure are precisely those where economic theory predicts the greatest need for public intervention and where the econometric evidence shows that substantial benefits will not only accrue directly to households but will also spill over to enhance the productivity of the private sector.[30]

Chapter 11 lays the foundations for an infrastructure plan for Australia.

CHAPTER 6

BEYOND PUBLIC VERSUS PRIVATE IN HEALTH AND AGED CARE

HEALTH AND AGED CARE IN A FAIR SOCIETY

A fair society provides quality health and aged care to all its citizens regardless of their financial capacity. Health care is a core government responsibility. Universality is a term commonly associated with health care. But what does it mean? Universality has in the past meant that all citizens are covered by public health insurance – nobody is left out in the cold, uninsured, to worry about how to pay for their health care if they get sick. More recently, universality has carried with it an expectation that all citizens – including the very wealthy – are entitled to free health care, including access to bulk-billed GP services. Confronted with an ageing population, we must reassess the sustainability of the health and aged-care systems, moving beyond the public versus private debate to ensure the delivery of quality health and aged-care services through a combination of public and private funds.

It is in the areas of health and aged care that the greatest strains on public finances will be felt in the coming decades. Government health spending as a share of GDP is projected to almost double over the next forty years, from just under 6 per cent to more than 10 per cent, while government spending on aged care is projected to more than double.[1] The number of older Australians in high-care residential aged care alone is projected to increase from less than 100 000 in 2003 to 337 000 in forty years' time.[2]

These official projections imply substantial increases in the income tax burden on those working Australians who will be expected to earn the incomes to pay the public health and aged-care bills of older Australians. But if the nation is to sustain and increase prosperity we will not be able to afford punitive income tax burdens on working Australians, since heavy tax obligations would reduce workforce participation, making the whole system unsustainable. We need to work out how to get more private money into the health and aged-care systems in a way that allows governments to meet their obligations to ensure affordable, quality health and aged care for all.

AUSTRALIA'S MIXED SYSTEM

Australia has a mixed system of universal public health insurance through Medicare supplemented by private health insurance, and a hospital system that caters for private and public patients. Around 57 per cent of Australians rely on the public health system, and 43 per cent are privately insured.[3] These figures understate usage of the public system, since many privately insured people use the public system for major surgery and to avoid having to make gap payments.

The public system, through Medicare, provides quality health care to all who need it. It is funded by general taxation revenue, which includes a separately identified Medicare levy that partially funds health spending. Private health insurance premiums are subsidised through the private health insurance rebate, set at 30 per cent for the general population and rising to 40 per cent for older Australians.

Private health insurance is only partly market-based. Though premiums are set at higher levels as the age of entry rises, and the insurer can refuse to insure against some pre-existing ailments,

BOX 6.1　THE EVOLUTION OF AGED CARE

During the last decade or so, formal aged care has evolved away from a system of hostels and separate nursing homes.

In the past, hostels were essentially a type of secured accommodation, without offering much in the way of aged care. These days retirement villages and independent-living units provide this sort of accommodation, and residents are likely to receive community-based care. And in place of nursing homes are low-care and high-care residential facilities, typically located on the same site. The movement from low care to high care is therefore usually a movement from one building to another on the same site, or even from one room to another.

discrimination according to health status is otherwise not permitted.

Australia's aged-care system is also a mixed system. The three main categories of formal aged care are community care, low-care residential (formerly known as hostels) and high-care residential (what used to be called nursing homes).

The Commonwealth provides around three-quarters of total funds, the remainder coming from aged-care residents. Two types of charges are applied in residential aged-care facilities: *accommodation payments* and *daily care fees*. Accommodation payments are designed to help provide a stream of capital for operators to build and maintain aged-care facilities. Daily care fees are a contribution to running costs.

Accommodation payments can take the form of deposits (bonds) for low-care places, but not for high-care places. A lump sum is deposited, and part of the capital amount and the income stream from the deposit is used by the provider for the upkeep of buildings, renovations, extensions or full rebuilding. When the resident leaves the aged-care service the balance of the deposit is refunded. Accommodation deposits can only be levied on residents who have assets valued at more than $30 000. The average accommodation deposit in mid-2004 was around $112 000.

In high-care residential facilities, where accommodation deposits are prohibited, accommodation charges apply. But the maximum accommodation charge is just $16.25 a day.

There are two types of daily fees: a basic fee and an income-tested fee. The maximum basic fee for pensioners is $27.86 a day; for non-pensioners it is $34.76 a day. The maximum income-tested fee is $21.27 a day for part-pensioners; for non-pensioners it is $48.82 a day. The highest possible daily care fee is therefore $83.58 ($34.76 plus $48.82) a day.

An innovation in residential aged care has been the creation of what are described as extra-service places. They provide not a higher level of care but a higher level of service, with additions such as extra menu choices, hairdressing and more outings. A daily fee is charged for these extra services. Accommodation deposits can be used for extra-service places in high-care residential facilities.

Extra-service places are more likely to be available in affluent and inner city locations.

The total number of extra-service places cannot exceed 15 per cent of all places in each state and territory. At mid-2004 less than 5 per cent of places were extra-service places.

Since operators of extra-service places receive extra fees from residents, the Commonwealth puts in less money for them than for conventional places.

RATIONING HEALTH AND AGED CARE

When the demand for health and aged care services is greater than the available supply they will be rationed one way or another: through prices or queues. Despite the gradual introduction of price signals in parts of the Australian health system, a fee-for-service philosophy still dominates. A provider who receives a fee for each service provided has an incentive to provide more services to earn more fees. And medical practitioners worried about the risk of litigation will tend to over-provide diagnostic and related services to protect themselves.

A user of health services who makes no financial contribution (co-payment) when obtaining that service has no financial disincentive against using more services. To illustrate, the number of medical services per Australian is more than 50 per cent greater than in the year before Medicare became operational, and it is unlikely that public health has improved commensurately.[4]

Where price is not used to help ration health and aged-care services, queues will form. They form as waiting lists for GPs, elective surgery, hospital emergency department treatment and high-care residential accommodation:

> even among many supporters of Medicare, there is a concern that a universal system of public health that is funded by taxpayers can only be sustained financially if there are better incentives to economise than at present ... Too often governments have felt forced to respond to excessive demand pressures by rationing access in a way that has led to unsatisfactory queuing and a decline in quality, both of which are also unsustainable.[5]

Those queues are *not* occupied by the wealthy. Wealthy people do not wait around in hospital emergency departments. Instead they go to a doctor and pay an up-front fee or, in an emergency, they pay for a doctor to come to their homes. Wealthy people pay private health insurance so that they do not have to join public hospital waiting lists. Wealthy people do not wait years for a high-care place. It is the poor who are disadvantaged by queues, not the wealthy.

A fair society should not be opposed to the use of properly designed prices in the health and aged-care systems, so long as their use is based on capacity to pay. Price signals, in the form of co-payments, already exist in the delivery of GP services, in hospital and medical services covered by private health insurance and in residential aged care. A GP who does not bulk bill a particular consultation is requiring a co-payment from the patient. A private health insurer who does not cover 100 per cent of the cost of a procedure is requiring a co-payment in the form of a gap payment. And an aged-care provider requiring a payment out of the age pension or an accommodation bond is seeking a co-payment from the resident.

Allowing, and encouraging, wealthier Australians to buy access to new, expensive health services is good for the general public, since it hastens the introduction of new services into Australia and contributes to bringing down the cost to the wider community.

We *must* insist that every Australian has a right to quality health and aged care. But we *must not* insist that where Australians want extra services they are always to be funded by taxpayers. Nor should we deny extra services to people who are prepared to pay for them. Wealthy baby boomers are approaching retirement, and a generation of younger Australians is enjoying unprecedented prosperity. Where they can make a contribution to the provision of these additional services, they should be encouraged to do so.

THE NEED FOR REFORM

When Labor came to office in 1983, almost two million Australians had no health insurance cover. The Fraser government had dismantled Medibank, and in its place introduced seven major health insurance policy variations in seven years.

Prime Minister John Howard favours a return to the pre-Medibank era when Australia did not have a universal health insurance system:

> I thought we had a very good system in the very early 1970s before there were some major changes made that I don't think made it better; I think it made it worse.[6]

But Australia has one of the best health systems in the world. It is not fundamentally flawed, though it does contain inefficiencies and inequities that are not sustainable in the face of an ageing population.

And yet population ageing is not the only – or even the main – driver of rising health spending.[7] As incomes rise, people understandably choose to spend more on their health to improve the quality of their lives. They want access to marvellous but expensive medical technologies that improve quality of life, save lives and extend lives. Since the old spend much more on their health than the young, the ageing of the population compounds the costs associated with better quality health care.

It has been argued that older people are likely to be healthier in the future, so that, although there will be more older people, they will not make a much greater call on funds than the present generation of older people.[8] This debate will be ongoing, and will not be easily resolved. The Productivity Commission considers that the ageing of the population, combined with rising health spending out of rising incomes, will greatly increase the proportion of the nation's income allocated to health and aged care over the coming decades:

> In sum, neither the possibility of a healthier older population in the future, nor evidence that costs are higher at the end of life, undermine the proposition that ageing of the population will place much greater pressure on health expenditure.[9]

The *Intergenerational Report* reaches similar conclusions. Even if the ageing optimists turned out to be partly right, it would be imprudent of governments to assume the best and maintain current inefficiencies and inequities in the health and aged-care systems.

In meeting the twin challenges of an ageing population and expensive new medical technologies, governments will need to rebalance the sharing of risks in the Australian health and aged-care systems. Responsibility for health and aged care must be shared between the community (through taxpayer-funded services) and the individual (through private contributions). Shifting the balance of risks towards personal responsibility is more acceptable in areas of genuine choice than in non-discretionary services. A system of shared responsibility would help ensure the long-term sustainability of Australia's health and aged-care systems.

Costly inefficiencies in the health and aged-care system also arise from the different responsibilities of the Commonwealth and the states for health and aged care. Hospitals are funded by the states, assisted by a predetermined amount of block funding from the Commonwealth. Aged care is funded by the Commonwealth. These split funding responsibilities create powerful incentives for cost-shifting; that is, one level of government pushing patients into the other level's area of funding responsibility. A prime example of cost-shifting is the rationing of aged-care places by the Commonwealth that causes elderly patients to be kept in expensive hospital beds instead of much less expensive aged-care beds.[10]

REFORMING THE HEALTH-CARE SYSTEM

POOLED FUNDING ARRANGEMENTS

In early 2005, federal health minister Tony Abbott invited the states to hand over responsibility for hospitals to the Commonwealth.[11] Soon afterwards the NSW premier made similar proposals. But the prime minister vetoed the idea. A Commonwealth government would not want to take on responsibility for all health and aged-care funding (even with the appropriate reductions in grants to the states), since it would then bear all the political opprobrium resulting from strains on the health system. Why would the Commonwealth want to take responsibility for public hospital waiting lists? The Commonwealth taking on responsibility for hospitals is not a feasible solution to the problem of cost-shifting between the two levels of government.

An alternative is a pooled funding arrangement involving the Commonwealth and the states. The federal health minister has alleged that pooled funding is part of a dangerous Labor agenda, describing it as a 'bureaucratic behemoth'.[12] Yet a series of pooled funding trials was conducted by the Howard government for a time from 1997. The trials suffered from a number of deficiencies, including a lack of financial incentives for cost efficiencies, heavy reliance on GPs for coordination, exclusion of vital services such as high-care residential accommodation, and small population sizes (less than 2500). Still, they demonstrated that Commonwealth–state pooled funding cooperation was possible. And, encouragingly, the trials for Aboriginal and Torres Strait Island people were among the more successful.[13]

One of the architects of Medicare, Richard Scotton, has floated a radical pooled funding proposal in which all relevant government programs are amalgamated into a single pool and allocated to competing budget holders who would purchase services from competing suppliers to cover all patients (not just the profitable ones). Every citizen would have a choice of budget holder. The budget holders would compete with each other on the range and quality of services provided, negotiating with competing suppliers for the best deal.

A somewhat more realistic proposal has been developed by the Allen Consulting Group, and advanced by Victorian premier Steve Bracks.[14] It is based on the US managed-care organisation, Kaiser Permanente, which aims to provide 'the right care in the right place at the right time' and integrates funding, patient care and prevention. In this model all doctors share a single budget; they design and manage services, and seek to avoid costly hospital services in favour of prevention and early detection. Patients are treated in multi-disciplinary health centres, with access to prevention services, GPs, nurses, diagnostic services and pharmacists. Patients move readily between hospitals, rehabilitation units and home and community care without having to navigate a maze of different agencies. At the heart of modern pooled funding systems like Kaiser Permanente is a strong emphasis on prevention and early detection.

An Australian version of Kaiser Permanente would be a system of regional health authorities, overseen by a joint Commonwealth–state funding body and providing integrated health and aged-care services. Each authority would have a mandate to purchase all health services for its defined population, negotiating performance-based contracts with health providers. Budgets would be allocated to each regional health authority on the basis of the health profile of its residents, adjusting for age, sex, socioeconomic status and location. Regional health authorities with a higher proportion of high-need residents would get bigger budgets. The budget-limited health authorities would have incentives for relatively low-cost prevention and early detection, and the most cost-effective accommodation of patients.[15] It has been suggested that the optimal number of regional health authorities for Australia might be between 18 and 30.[16]

As a first step, funding could be pooled for the provision of primary health care, involving health promotion, early detection and disease management. The Commonwealth and states could pool their primary health-care funds to develop local health promotion plans, administered by local GPs, community health centres and hospitals. More generally:

> The options for health reform invariably involve the pooling of funds to allow the rationalisation of programs and the introduction of some form of managed competition. This managed competition would seek to use market incentives to improve services and increase efficiency, but within a framework which maintains equity and universal access for health care services.[17]

But if large efficiencies are to be achieved while retaining equity, any pooled (or non-pooled) funding system should contain price signals for those with a capacity to pay. Most pooled funding models do not; although, importantly, the New Zealand pool-funded *primary health organisations* can charge co-payments for specific services. These organisations always include a GP, and can also include nurses, pharmacists, dieticians, mental health workers, community health workers and dentists. They cover almost half of New Zealand's population.

Pooled funding systems without price signals for patients can achieve efficiencies from avoiding cost-shifting between government jurisdictions and from emphasising prevention and early detection. But patients themselves will want the highest possible levels of service regardless of cost-effectiveness, since, for them, the service is free. Ultimately this will put extra pressure on government budgets or increase waiting lists or both. And, in the Australian context, doctors and their representative body, the Australian Medical Association (AMA), will strongly object to any suggestion of being on the government payroll.

A pooled funding system without appropriate price signals is not the best response to the challenge of adapting Australia's health system to the realities of population ageing and rising costs associated with advances in medical technologies.

MEDICARE PLUS PRIVATE FUNDING

Medicare is popular, fair and, by world standards, an efficient and affordable health-care system. But those who champion Medicare need to acknowledge the challenges to its long-term sustainability in the face of population ageing and costly technological advances.

One model for strengthening Medicare while inserting more price signals for those who are able to pay is to build on the emergence of GP corporate groups in Australia. Around 15 per cent of all GPs in Australia have linked up with a corporate group. The corporate group provides management, administrative and clinical support services, including nursing and operations staff. In return, the GP typically contributes 30 to 40 per cent of billings to compensate the corporate group for management of the practice. Though this might seem a large amount, it allows the GP to practise medicine and not be bothered with financial and administrative matters.

GP corporate groups have grown up under Medicare. They offer the prospect of combining the best the private and public sectors have to offer – the coexistence of a high quality, publicly funded health and aged-care system with private sector arrangements for those willing and able to pay for extra services.

Under the proposed model, GP corporate groups would be encouraged – though not required – to provide a minimum range of primary-care services: GP services, pathology, radiology, hospital care and aged care. Many GP corporate groups already provide a number of these core services. This range of services would constitute a standard package.

The standard package could be supplemented by other services such as physiotherapy, occupational therapy, chiropractic and dental services, psychology and counselling as well as core services of higher quality than those provided in the standard package.

Medicare would underwrite the standard package. In addition, the Commonwealth dental service would be restored.

Extra services and higher quality services would be privately funded through patient co-payments and/or private health insurance. A patient entering a local GP surgery would be invited to sign up to the range of services offered by that GP's corporate group, including the option of taking out private health insurance for extra services. Providers of these integrated services would compete on both the quality and timeliness of services offered, and the range of available extra services funded by private health insurance.

GPs who wanted to stay outside of a corporate group would be free to do so, though they would inevitably be limited to offering a narrower range of services. But they might offer higher quality services and more personalised services over a more limited range, and be able to carve out for themselves a market niche in a particular location or a particular specialisation. Patients who prefer this type of service would be free to choose it.

A GP corporate service could offer the attraction of an integrated health and aged-care system by contracting with regional providers of the various health services. Patients would not have to make inquiries and decisions at each stage and for each type of health care. Once they signed up they would receive integrated health care in a system where there was a strong private incentive to achieve both quality care and efficiency. These networks would be ideally suited to deliver comprehensive disease management.

It would need to be decided whether the GP corporate groups should be funded through pooled funding arrangements on the basis of a risk-weighted assessment of their signed-up population, or through fee-for-service arrangements that include co-payments for those patients with a capacity to pay.

Preventative health care could be incorporated into this model of coordinated health care to reduce acute presentations and hospitalisations. Health promotion and prevention campaigns and medical research possess the features of public goods. They would continue to be provided, or subsidised, by the public sector.

BULK-BILLING

In a fair society no one should be denied access to a doctor. Those Australians who do not have the money to pay for a GP consultation should not be turned away or deterred from seeing a doctor when they or their families need medical attention. But Australians with ample capacity to pay for GP services do not expect to be bulk-billed; they are willing to pay for timely access to GP services.

It should not be a priority of governments to provide incentives for bulk-billing in affluent neighbourhoods. Any bulk-billing incentives should be directed to disadvantaged communities. This does not amount to the means-testing of Medicare. Better-off Australians who want to consult a bulk-billing doctor and are prepared to travel and wait to see one would be free to do so (though very few would).

THE ROLE OF PRIVATE HEALTH INSURANCE

Under the present hybrid system of health care, private health funds cover hospital services that are also available without charge in public hospitals. But they also cover services that are not publicly funded, such as dental, optical, chiropractic and podiatry services, some pharmaceuticals not subsidised by the pharmaceutical benefits scheme, and some preventative health services. And private funds can offer to cover the cost of medical gap payments. Consequently, private health insurance neither fully substitutes for nor fully complements the public system. Privately insured patients can and do use the public hospital system free of charge when it suits them. And why not? They pay for it through their taxes and the Medicare levy.

A more efficient system would be one in which private health insurance played a much more complementary role in relation to the public system.[18] Medicare would offer quality hospital care without charge for all Australians. Private health insurance would then provide a top-up of the public system for those who choose to purchase extra care in the form of better facilities, speedier elective surgery and services not covered under Medicare. In moving beyond the public versus private debate, governments should also have the flexibility of contracting Medicare-guaranteed free hospital care with private providers.

THE PRIVATE HEALTH INSURANCE REBATE

The federal government has introduced a set of incentives for Australians to take out private health insurance. These are a 30 per cent private health insurance rebate, rising to 40 per cent for older Australians; Lifetime Health Cover, which imposes an additional premium for those patients who fail to take out private health insurance until they are over 30; and an additional 1 per cent tax surcharge for middle and higher income earners who do not have private health insurance. Lifetime Health Cover was designed to prevent the 'hit and run' behaviour of people joining a private health fund when they anticipate the need for private hospital treatment, only to withdraw from the fund when the treatment had been completed.

The proportion of Australians with private health insurance has risen from a low of 30 per cent in 1998 to a peak of just under 46 per cent in 2000, falling back to 43 per cent in 2005. But the private health insurance rebate appears to have been, at best, only mildly successful in taking the pressure off public hospitals.[19] To avoid gap payments, a large number of patients with private health insurance choose to be admitted free to public hospitals as public patients. And private patients tend to prefer the public hospital system for complex and urgent procedures, using the private system for less complex and less urgent procedures.[20] Most of the increase in private health insurance appears to have been due to Lifetime Health Cover, not the private health insurance rebate.[21]

And it appears that most of those who claim the private health insurance rebate would have purchased private health insurance anyway.[22] It is estimated that two-thirds of single people who have private health insurance and more than 80 per cent of families with private health insurance would have taken it out regardless, without the incentive of the private health insurance rebate.[23] About 80 per cent of the wealthiest Australians have private health insurance while only about 25 per cent of the poorest have it,[24] supporting a conclusion that 'households with high income and socioeconomic standings are the main beneficiaries of the policy changes'.[25]

It is estimated that abolition of the private health insurance rebate would cause little change in the proportion of the population with private health insurance.[26] The rebate costs Australian taxpayers more than $2.5 billion a year. It is ineffective in achieving its stated goal of taking the pressure off the public hospital system. However, older Australians, especially, use and rely on it. And the rebate has been factored into the household budgets of many lower and middle-income Australians who, under Lifetime Health Cover, feel that they must have private health insurance. Given these circumstances the rebate should be retained, while acknowledging that, for wealthy Australians who would have taken out private health insurance anyway, it is a gift.

WORKFORCE ISSUES

One of the most pressing issues in Australia's system of health care is the shortage of medical professionals. Australia faces shortages of GPs, specialists, nurses, speech therapists, occupational therapists, physiotherapists, dentists and just about every other kind of medical professional. Governments need to rethink the role of nurses in administering primary health care. Are there not restrictive work practices that maintain doctor shortages in order to keep fees high? Couldn't nurses do some of the standard work that only GPs are permitted to do at present?

Maybe we should also consider the possibility of pharmacists being allowed to provide some of the routine services that GPs currently provide, in the prescription and repeat prescription of particular medicines.

These are controversial issues, but they need to be addressed in assuring the sustainability of Australia's health system.

REFORMING THE AGED-CARE SYSTEM

Australia already suffers a shortage of high-care residential accommodation, and this can only get worse with the ageing of the population. Through accommodation deposits, providers of low-care facilities are able to raise enough capital to meet the rising demand associated with population ageing. But the prohibition on accommodation deposits for high-care places limits providers to receiving a capped accommodation charge only – only about half the income stream that can be generated by an accommodation deposit.

The accommodation deposits provided by low-care residents are being used to fund the accommodation of high-care residents at the same location. The ban on accommodation deposits for high-care accommodation is obliging low-care residents to subsidise wealthy high-care residents. Yet around 65 per cent of all residents in residential aged care have high care needs. This ratio will continue to rise as increasing numbers of older Australians are cared for in their own homes through community aged-care packages and extended aged-care-at-home packages. When these residents are no longer able to be cared for in their own homes they will need high-care accommodation, bypassing low-care accommodation.

Perversely, the Commonwealth has been approving almost twice as many low-care beds as high-care places. The reason is financial: private providers are allowed to apply accommodation deposits in funding low-care places, but not high-care places.

The argument previously used against accommodation deposits for high-care places is that moving into a high-care residential facility is traumatic enough for all concerned without having to go through the added trauma of selling the family home. But under present laws accommodation deposits cannot be levied where the resident has a spouse, relative or other carer living in the resident's former home.[27] These restrictions ensure that a prospective resident in an aged-care facility is not forced to sell a home where it is occupied by a spouse or by a relative or friend who has been providing care in recent years.

Residents in low-care accommodation who have contributed an accommodation deposit are able to carry the arrangement into high-care accommodation. But absurdly, residents who have bypassed low-care residential aged care cannot contribute accommodation deposits for high-care residential aged care.

There is no valid philosophical basis for supporting accommodation deposits for low-care places and extra-service places but opposing them for high-care places. If families with the financial capacity to pay decide that they want to accommodate an ageing parent in a better quality high-care facility, why should they be prevented from doing so? And if some of the proceeds of a high-care accommodation deposit from a wealthy family can be used to cross-subsidise high quality care for poorer residents, surely it should be done.

Imagine the furore if the Commonwealth were to insist that private hotels could not build accommodation beyond a specified maximum standard of quality, so that those who wanted to avail themselves of higher quality rooms would be prevented from doing so. Yet this is precisely the situation in Australia's high-care residential facilities. The Commonwealth justifies this ridiculous regulation on the basis that it is a major purchaser of aged-care services. But so are private individuals, and many would purchase more services if they were allowed to do so.

In moving beyond the public versus private debate, the Commonwealth should take direct responsibility only for those older Australians who genuinely lack the financial means to pay for their care. The Commonwealth should specify the quality of care for those for whom it has responsibility, using its purchasing power to advantage in contracting with private providers in delivering that standard of care. Those able to contribute to the cost of their own accommodation should be free to do so, at a quality that suits them.

For those who are asset-rich but income-poor, access to quality high-care accommodation could be gained by agreeing to pay off some or all of the fees accumulated, with interest, from the proceeds of the resident's estate. The call on the estate by the aged-care provider would need to be a first-ranking mortgage, to minimise both the risk to the provider and the interest rate charged to the resident. High-care accommodation providers would bear risks such as the resident's longevity, sharp falls in house prices and mis-selling risks – which could arise where beneficiaries of a resident's estate feel aggrieved about the level of estate proceeds flowing to the accommodation provider. Financial intermediaries might be required to facilitate trans-actions – perhaps the same intermediaries who already manage the embryonic but growing reverse-mortgage market in Australia.

Another way of increasing private funding for high-care accommodation is to relax some of the limitations on extra-service places. The 15 per cent cap on the number of extra-service places in any state or territory could be lifted. The increased income from accommodation deposits for better-off residents would then be available for cross-subsidising services to poorer residents through improved common facilities such as lounge rooms, recreation areas, kitchens and grounds.

A third way to inject more private funding into high-care facilities is to lift, or remove, the ceiling on the means-tested accommodation charge that can be applied to residents. At the very least, residents should be permitted by government to enter voluntary agreements with providers of high-care residential services to pay extra for their accommodation.

The former federal minister for ageing, Julie Bishop, has floated the option of a competitive model of aged-care provision in which public and private dollars would follow the person rather than the provider.[28] This model is pejoratively called a *voucher system.*

There is nothing intrinsically wrong with a competitive system, and much that recommends it, since it is more likely to keep costs down and quality up.

But an important consideration in assessing the sustainability and fairness of this proposal is the question of whether the same number of public dollars would follow each person. If each person was allocated the same number of public dollars regardless of their wealth – such that the voucher was, in effect, a birthright – the system would not be fiscally sustainable unless the number of dollars was reduced to the extent that poorer people were deprived of quality aged care.

This could be overcome by allocating money on the basis of a person's wealth. The allocation would not then be a voucher in the conventional meaning of the term; but the idea nevertheless warrants serious consideration. A needs-based voucher system has been proposed by Professor Warren Hogan.[29]

Bishop further suggests that the dollars allocated could be used by the person to purchase in-home care, including personal care by a spouse, relative or friend. Again, this idea has merit. But it needs to be recognised that older Australians who are cared for longer in their own homes, highly desirable as this is, typically have more serious health problems if and when they enter formal aged care. That is, they are more likely to enter high-care than low-care accommodation. Bishop does not propose to do anything about the funding problem for high-care accommodation; and, on its own, her proposal could make the problem worse in the absence of accommodation deposits for high-care places.

THE PROPOSED REFORMS IN SUMMARY

New private financing initiatives will need to apply for high-care residential aged care if we are to meet the sharply increasing demand for these services from an ageing population. At present, low-care residents are cross-subsidising wealthy high-care residents. Extra private funds should be made available for high-care places through any or all of accommodation deposits, the greater provision of extra-service places (for which accommodation deposits can apply) and lifting the ceiling on accommodation charges for better-off residents.

Any new measures would need to pass the following tests. First, the extra private funding must be asset-tested, so that it is not drawn from those residents with the least capacity to pay. Second, part of the extra private funds must be used to cross-subsidise services for the poor. Third, any payment of accommodation deposits for high-care accommodation should not apply to what are clearly going to be short stays, such as palliative care.

THE PHARMACEUTICAL BENEFITS SCHEME

Co-payments should be retained for the pharmaceutical benefits scheme. This increases the financial viability of the scheme in the face of greater refinements in pharmacology and the ageing of the population. It will also allow more pharmaceuticals to be listed, increasing their availability to all Australians. Income-tested co-payments for the PBS meet two of the key objectives of co-payments: a contribution to the funding of pharmaceuticals, and the use of price signals to ration use by the better-off.

HEALTH AND AGED-CARE
ACCOUNTS?

There are proposals for *medical savings accounts*[30] – which are advocated by the AMA.[31] Medical savings accounts would be an alternative to private health insurance, with people building up their own savings to pay for their health expenses rather than paying private health insurance premiums.

Insurance would still be needed for catastrophic health events; part of the savings in the accounts could be used to pay the premiums. A government-funded safety net would be needed for those whose incomes are too low for them to be able to accumulate savings in a medical savings account.

Questions that would need to be resolved in designing medical savings accounts include whether they would be voluntary or compulsory; eligible uses; and the apparatus for administering them.

Labor in government spread superannuation through most of the Australian workforce. Recognising that access to health and aged care is a crucial determinant of security in retirement, a variation of the medical savings account proposal could be to augment superannuation contributions with contributions for post-retirement health and aged care.[32] These health-care accounts could be added onto superannuation accounts, subject to a cap on amounts that can be contributed while remaining eligible for the concessionary tax treatment that applies to superannuation. Proceeds of the funds could be used in retirement to finance patient co-payments for services received, or to pay private health insurance premiums.

Integrating health-care accounts with superannuation would have the practical advantage that the superannuation industry already has established systems for collecting contributions.

Consideration should be given to the development of medical savings accounts for lifetime health care, or health savings accounts for post-retirement health and aged care.

CHAPTER 7

BEYOND PUBLIC VERSUS PRIVATE IN EDUCATION AND TRAINING

OUR CHILDREN ARE OUR FUTURE

Never has it been more true that Australia's children are our future. In many ways, they are more precious than ever before. Australia in forty years' time is projected to have 4 300 000 more people over the age of 65, but less than 550 000 more children.[1] Australia's children will be the source of much of the happiness and prosperity in our nation over the next four decades.

For the sake of our children, and for Australia's sake, the present and coming generations of parents have an obligation to provide the best possible education that gives every child an equal opportunity to lead a happy, creative and productive life.

Education delivers higher earnings. Early school leavers earn around 20 per cent less than those completing year 12 – who earn on average 20 per cent less than those who complete a vocational education. They, in turn, earn around 40 per cent less than university graduates.[2] Looked at another way, Australian university graduates on average earn at least 50 per cent more than those who complete high school, and at least 70 per cent more than high school drop-outs.[3] The chances of being unemployed are three times greater for a high school drop-out than for a university graduate.[4]

The nurturing of intellect and the acquisition of skills are by far the most potent sources of productivity growth in the modern world.[5] Arguably, knowledge and skills stand alone as the only sources of comparative advantage.[6] Investing in skills offers the double benefit of raising productivity and lifting lifetime workforce participation rates:

> Education is increasingly becoming the 'engine room' of modern economies. If we get this part of the economy right, most other things ought to fall in place (or be better placed), because increased investment in education boosts both productivity and participation.[7]

Education also improves health outcomes, further helping to combat the adverse effects of population ageing.

Giving all young Australians a quality education would set the nation onto a virtuous upward spiral of ever increasing prosperity, providing opportunity for all.

THE AUSTRALIAN EXPERIENCE WITH SKILLS DEVELOPMENT

The acceleration in skills formation of the 1980s and early 1990s under the Labor government has slowed in recent years. As a result, the contribution of skills formation to Australian productivity growth has slackened off. A Productivity Commission review of the Australian evidence8 concludes that the increase in average length of schooling in the working-age population slowed sharply in the 1990s compared with the 1980s. When experience is taken into account as well as educational attainment, the evidence remains that the accumulation of skills slowed during the 1990s compared with the rapid pace of the 1980s. The Productivity Commission concluded that there was a slower rate of accumulation of human capital in the Australian workforce in the 1990s, which would have detracted from a productivity acceleration in the 1990s.

The Productivity Commission further concludes that

there appears to have been no significant acceleration in workforce skills in the 1990s. In fact, the evidence shows a faster increase in skills in the 1980s.[9]

These conclusions are supported by the OECD's empirical work, which suggests that skill upgrading made no contribution to Australian productivity growth between 1990 and 2000.[10]

Drawing together the work of the OECD and the Productivity Commission, Eslake asks:

> So why has education apparently not made any discernible contribution to the improvement in Australia's economic performance over the past decade? The answer, unfortunately, seems to be that there has not been any discernible improvement in Australia's educational outcomes – at least insofar as they impact on productivity growth during this period.[11]

Australia ranks around the middle of the OECD in the proportion of 15 to 19-year-olds enrolled in secondary education beyond the compulsory attendance age.[12] A range of indicators of educational attainment has been used to draw comparisons between Australia and other OECD countries, leading to the conclusion that:

> These international comparisons suggest that Australia's educational report card should be marked: 'Started well, but slackened off. Substantial room for improvement'.[13]

International forecasts of the percentage change in years of education between 2005 and 2020 prepared by Deutsche Bank put Australia *last* among 33 countries.[14] Countries with faster expected growth rates in average years of education include not only developing countries coming from a low base like India and China; they also include other rich countries such as Belgium, France, Japan, Sweden, Denmark, Germany, Britain, the United States, Norway, Canada and Switzerland. Australia's appallingly slow improvement in average years of education is expected to leave us languishing behind 19 countries in workforce education levels by 2020.

A saving grace is that the benefits of the sharp increase in educational attainment by females during the 1980s and early 1990s have yet to be fully unleashed on Australian productivity growth. As these generations of highly educated women replace generations of less well educated women and men, Australian productivity growth could be expected to improve.

Those effects will help to counteract the deceleration in skills formation from the 1990s.[15] The flow-through effect of good policy decisions in the 1980s and early 1990s that sharply lifted school retention rates and tertiary education participation rates will be a valuable offset to the ageing of the population, perhaps causing per capita GDP growth to slow to 1.74 per cent a year[16] instead of the 1.5 per cent per annum projected in the *Intergenerational Report*.

The conclusion of ageing optimists[17] is that in forty years Australians will have almost double the incomes they enjoy now, and will therefore be able to afford to care for an ageing population through higher taxation:

> We conclude that rising educational attainment, the factor that has driven the fall in fertility, is also acting to mitigate the effects of rising dependency rates by raising the growth rate of productivity.[18]

Separately, the Productivity Commission[19] projects growth in per capita GDP to bottom out at less than 1.3 per cent per annum in the mid-2020s, recovering to a little over 1.5 per cent per annum by 2042. Though these projected growth rates are down from the 2.15 per cent of the 1990s owing to the ageing of the population, they, too, would lead to a real GDP per person in forty years' time that is almost double present levels.

Does this mean that present generations of working Australians have done enough to secure the future prosperity of their children and grandchildren, and to ensure that they themselves can be looked after in their old age? The answer is, almost certainly, no. Recall that past official projections of population ageing have all underestimated increases in life expectancy, and that current projections may suffer from the same shortcoming. And Australia must recognise that much of the rest of the world is investing heavily in education. Australia's educational attainment levels will need to continue improving if we are to be globally competitive in the coming decades. To stand still is to fall behind. To go backwards, as Australia is doing, is downright dangerous.

Seen in this context, the deceleration in skills formation in Australia from the 1990s is a tragically wasted opportunity. Total government spending on education fell from 4.3 per cent of GDP in the early 1990s to 3.8 per cent in 2002–03, and to 3.5 per cent in 2003–04. An increase in private spending on education was not enough to prevent an overall reduction in national spending on education over the period.[20] The privately funded share of education spending has risen more quickly in Australia since 1995 than in any other OECD country. Australia has been virtually alone among OECD countries in failing to increase public funding commensurately with increased private funding.[21]

As population ageing continues, the *Intergenerational Report* projections are for a *fall* in Commonwealth spending on education from 1.8 per cent of GDP in 2001–02 to 1.6 per cent in 2041–42.[22] In an ageing population, a new approach is needed that focuses not on education spending as a proportion of GDP, but on real spending per student. A dramatic slowing in the rate of increase of Australia's young population, though not desirable, provides an opportunity for increased real spending per student. Australia needs to invest heavily in our children as never before:

> Whatever the explanation for the apparently minor role played by education in Australia's good economic performance over the past decade, education will almost certainly need to make a much larger contribution in coming decades if that performance is to be sustained, particularly in view of the impact that demographic change will have on the principal drivers of economic growth.[23]

Obviously it is not only the quantity of investment in education and training that is important but also the quality, and getting the best value for money spent. As in other areas of major expenditure, we must move beyond the stultifying debate over public versus private provision of education to find ways of providing a quality education for every young Australian.

EDUCATIONAL DISADVANTAGE IN AUSTRALIA

Though the Australian student population performs well in reading overall compared with students from other OECD countries, it exhibits above-average disparities in reading performance.[24] Thirty-six per cent of Australian students from low socioeconomic backgrounds leave school before completing year 12 compared with only 12 per cent from high socioeconomic backgrounds.[25] And the average university entry score for low-socioeconomic status students is 66, compared with 80 for high-socioeconomic status students.[26]

A deeply worrying finding is that over the last quarter of a century there has been no improvement in average literacy and numeracy among 14-year-olds, despite a doubling in real spending per student.[27] The extra resources have mostly been directed to reducing student–teacher ratios, an ineffective response to the challenge of improving these particular educational outcomes – one in five adult Australians is functionally illiterate.[28]

At present, around 50 000 young Australians drop out of school each year and never complete year 12. It is estimated that if they completed year 12 Australia's GDP would rise by 1.1 per cent by 2040 – or around $500 a year per person in today's dollars – and the extra budgetary costs would be more than recovered by extra taxation revenue generated in the future.[29]

Australia's poor performance in educating disadvantaged children is a blight on our society and a huge lost opportunity for the nation. Australia can never be a great society while it continues to entrench disadvantage by refusing to make the extra effort needed to give these children the same chance in life as their more privileged peers.

WHY WE NEED SCHOOL EDUCATION REFORMS

Australia's school system badly needs reforming. While it functions well for children from privileged backgrounds and adequately for children from middle Australia, it is neglecting children from disadvantaged communities. The reform proposals advanced here are designed to lift the educational performance of disadvantaged young people while maintaining a quality school education for all young Australians.

WHO PROVIDES THE FUNDS?

In the early 2000s around 80 per cent of total government recurrent schools spending was on government schools. State governments provided more than 90 per cent of the recurrent funding for government schools, and the Commonwealth less than 10 per cent. In contrast, the Commonwealth provided more than 70 per cent of government spending on private schools, and state governments less than 30 per cent.

These figures disguise a major shift in funding patterns over the last few years. The Coalition government has shifted funding towards private schools. In the five years to 2002, real Commonwealth funding per student increased by 12 per cent in government schools, 32 per cent in Catholic schools and 47 per cent in independent schools.[30]

Private schools are receiving increasing amounts of government funding, and government schools are relying more and more heavily on the fundraising activities of parents' associations, voluntary contributions from parents and financial support from local businesses and gambling benefit funds. No private school is purely privately funded anymore, and no government school is purely publicly funded.

STUDENTS ARE LEAVING GOVERNMENT SCHOOLS

Around two-thirds of students were enrolled in government schools in the mid-2000s. But virtually all the enrolment growth in the twenty-year period from 1984 has been in private schools. Enrolments in Catholic schools increased by around 17 per cent over the period, in independent schools by a massive 118 per cent, and in government schools by less than 1 per cent.[31]

As parents move their children out of government schools into private schools the students remaining in many government schools are increasingly from disadvantaged backgrounds. Analysis of the performance of students from the different categories of schools suggests that independent schools outperform Catholic schools, which outperform government schools. But these differences are largely explained by differences in the student population – government schools have the highest proportion of students from low socioeconomic backgrounds, independent schools have the lowest.[32]

After adjusting for the differences in student population the overall performance of the three sectors is similar, and many government schools are performing very well compared with private schools.[33] The observation that the performance of different schools is strongly influenced by the socioeconomic status of their students has very important implications for reform of Australia's school system. The need for reform is pressing:

> Left unchecked, this situation is likely to worsen. The increasing concentration of students from disadvantaged families in some schools and regions is making the job of those schools more difficult. They already have a significantly higher concentration of students from disadvantaged backgrounds and sometimes have more students with behavioural problems. As students move away the school often loses those families better able to contribute to school life and school resources.[34]

The exodus of higher performing students from many government schools is leaving them vulnerable and poorly placed to lift their

standards. Australia is headed for a period of squandered opportunity and much greater inequality unless a new funding model is
put in place.

I asked the principal of a disadvantaged government school in
Logan City near Brisbane to write down what she saw as the
issues facing her school. Her heart-breaking account of life at this
poor school is summarised in box 7.1. Can this be twenty-first
century Australia?

A NEW SCHOOL FUNDING MODEL

Schools should be funded according to the needs of the child. It is
the children who are important, not whether they are attending a
government or a private school. Let us declare an end to the class
war and abandon distinctions between government and private
schools for funding purposes.

Various proposals have been advanced for funding students
rather than schools, adjusted to take account of revenue raised
through private fees.[35] Schools with large numbers of children
from disadvantaged backgrounds would receive more government
funding than schools with children from more privileged backgrounds. A funding model based on the needs of the child would
recognise that:

> Those schools with a high proportion of disadvantaged students
> are in a particularly difficult situation: they have a need for tai-
> lored, individual approaches for many of their students and, at
> best, have a very standard budget with meagre supplementary
> funds to finance additional effort for these students and little scope
> to add much resources from parent contributions.[36]

Commonwealth and state funding should be pooled, and a standard amount per student notionally allocated regardless of
whether the school the child attends is a government or private
school. Extra funding would be allocated for each student who is
disadvantaged – whether because of socioeconomic status or

BOX 7.1 ISSUES FOR OUR SCHOOL

'If I had to say what our biggest headache was it would have to be the frustration we all feel in not being able to get stuck into learning and teaching because of the huge amounts of time we have to spend dealing with issues that seem to be escalating, particularly in a complex, low socioeconomic community such as ours.

Working a 10 to 12 hour day is the norm because it is very difficult to deal with the things that should be dealt with during working hours. This time is spent dealing with student behaviours and with a wide variety of concerns that children bring into the school with them.

The life circumstances for many of our kids are quite traumatic. We are seeing an increasing number of children who are really 'screwed up' because of what is happening in their lives. Some have behaviours that are pathological and these kids need ongoing intensive help and support from people who are qualified to provide it, rather than the occasional 30-minute session some receive.

While we try to ensure that children are getting a fair deal in terms of literacy and numeracy learning at school, this is frequently disrupted because of the behaviours of kids who cannot concentrate on learning because in their personal lives they are not being provided with the security, care and love they need.

We try to provide a safe haven for children at our school. However, this means that our major focus is on trying to help kids develop skills that will enable them to deal more effectively with the problems they are encountering in their everyday lives. This includes trying to get them to resolve problems using strategies other than violence. This is really hard as violence is the only method of problem-solving many of them see being used at home from when they are tiny babies.

By the time some of our kids reach school, retrieval in terms of emotional wellbeing is often really difficult. It seems to me that one little-used mechanism we have for helping future parents to become good parents is through parenting programs at school. If young people are taught the skills of parenting before they even become parents, we may be able to turn around some of the difficulties teachers are now facing in schools.'

physical or intellectual disability. Further adjustments could be made for circumstances of the school, such as remoteness or small size. Then a final adjustment would be made to take account of the school's access to private income.

An alternative to adjusting funding per student according to a school's access to private income is to enter into agreements with wealthier private schools to take specified numbers of disadvantaged students whose parents cannot afford private school fees. Since poorer schools are being disadvantaged through having to take students with emotional and behaviour management problems, contracting with well-resourced schools to take some of these children and support them at school would allow the poorer schools to concentrate more on teaching.

Private schools that did not wish to participate in the new funding arrangements would not be obliged to, but they would not receive government funding.

Extra funding for disadvantaged schools is likely to cost up to $1 billion a year, and funding of around $1.5 billion a year would be required to lift the per student funding of poorer private schools with little private income to the level of government schools.[37] Catholic schools that charge low fees would be the main beneficiaries of this second category of funding; needy government and private schools would benefit from the first.

Since avoiding early school leaving is expected to be self-financing in budgetary terms over time[38] and would offer large benefits to the wider community, these outlays are best thought of as investments in Australia's economic and social future. Extra funding for each disadvantaged student in government and private schools would be spent on programs such as remedial learning, nutrition, school nurses and securing the best teachers for the most disadvantaged schools.

LITERACY AND NUMERACY SUPPORT

There is compelling evidence that the life chances of young people are determined at a very early age. The development of a child's brain is heavily influenced by how much nurturing and physical and mental stimulation the child receives at home. Children who do not receive adequate nutrition and adequate stimulation in infancy have great difficulty in overcoming these deficits in their school years. Children in dysfunctional and violent families are much more likely to develop emotional and behavioural problems later in life.

Extensive research[39] confirms that children from disadvantaged backgrounds gain the most from quality early childhood education programs, with the benefits being greater the earlier the intervention:

> There is hardly a better researched and documented aspect of education than these significant early childhood years ... investment in children at this level will pay off in myriad ways, helping to prevent child abuse, lack of thriving, ill health, school failure, early dropout, poor job chances, delinquency and crime in later life.[40]

Ideally early intervention should occur at birth, or even with pre-natal support for the mother and her family. Certainly taking action before the child reaches the age of five is crucial.[41] Returns per dollar invested in successful early childhood programs have been estimated at between $7 (for a Chicago program) and $17 (for the Perry Preschool program in the United States), with well above half the returns accruing to society as a whole. A more recent generation of early intervention programs, mostly in the United States, has been yielding similarly good results.[42]

However, not all appealing ideas work. Programs like home visiting do work, but not consistently across all settings; and engaging with families can be very difficult, especially without the support of the local community.[43] Large-scale, formula-driven early intervention programs are less likely to work than smaller scale programs tailored to the particular circumstances and needs of the local

BOX 7.2   EARLY INTERVENTION IN INALA

One component of the program in Inala is a *family indepen-dence program*, which employs community workers from local ethnic communities.

On a routine visit to one of the preschools to introduce herself to parents, a Vietnamese community worker started talking with a Vietnamese mother (who was unable to speak English). The mother asked the worker to help her understand a form she had received from the school. The worker arranged a home visit to do the translation. During the home visit the community worker became aware that the mother was suf-fering from depression after recently giving birth to a baby who had died. She also became aware that the family was living in poverty, subsisting mostly on vegetables grown in their garden and sleeping on clothes on the floor.

The father initially rejected offers of assistance as a threat to family pride. But the worker maintained contact with the family, and the father eventually agreed to accept beds for the children in exchange for home-grown vegetables. He also agreed that the mother should attend the family independence program playgroup with the youngest child, who was very quiet and withdrawn.

Since regularly attending the playgroup the child has become more confident, and the mother expresses her under-standing of the importance of spending time with her children: 'I wanted to know more so I could help my daughter. Now I pay more attention to what my children are doing. I ask them about homework and what they are doing at school. I know the songs from playgroup ... so I can sing along with them.'

community. For example, a community-based early intervention and crime prevention program in the disadvantaged multicultural outer Brisbane suburb of Inala is achieving encouraging results with the support of local ethnic communities (see box 7.2).[44]

All states now have procedures for the early identification of students who are struggling with reading and numeracy. Having identified students in need of remedial learning, the different states then apply various early intervention programs. A battle has been raging for some years overseas and, more recently, in Australia over the most effective forms of remedial support. Categorised as a debate between phonics and whole language learning, these 'reading wars' are over whether children in need of extra support should be given text from stories to read with the support of a specialist teacher or taken back to the basics of identifying and sounding groups of letters in forming and understanding words.

Reading Recovery, adapted from New Zealand, is used in several states, and is labelled by advocates of phonics as a whole language approach. Their critique is that struggling students need to be taken back to the basics, and that Reading Recovery fails to do this.

Disadvantaged children would be the big winners if the protagonists in this debate called a ceasefire and developed the best possible remedial literacy programs for Australian schools. A report by literacy experts on Reading Recovery in New Zealand recommends that the program should place greater emphasis on explicit instruction in phonological awareness and the use of spelling-to-sound patterns in identifying unfamiliar words in text.[45]

As a matter of commonsense, surely children need both the basics of phonics and the contextual benefits of whole language so that they not only can sound out words but can understand their meaning and have their imaginations stimulated by what they read.

A PRESCHOOL EDUCATION FOR ALL AUSTRALIAN CHILDREN

Preschool equips three and four-year-old children with the skills to participate meaningfully in the classroom from the first day of formal schooling. It provides basic learning skills, and an environment in which children can acquire the social skills to be able to interact positively with other children. There is compelling evidence that children who miss out on a preschool education are at a distinct disadvantage compared to children who receive a preschool education.[46] As the OECD points out:

> Investment in early childhood education is of key importance in order to build a strong foundation for lifelong learning and to ensure equitable access to learning opportunities later in school.[47]

Yet Australia spends just 0.1 per cent of GDP on preschool education, less than any other OECD country.[48] In fact, Australia does not have a system of preschool education. Arrangements for providing early childhood education are different in each state and territory, the age at which children participate differs and, as if to highlight the fragmentation of preschool education in Australia, there is not even agreement on a name for formal education before beginning primary school. It can be kindergarten, prep or preschool, depending on the state or territory. And the first year of formal schooling is variously known as kindergarten, pre-primary, transition or reception.

So what is preschool? A good definition is provided by Walker:

> Preschool is a planned educational program for children in the year before the first year of school. Children are usually aged between 4 and 5 years of age. A qualified early childhood teacher, who has completed a degree in education, plans the program and is usually supported by a teacher assistant.[49]

Not only is there no national policy on preschool education and no national consistency, but the Commonwealth – though providing assistance to all other levels of education – has provided no financial support for preschool education since 1985 (with the exception of some indigenous preschool programs).

Official data, such as it is, overstates preschool attendance, with some states reporting attendance of 99.8 per cent and even 101 per cent.[50] The best available estimate is that 83.5 per cent of four-year-old children participate in some form of preschool education in the year before formal school, and around 17 per cent of three-year-olds participate.[51] It appears that more than 58 000 four-year-old children miss out on a preschool education every year.[52] Children from the most disadvantaged families, including children from low socioeconomic groups, non-English speaking backgrounds and indigenous children, are the ones who miss out.

Different government departments, including education, family and health departments, administer preschool in different states and territories. In some states responsibility for delivering preschool education is shared with childcare centres administered by children's services departments. Some states fund only four-year-old children, while others also fund three-year-olds. Some states charge parents for preschool, while in others it is free or subject to a voluntary contribution. Government involvement in the provision of preschool education ranges from 18 per cent of services in Victoria to 100 per cent in Western Australia. Government spending per preschool student ranges from $1260 in NSW to $5810 in the Northern Territory.[53]

The Commonwealth's early childhood strategy, released in 2004, excluded preschool education from the government's plans. The Commonwealth is failing to show any leadership in developing a national approach to preschool education within an overall early childhood development strategy. While the Coalition government pursues an obsession against university student unions, it has abrogated all responsibility for preschool education, vital in determining the life chances of our children.

The total cost of providing a preschool education to all four-year-old children in Australia is estimated at between $828 million and $1422 million per year.[54] The Commonwealth, state and territory governments should work together to create a nationally consistent preschool education system, with common starting ages and quality assurance. It should specifically aim to lift preschool participation by children from disadvantaged families.

Family payments to parents with four-year-old children could be made conditional on the children being enrolled in a formal preschool or a child-care centre that offers accredited early childhood education. Most financially better-off parents already send their children to preschool or an equivalent standard of childcare. The big advantage of making family payments conditional for children in this age group is that it would lift the participation of children from disadvantaged families. Access for disadvantaged children to a preschool education would need to be free of charge. Where necessary, parents should be supported by parenting programs and other early intervention measures to ensure regular attendance by their children. There is a precedent for this sort of mutual obligation – eligibility for child-care benefits is conditional on parents having their children immunised.

The purpose of making family payments conditional on preschool attendance is not to deny disadvantaged families government income-support payments. It is to act as an alert and a point of contact between government support agencies and disadvantaged parents whose children are not attending preschool. Having made contact and identified any problems, the government agencies would then offer transport and other necessary support to enable the child to participate in preschool.

FULL-SERVICE SCHOOLS

State and territory agencies with responsibility for the health, education and overall welfare of disadvantaged families could make a big difference by moving towards full-service schools and preschools. Full-service schools assemble on the school campus a range of professionals in physical and emotional health, law and order and, in the case of high schools, career guidance and pathways to vocational education.

A full-service school would have a school nurse, a visiting dentist and (desirably) a visiting GP, a conflict resolution officer, a counsellor and a police officer. Marsden State High School in

BOX 7.3 MARSDEN STATE HIGH SCHOOL'S STUDENT AND COMMUNITY SERVICES CENTRE

'The centre aims to draw professionals and community members into the school to support students and the community in which they live. The staff at the centre will include counsellors, career advisers, a school nurse, a student liaison officer, a school police officer and, from time to time, community organisations such as the Smith Family.

The centre will change the way Marsden High School operates. Fifteen-year-olds in the local community now balance part-time work with school and family commitments. Frequently, in this setting, school loses some meaning. In the services centre, students will find a collection of professional people who care and who can help them to find balance in their lives.

More often than not, young people find the pressures of home life difficult to manage. The services centre will draw parents into the school to help them understand better how the school operates and, more importantly, to offer training for the parents so that they can be more successful in their families and their community. Schools often talk of connecting with parents: the services centre will make this link happen.

As Marsden High moves more to become a community-based school, its training role in the broader community will increase. *Career Keys* will operate from the centre. It is a registered training provider and already, parents and community members are coming back to school to improve their qualifications.'

– Don Whitehouse, Principal, Marsden High School

Logan City near Brisbane, with a student population of almost 1600, has constructed a student and community service centre that will eventually offer this range of services (see box 7.3). Through the operation of the centre the school hopes to attract more parents onto the school campus to improve the school and home lives of disadvantaged children.

The advantage of full-service schools is that they can better integrate home and school life, offering services to students beyond the classroom and leaving teachers to concentrate on what they are trained to do – teach. The full-service model can be expanded to incorporate initiatives undertaken jointly with the private sector, including school-based apprenticeships and traineeships.

The Blair government's *education action zones* combine public and private resources to lift academic standards and improve career opportunities in disadvantaged communities. Labor took a policy of education priority zones, based on the Blair model, to the 2001 federal election. A policy of establishing education priority zones that incorporate full-service schools should be revived.

ATTRACTING – AND RETAINING – THE BEST TEACHERS

The quality of teachers has been shown to have a profound influence on the performance of students, arguably greater than the influence of their socioeconomic backgrounds.[55] Large improvements could be expected in educational outcomes for disadvantaged students from lifting teacher quality.[56]

Although the starting salaries of Australian teachers of around $40 000 per annum seem reasonable, the rewards for experience and excellence appear to be very low: the salary scales for experienced government school teachers other than principals and their deputies top out at around $60 000 in most states. Disturbingly, there has been a heavy compression of pay scales for Australian teachers since 1996. In the period from 1996 to 2002 starting salaries for teachers in Australia increased by 27 per cent in real terms, but for teachers at the top of the scale the real increase was only 3 per cent.[57] Starting salaries in Australia have increased faster relative to the salaries of experienced teachers than they have in any other OECD country.[58]

To achieve the best outcomes for disadvantaged students, the

Australian teaching profession will need to move to a system of professional development and pay based on quality of teaching.[59] And since the quality of school principals has a powerful influence on the quality and performance of teaching staff, the best school principals should be paid more. Their salaries should be boosted over time by an average of at least 25 per cent (with pay variations according to quality), at a total cost to the nation of around $200 million a year.[60]

Under the funding model advocated here, schools with large numbers of disadvantaged students would receive extra funding to allow them to attract the best teachers and school principals by offering better pay.

UNIVERSITY FUNDING

The Whitlam government opened the doors of the nation's universities to the children of working Australians. The Hawke and Keating governments expanded access to education, more than doubling the proportion of students completing high school and creating a system that allowed all talented high school students who worked hard to go on to a university education. The Hawke government introduced the *higher education contribution scheme* (HECS), a loan to students repayable out of future income designed to enable them to make some contribution to the cost of their university education. The funding generated from HECS was used to expand the number of university places. Repayment of the HECS loan was conditional on the graduate earning a specified minimum income. Those who earned less than the minimum level would not have to repay the loan. The level of HECS fees was set so as to only partially cover the full cost of a university degree – around 20 to 30 per cent of recurrent costs. Limiting cost recovery to only part of the cost of a university place recognised the wider benefits to the community of a better educated population.

The government has described the Labor Party as 'obsessed

with higher education'.[61] Yet international research conducted by Deutsche Bank concludes that:

> Successful countries share ... the goal of bringing as many children as possible into higher education – without jeopardising quality. Private financial resources are an important ingredient in these systems. These countries understand that education is an investment.[62]

The Coalition government is deliberately making access to a university education much harder for all but the financially well-off. University places are increasingly being rationed according to capacity to pay full fees. The prospect of massive HECS debts for those fortunate enough to gain a HECS place is reducing the returns from a university education, and reducing its attractiveness to prospective undergraduates.

In 1997 the Howard government increased HECS charges by between 31 and 119 per cent, depending on the course.[63] At the same time the government reduced the income level at which repayments of HECS begin by more than 30 per cent. The government also provided for full-fee paying Australian students but without a loan scheme. The take up was small, presumably because most students did not have the money to pay full fees up front.

An analysis of the socioeconomic composition of university enrolments from 1988, just before the introduction of HECS, to 1999, well after its introduction, finds that 'HECS did not act to discourage university participation in general or among individuals from the lowest wealth groups'.[64]

Since coming to office in 1996 the Coalition government has increased funding for university running costs more slowly than actual cost increases. By 2008 the government's indexation formula will be short-changing Australian universities by an estimated $337 million a year.[65]

The Coalition made further, major changes to university funding arrangements, effective from 2005. First, universities were allowed to increase their HECS fees by up to 25 per cent. Second, the HECS repayment threshold was lifted from about \$25 400 per annum to just over \$36 000 per annum. Third, universities were permitted to fill up to 35 per cent of places for Australian students with full-fee paying students. And fourth, to assist full-fee paying students, an income-related loan scheme like HECS, called FEE-HELP, was introduced, with a loan cap of \$50 000.

Of these four measures the lifting of the income repayment threshold for HECS is a progressive move, since it benefits those students – especially women – who might expect their incomes following graduation not to exceed \$36 000 per annum. In these circumstances graduates would not have to repay their HECS debts.

But the other changes will be damaging. Cash-starved universities will need to avail themselves of alternative funding sources such as HECS fee increases and full-fee paying students. Most universities took the opportunity to increase their HECS charges by the full 25 per cent from 2005. FEE-HELP will encourage a much bigger take-up by full-fee paying Australian students. The effect of capping FEE-HELP at \$50 000 per student is that students taking courses that cost more than this must make an up-front contribution before they have completed their university education.

An analysis of the HECS fee increases concludes that:

> the government will be transferring the problem associated with indexation shortfalls away from taxpayers to students [and] ... the 2005 HECS increases rest ... uneasily with the economic rationale for public sector additional financial support, which suggests that activities associated with spillover social benefits should be subsidised by taxpayers; in other words that students should pay less than the full costs of the activity.

The same analysis of the capping of FEE-HELP concludes that it has the potential to jeopardise access for those who expect to receive relatively low future incomes, which is 'very regressive when viewed in a lifetime context'.[66]

Since cash-starved universities have every incentive to lift the proportion of their students who are paying full fees, Australia now has a queue-jumping system whereby full-fee paying students with lower tertiary entrance scores can displace HECS students with higher scores. Education Minister Brendan Nelson has acknowledged the unfairness created by a capped FEE-HELP scheme,[67] but the government has persisted with it.

An international comparison of the affordability of a university education finds that Australia ranks a lowly 11th out of the 15 developed countries reviewed.[68] Australian university students must find an average of more than $14 000 a year to meet education and living costs, making Australia the fifth most expensive place to study. Of more than passing interest, all the countries ranking above Australia on the affordability index also rank above Australia on the productivity table.

Australia stands out among OECD countries as one of the very few in which increases in private spending on higher education have replaced rather than complemented extra public spending:

> In fact, many OECD countries with the highest growth in private spending have also shown the highest increase in public funding of education. This indicates that increasing private spending on tertiary education tends to complement, rather than replace, public investment. The main exception to this is Australia, where the shift towards private expenditure at tertiary level has been accompanied by a fall in the level of public expenditure in real terms.[69]

The number of HECS places at Australian universities for Australian students must be increased if Australia is to achieve the productivity gains needed to meet the economic challenge of an ageing population. And to ease the financial pressure on universities, operating grants should be increased – and indexed according to a wage–cost index, rather than the general consumer price index.

If Australia is to increase its prosperity and improve opportunities for young people in this the Asian century, the proportion of high school students completing a university degree needs to rise sharply. More than 500 million Indians are under the age of 25, and India is churning out 2.5 million university graduates annually.[70] China is producing around 2.8 million graduates a year.[71] Absolute numbers of university graduates are not an entirely relevant point of comparison; but neither is the number of graduates as a proportion of the population. Though Australia has a small population compared with India and China, the sheer number of university graduates from those two countries alone constitutes an enormous pool of creative talent. Australia needs its own pool of talent to be able to compete successfully with these much larger pools in India, China and other Asian countries.

In 1970, only 8 per cent of Australian high-school leavers went on to higher education. The introduction of HECS allowed the number of university places to be expanded, helping to double

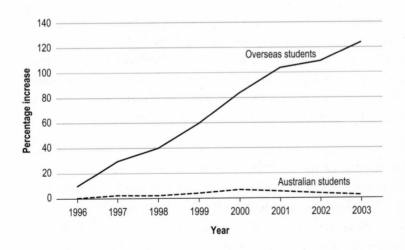

FIGURE 7.1 CUMULATIVE CHANGE IN STUDENT LOAD
FOR COMMENCING UNDERGRADUATE STUDENTS, 1996–2003
(BIRRELL ET AL. 2005, P.65)

the proportion of school leavers going on to university from 15 per cent in 1983 to 30 per cent in 1999.[72] But following the Coalition government's changes to HECS and its unwillingness to fund universities adequately, growth in university attendance by Australian students has virtually stalled.[73] Almost all the growth in first-year undergraduate numbers since the change of government in 1996 has been among full-fee paying foreign students; growth in commencements by Australian students has pretty much flat-lined (see figure 7.1).

While educating foreign students has become a big export industry for Australia, with all the domestic and international benefits this brings, universities are relying on full-fee paying foreign students to balance their budgets. The OECD finds that, of OECD member countries, Australia and Switzerland receive the largest proportion of foreign students relative to their total tertiary enrolments, with more than one in six enrolled tertiary students being a citizen of another country.[74] Heavy reliance on full-fee paying foreign students is making Australian universities vulnerable to sudden declines in overseas enrolments – an emerging possibility as source countries change their preferences or improve their own higher education systems.

Over the period of the Coalition government Australia has experienced strong employment growth among professionals, opening up a huge gap between demand and supply that is being filled by skilled migrants:

> there has been a substantial increase in the employment of profes-
> sionals since the Coalition came to power in 1996. Yet over the
> same period, the number of domestic students has hardly increased
> at all. All of the increase in professional training at the undergrad-
> uate level in Australian universities has been directed at overseas
> students. Partly as a consequence, there has been a rapid increase in
> the intake of professional migrants to satisfy employer needs ...
> there is a need for more training of domestic undergraduate stu-
> dents, not less.[75]

Yet the government has predicted a decline in the number of university places for Australian students by 2015.[76] Australia produces less than 160 000 Australian university graduates a year. And in the mid-2000s university enrolments have fallen for only the second time in fifty years. In 2004, the year before the big relaxation in limits on full-fee paying Australian student places, the number of full-fee paying places increased by more than 3000 while the number of HECS-funded places fell by almost 10 000. Following the changes of 2005, universities responded in the expected way, reducing the number of HECS places by more than 8000 while increasing the number of full-fee paying places by 2500.

It's time again to take a big step forward towards mass participation in higher education and training by ensuring that every school student has quality schooling and that finance is no barrier to a university education. Australia should aim to double the proportion of young people going on to university by 2020, from around 30 per cent to 60 per cent.

The British government has set a target of 50 per cent of young Britons participating in higher education by 2010. An Australian target of 60 per cent to be achieved ten years beyond this is not 'madness', as the government claims, but a worthy, realistic goal.

AUSTRALIAN STUDENT EQUITIES

The Commonwealth will not be in a position to provide all, or most, of the necessary extra financing to double the number of university places, since Australian tax rates will need to be globally competitive. The present government's solution is to require ever increasing contributions from students themselves – reducing the incentive to undertake higher education, and excluding well-performing high school students from disadvantaged backgrounds. Neither funding approach will deliver the financial resources required to achieve mass participation in higher education. Australia needs more of both public and private funding of extra university places for Australian students.

A new funding vehicle should be developed that harnesses private resources for the public good. HECS is a form of *debt* financing of higher education. Perhaps private *equity* financing of higher education could also be introduced in Australia. Superannuation funds and other financial institutions could offer to pay a student's fees and living expenses in return for an agreed share of future earnings over an agreed number of years.

These *Australian student equities* would effectively allow young people to gain access to their own future earnings during their student days. If future earnings were large, the return on equity funds invested in the student would be large – making it potentially attractive for private financiers.

Our financial institutions are familiar with investing in *physical* capital like buildings, roads, ports and equipment. Why not invest in the *human* capital of young people?

Australian student equities build on the idea of *human-capital contracts*, which have been implemented in the United States since 2001 by Vishal Garg and Raza Khan – the founders of Iempower Inc, the company behind the MyRichUncle trademark. They offer finance with repayment periods of ten or 15 years, and a maximum repayment of 15 per cent of income.[77] Actual terms depend on the university being attended and the course being undertaken.

One of the difficulties in implementing human-capital contracts overseas has been the absence of a collection and enforcement mechanism. But on both counts Australia is well placed, having the administrative infrastructure in place already for the implementation of HECS. The Commonwealth could create the legal framework for Australian student equities, to reduce uncertainty concerning the enforceability of contracts and the high cost to a private equity provider of collecting payments. For ease of administration, the legislation could specify that the same percentage of income is collected from each participating student, and it could set a standard time period over which repayments were made. Students could then shop around in a competitive market of human-capital funds for the fund that offered to invest the most in them, given these legislated parameters. That is, the only variable – to be determined by the forces of competition – would be the amount financed in each case.

Alternatively, legislation could establish a maximum percentage of income and a maximum repayment period, and competition could occur on both the amount of finance offered and the share of income up to the legislated maximum.

The amount financed need not be restricted to tuition fees; it could also cover living expenses, allowing students to spend more of their time on university studies and participation without needing to work long hours in casual jobs to cover the cost of living while at university.

Australia's superannuation funds tend to allocate a share of their capital to ethical investments. There could be no more ethical investment than the higher education of Australia's young people. Superannuation funds are turning more towards investments that produce income streams rather than capital growth, to pay the superannuation annuities of retiring baby boomers. Australian student equities would provide income streams.

There are two further problems for the design and implementation of human-capital contracts: adverse selection and moral hazard. *Adverse selection* means that those students who consider themselves unlikely to earn a good income from their higher education efforts would be the most attracted to the system. They would seek up-front finance without expecting to repay any or much of it. *Moral hazard* arises when a graduate earning a large income from a university education seeks to negate the contract to pay the equity provider by falsifying and hiding income, or by leaving the country.

In a private student equity market, financiers will have a strong incentive to select those courses, universities and individuals offering the largest expected returns – the opposite of adverse selection. They would employ staff skilled in assessing risks and prospective returns. And they would write contracts that were not easily negated.

In due course, based on the American experience, a human-capital equity market is likely to form naturally in Australia. But it would probably take up to twenty years. The Australian government could bring it forward. In the initial period of a student equity market private financiers would find it almost impossible to price the risks of the equities, since there would be no history of yields and defaults. And there would be no experience of what is called 'mis-selling risk' – in this case, the risk that popular media would run stories about naïve teenagers lured into student equity contracts and then obliged to pay lots more money to the financier than was provided in the first place.

As the human-capital equity market matured these risks would abate, but in the early years they would either prevent the formation of a market, or would add such a large risk premium as to make the contract unattractive to most students. Bringing forward the formation of a human-capital equity market would require some early risk-sharing by the Commonwealth. For example, to avoid mis-selling risk the Commonwealth could pool funds from private financiers. Early pooling would have two other advantages. First, it would enable the development of a secondary market of buying and selling in the bonds and associated innovations in risk management and development of better products. And second, the use of the tax system to collect income from graduates would be more readily acceptable to the general community where the government was directly involved in arranging student finance.

Since competition among student equity providers would direct the market to those students offering the highest expected returns at the lowest risk, the market would gravitate towards students with strong records of academic achievement at school seeking to enrol in degrees leading to the highest salaries. HECS-funded places would then be determined according to two criteria: wider (spillover) benefits to the community but low expected private returns; and considerations of fairness. Commonwealth-subsidised HECS places would be concentrated on courses such as pure science (basic research rather than applied research) and the education of artists, historians and other creative people. HECS funding would also be available on the basis of a lack of financial capacity to pay full fees and living expenses while at university – an effective return to the system of Commonwealth Scholarships that applied before 1972.

As the student equity market matured, private financiers would increasingly work directly with public universities of their choosing to increase the number of university places in degrees offering large private returns, such as dentistry and medicine. Though this would be good for Australia, traditionalists would brand it as the privatisation of public universities. Yet public universities already derive more than half their income from non-government sources, including student fees. As in all areas of public policy, the challenge is to harness private resources for the public good, and combine them with public resources to produce the best results for Australia.

A combination of public funding for universities, HECS and Australian student equities could provide the financial resources to take the step up to mass participation in higher education that Australia needs. It would provide opportunities not currently available to well-performing students from disadvantaged backgrounds, giving effect to the ideal of opportunity for all.

VOCATIONAL EDUCATION FUNDING

Australia has an acute shortage of trade skills. Skill shortages have been identified as a key constraint on Australia's productive capacity. In response to these shortages, the federal government has greatly increased the number of places for skilled migrants. While extra immigration is a welcome contribution to sustaining Australia's prosperity, the sudden, large increase in the skill category is an admission of a national failure to turn out sufficient numbers of Australian tradespeople.

The case for increased public funding of vocational education is compelling. But the story is the same as for universities – the number of extra places required is likely to exceed the willingness of taxpayers to fund them.

Philosophically and practically there is no sound reason for limiting HECS and Australian student equities to university degrees. In fact, student equities might be especially well suited to vocational education, and could be provided by employers in a radically revamped apprenticeship system. Employers could be permitted to enter into contracts with apprentices, paying training costs and a more attractive wage during the period of the apprenticeship in return for an agreed share of income after completion of the apprenticeship.

Voluntary bonding could be a feature in the scheme, where the apprentice agrees to stay with the employer for a specified period after gaining the training qualification. If the employer and the apprentice agreed to a bonding arrangement, the employer would be able to capture a larger share of the benefit of training the apprentice. The terms of the equity arrangement in these circumstances would be more favourable to the apprentice than if no bonding arrangement were included.

CHAPTER 8

ENCOURAGING AUSTRALIAN IDEAS

AUSTRALIA'S RESEARCH AND DEVELOPMENT EFFORT

National returns from extra investment in R&D are estimated at around 60 per cent.[1] At these high rates of return Australia would clearly benefit from more investment in R&D.

Australia's business spending on R&D as a share of GDP peaked in 1996. The gap between Australia and the OECD narrowed consistently from the mid-1980s through the early 1990s. But following the incoming Coalition government's cut in the 150 per cent R&D tax concession to 125 per cent, the gap between Australia's business R&D spending and that of the OECD has widened.

Australia's R&D intensity – as measured by business spending on R&D as a proportion of GDP – is below that of 15 other OECD countries (see figure 8.1).

A broader measure of Australia's R&D effort – a measure of investment in knowledge – aggregates public and private spending on R&D, higher education and computer software. On this measure, Australia ranks a mediocre 14th out of 26 OECD countries surveyed.[2]

The introduction in 2001 of a 175 per cent premium rate

concession on eligible incremental R&D spending does not appear to have caused any significant increase in spending. Budget projections of the cost of this concession to 2008 imply no significant increase on 2004 spending levels.[3]

Yet Australia appears to have relatively generous tax concessions for spending on R&D by large firms compared with other

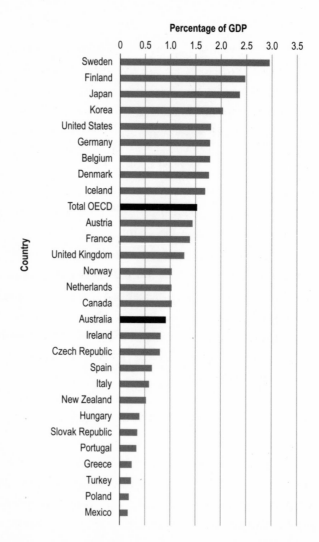

FIGURE 8.1 BUSINESS SPENDING ON RESEARCH AND DEVELOPMENT, 2004 (OECD (2005E); ABS (2005A)

OECD countries,[4] which raises the question of whether these tax concessions are a wise public investment. R&D tax concessions may be an afterthought in business decision-making; often businesses appear to decide on their R&D spending on other grounds, and claim a deduction at the end of the tax period for decisions that would have been taken anyway.[5]

OVERSEAS EXPERIENCE

Most OECD countries provide enhanced tax deductions, tax credits or direct subsidies for business spending on R&D. Tax deductions of around 125 per cent and 150 per cent are common, as are tax credits for all R&D or for extra R&D above a firm's recent historical levels. Recognising that most private R&D is carried out by large companies – and probably would be undertaken regardless of tax concessions – OECD countries are increasingly favouring small businesses in the design of R&D incentives.

Several countries, including the United States, Japan, Britain, the Netherlands and New Zealand, have been examining new ways of enhancing the tax treatment of R&D, while that bold R&D experimenter, Ireland, discontinued its R&D tax allowance in 2001. Other countries are considering phasing out their R&D tax concessions to increase the neutrality of their tax systems. A number of OECD countries target their incentives to R&D projects undertaken in collaboration with universities and other public research institutions.[6]

REFORMING AUSTRALIA'S R&D INCENTIVES

Australia's system of encouraging R&D needs a total overhaul. The subsidy value of the R&D tax concession, including the 175 per cent premium rate, is so low for businesses, and the base of eligible expenditures is so narrow, that the concession appears to be at best marginal to business R&D spending decisions.[7] The government's R&D tax concession appears to be a $400 million

annual gift to businesses that elicits little or no extra R&D investment. And the imputation system of company income tax means
that concessions claimed by Australian companies, while reducing
company tax, correspondingly increase the personal tax liabilities
of most shareholders. That is, the government claws back a large
part of the subsidy from Australian shareholders.

The Productivity Commission has floated the idea of converting the R&D tax concession into a non-taxable grant, and
applying it only to incremental investment.[8]

The tax concession could be cashed-out to create a pool
of public funds for encouraging private sector R&D. It could be
combined with other, smaller R&D programs to create a large
Australian innovation fund of up to $3 billion.[9] At least some of the
funds could be made available as loans, with repayment contingent
on the private innovator achieving specified minimum returns on
investment. If the minimum returns were not achieved the loan
would not be repaid; if they were, the loan would be repayable over
time, with interest. Such a loans system, modelled on HECS for university fees, could ensure the replenishment of the fund while encouraging the commercialisation of Australian ideas and inventions.

In determining the merit of applications for Australian innovation funding, regard should be had for Australia's prospective
competitive strengths. Australia's biological diversity is unique,
and the richest among all the continents. Biotechnology might
therefore be an area of competitive strength. So, too, might
research into cures for sun-induced melanoma. Indeed, it has been
estimated that annual rates of return to Australian health R&D
have historically been up to five dollars for every dollar expended,
including eightfold returns to cardiovascular R&D, sixfold
returns to respiratory R&D and fivefold returns to R&D
involving research into the digestive system.[10]

A common complaint about R&D tax incentive schemes is that
governments change them too often, altering the eligibility criteria
and the rates of concession. The argument is that a lack of cer-

tainty about future government support hinders private R&D investment. These criticisms have some validity. But if, as seems probable, the present tax concessions are eliciting little extra private R&D, the creation of a merit-based grant scheme would be a real improvement.

To impart a degree of transparency and predictability in a grant scheme, clear selection criteria would need to be laid down. The scheme should be oriented towards smaller firms, business collaboration with public universities and research institutions and R&D activities that make intensive use of researchers. Large-scale, capital-intensive R&D projects, like work on synchrotrons, would be funded separately, as at present.

USE IT OR LOSE IT

Australian universities and other public research institutions generate very large amounts of potentially valuable intellectual property, but much of it is locked up and never sees the light of day. Public and private researchers could augment some of that intellectual property and create commercial value from it, but are prevented from doing so by patent laws. At the same time, the vesting of parts of intellectual property rights in the array of bodies that fund public university research weakens the incentive for researchers to continue a line of inquiry, since they may gain no benefit from the intellectual property rights created along the way.

Policy-makers in the United States recognised these problems more than a quarter of a century ago, and in 1980 introduced the *Stevenson-Wydler Technology Innovation Act* and the *Bayh-Dole [Patents and Trademark] Act*. These acts allow non-profit, publicly funded researchers to keep the intellectual property they generate and to apply for patents in their own names, while setting maximum time limits on the ownership and commercial development of intellectual property held by universities and public research laboratories.

The effect of the legislation is to confer intellectual property rights in innovations on publicly funded researchers who create them, but then to require their further use within specified time periods so that they are not locked away from other researchers for an inordinate length of time.

Reviews of the US legislation have concluded that it has been highly successful in increasing technology transfer from universities to industry, and on to the general public, while encouraging scientists to continue using and building on specific lines of inquiry. This is seen as crucial in typical circumstances of multiple funding sources.[11]

AUSTRALIA AS A FREE-RIDER?

Investing more in R&D is a different proposition from Australia developing its own home-grown ICT production industry. Visiting Melbourne for the World Economic Forum in 2000, Bill Gates criticised Australia for failing to develop major ICT production industries. But there is no reason to believe Australia would have a comparative advantage in ICT production. During the 1990s the price of IT hardware in the United States declined by a staggering 21 per cent per annum, and in Australia it declined by 18 per cent.[12] Australia received huge benefits from these price reductions without bearing the costs of investing in IT hardware.

Pointing to the folly of Australia trying to establish its own computer hardware production industry is not to suggest that Australia should be a total international free-rider when it comes to R&D. We should position ourselves to be able successfully and quickly to adopt and adapt overseas advances in ICT and other innovation. The international evidence clearly shows that a country's success in adopting foreign technology is enhanced by its own investment in education and R&D:

> although the rest of the world provides a huge source of ideas and technologies, a country like Australia cannot rely on a strategy of

passive absorption to maintain strong productivity performance. In order to benefit from the global public good of world knowledge, countries need to have well trained scientists, a technologically capable workforce and active engagement in cutting edge research.[13]

Australia is a proven leader among OECD countries in absorbing ICT developed overseas,[14] having few regulatory restrictions in comparison with other OECD countries. The creation of the open, competitive economy has greatly assisted Australia in absorbing overseas technologies. It has been estimated that domestic R&D and the spillovers from foreign R&D absorbed into Australia are of roughly equal importance to Australian productivity growth.[15]

Australia cannot simply be an international free-rider, utilising ICT developed overseas; but nor should we seek to invest heavily in replicating the ICT production effort of countries like the United States. We should identify our own competitive advantage in R&D, lifting both private and public sector investment in R&D, and targeting smaller firms and collaborative research with universities and other public research institutions.

CHAPTER 9

REWARDING AUSTRALIAN INITIATIVE

A REWARD FOR EFFORT AND RISK-TAKING

Modern Australia is built on the hard work and entrepreneurial spirit of its people. But as the welfare state has advanced through middle Australia and onto the wealthy, the increasing tax burden has stifled the incentive to work. And as the tax system confronting small business has become ever more complex under a government that purports to be pro-business, the crushing compliance burden is diverting businesses away from creating wealth and jobs. It's time to restore incentives for work and risk-taking.

THE WORKFORCE PARTICIPATION RATE

High taxes on income can depress the proportion of the working-age population in work or actively looking for it (the *workforce participation rate*). Among 28 OECD countries, Australia has the 11th highest participation rate. More than 73 per cent of Australians aged from 15 to 64 participate in the workforce, compared with an OECD average of 70 per cent and highs of around 80 per cent for the Czech Republic and Scandinavian countries.[1] Claims that Australia has low workforce participation are exaggerated; but there is obvious room for improvement. The workforce participation of Australian women in the 25 to 49 age group ranks around 20th in the OECD; the participation of Australian men in the same age group ranks second lowest, though their participation rate is still 90 per cent.[2]

By better rewarding effort we can lift the participation rate of working-age Australians and increase the number of hours they choose to work, creating a valuable counterbalance to the harmful economic consequences of population ageing.

INCREASING WORKFORCE PARTICIPATION

WHERE DO WE START?

More than one in five working-age Australians – around 2.7 million people – receives some form of government income support.[3] Each working-age Australian who moves from welfare to work contributes a double benefit to the nation: a reduction in tax-payer-funded government spending, and an increase in national income. These national benefits are additional to the personal benefits arising from working – improved self-esteem, social interaction with colleagues, a sense of personal fulfilment, and financial independence, as well as reductions in crime, domestic violence and ill health. These, too, offer broader benefits for the nation.

In meeting the challenges of an ageing population and faltering productivity growth, sensible government policy for lifting workforce participation should focus on those whose workforce participation offers the greatest benefits to society. Yet the federal government's main response to the problems identified in the *Intergenerational Report* has been directed at arguably the least productive option – increasing the workforce participation of Australians close to retiring age. The treasurer declared 'there is going to be no such thing as full-time retirement',[4] and set about reducing disincentives for ongoing participation in the workforce by older Australians. While reducing work disincentives for older

Australians is a worthy policy objective in its own right, it will achieve the smallest payoff in combating the ageing of the population, since it will have a very short payoff period compared with policies directed at increasing the participation of younger Australians. The Productivity Commission points out that policies that elicit increased participation only for older people cannot, by themselves, act as an antidote to the poor labour supply growth arising from ageing.[5] These conclusions are supported by the *Intergenerational Report*, which concludes that even large increases in the participation rates of older workers would have only a small impact on the overall participation rate.[6]

Selecting the end of the working lives of Australians as a place to lift workforce participation seems relatively unproductive in view of the short period during which returns can be achieved. Focusing on the disability support pension as a point at which to reduce welfare spending might not be very productive either. True, the number of recipients has ballooned since the early 1980s, especially among males aged from 40 to 49.[7] Perhaps this reflects the attractiveness of the disability support pension relative to the unemployment benefit.[8] But this trend appears to be coming to an end. Disability support pension rates are already dropping for men over 50, and are likely to stabilise for younger men and women over the longer run, such that one of the major drivers of falling participation rates for men is set to play a much less significant role in the future.[9]

Cajoling older men off the disability support pension and into the workforce might ease budgetary pressures but it would *reduce* average labour productivity, since these Australians with a disability are only marginally attached to the workforce. Measures to reduce the risk of retrenchment for older men would be far more productive.

Consideration could be given to encouraging, and financially rewarding, volunteering by older men on disability pensions (and age pensions). Since older Australians tend to volunteer more than younger people, the ageing of the population over the next forty years will have the beneficial side-effect of increasing the number of volunteers, perhaps by more than one-third.[10] Encouraging and subsidising volunteering work by older Australians, including those on the disability support pension, would be a valuable contribution to the task of combating the impacts of population ageing, and would benefit the volunteers themselves.

The third priority group targeted by the federal government in raising workforce participation is sole parents. More than 80 per cent of sole parents receive income support, and almost all the increase in the number of jobless households since the early 1980s has been due to an increase in jobless households headed by sole parents. The high incidence of such households is a big social problem for Australia, since it perpetuates the cycle of dependency, creating second and third generation unemployment.

But is ever tougher work-testing the answer? Forcing sole parents into the workforce against their will might make some difference to overall workforce participation rates, but who is going to look after the children left at home? Crucially, who is going to ensure that those children are well adapted to learning? A latchkey approach to getting sole parents into work is classic short-term thinking that is bound to have long-term costs for those children, and for society as a whole. More than half of single parents receiving sole parent benefits have no tertiary qualifications, compared with around 40 per cent of partnered mothers.[11] Far more productive approaches would involve raising the workforce skills of sole parents and removing impediments to their participation in the workforce, such as loss of government benefits from working and problems in accessing affordable, quality child-care.

Better educated Australians participate more heavily in the workforce.[12] The best prospects for lifting workforce participation therefore lie with young people entering the workforce. The greater the proportion of these young people who have skills, the greater will be the overall participation rate, and the longer lasting will be the benefits to Australia. This again points us in the direction of improving high-school retention rates:

> the significant increase in year 12 retention rates that has occurred since the 1970s is likely to have a positive effect on participation regardless of whether these people obtain additional qualifications. Further ... policies that increase education retention are likely to increase labour force participation and promote improved labour market outcomes.[13]

Not only will these young workers lift the aggregate workforce participation rate over the longest possible time, the skills they possess will also raise productivity growth – improving two of the P's in one go.

Government policy should concentrate on raising the skills of all working-age Australians, and especially those who have a full working life ahead of them. Breaking the cycle of poverty and despair must involve a conscious investment in the coming generations, rather than simply coercing those in the present generation who lack the skills to participate fully in the workforce.

DISINCENTIVES TO MOVING FROM WELFARE TO WORK

Much has been made of the disincentives to moving from welfare to work created by the interaction of the income tax and social security systems.[14] A combination of phasing out government cash benefits as earned income increases, together with the application of higher rates of tax in a progressive income tax system, can produce high effective marginal tax rates. (An *effective marginal tax rate* is the proportion of a one dollar increase in private income that is lost to income tax and income tests on social security and family assistance payments.)[15]

The withdrawal of family payments if mothers return to work after having a baby can deter them from deciding to do so. Labor in government began means-testing the family allowance, introduced an extra means-tested family allowance supplement and later brought in a parenting allowance. The Howard government introduced a family tax initiative in 1997 that added complexity to the system of family payments. In association with the introduction of the GST in 2000, the government then simplified the family payments system by introducing an income-tested payment for each dependent child – Family Tax Benefit Part A – and a payment for parents who stay at home to care for children – Family Tax Benefit Part B. The government extended payments up the income scale as partial compensation for the GST.

In 2004, the government reduced phase-out rates on Family Tax Benefit Part A and Part B from 30 per cent to 20 per cent, and increased the income level at which Family Tax Benefit Part B was fully payable. Although these measures reduced effective marginal tax rates for the households, they took the family payments system even further up the income scale.

Before the 2004 changes, only 8 per cent of the working-age population faced effective marginal tax rates greater than 60 per cent, almost all of these being in the 60 to 80 per cent range.[16] But among households earning an income, around one-fifth of couples with children and more than half of sole parents faced high effective marginal tax rates.[17]

Contrary to the popular belief that high effective marginal tax rates are mainly confined to low-income earners, they are very prevalent in the middle-income ranges.[18] Nevertheless, low-income couples with children often gain little or no extra family income when the mother increases her hours of work; and for some increases in hours worked they can actually be worse off after counting child-care costs.[19]

There is no magical way of further reducing effective marginal tax rates for sole parents and for couples with children without undesirable consequences. High effective marginal tax rates can be reduced only by reducing income tax rates or slowing the phase-out rates on government income-support payments. In a progressive income tax system and a needs-based income-support system this is like squeezing a hose – the effective marginal tax rates will not disappear but will pop up somewhere else along the income scale.

Reducing phase-out rates for family payments would take Australia further into the realms of upper-class welfare. An alternative approach is to identify variables that are not income-related but that correlate closely with need and with work decisions. One such variable is the age of children. Key decisions by mothers about returning to work are typically made when the child they are caring for is under the age of three. It might therefore be highly efficient to base family payments on the age of children.[20]

The family payments system could be made universal in respect of children under three. Such a system would take 20 percentage points off effective marginal tax rates over a very large income range – a big improvement in work incentives. A universal family payment for children under three could form a stepping-stone to a more ambitious reform program, such as that proposed by Garnaut,[21] that would greatly reduce effective marginal tax rates and improve work incentives.

While making family payments universal for children under three might seem to violate the principle of needs-based welfare, the present system is getting close to universality. Almost 90 per cent of families with dependent children receive family payments.[22] And the number of children in a family is probably correlated with need anyway – bigger families are often the neediest. Parents of young children are usually in the early stages of their careers, and one parent – typically the mother – will have been out of the workforce during the children's infancy.

Mothers with children aged three and older have typically already made their key decision about returning to work. For them, the loss of family payments is likely to have less influence than for mothers of very young children. For parents with children aged three and above, Family Tax Benefits Part A and Part B could be combined into a single payment, and means-testing tightened by 10 per cent. The savings would be about enough to finance the universal payment for children under three.

A family payments system developed along these lines would recognise the key decision points for women in balancing work and family life, and therefore would support higher rates of work-force participation by women.

WOMEN AT WORK, AND FERTILITY

Countries with high female workforce participation rates also tend to have higher fertility rates. Maintaining an attachment to the workforce through the connector of part-time work seems to be the key to avoiding trade-offs between participation and fer-tility. An affordable, flexible child-care system can act as the con-nection between fertility rates and workforce participation by mothers. A fair and efficient child-care system that helps women balance work and family life is better thought of as an investment in Australia's future than simply as a social spending program.

Research conducted for the OECD points to potentially very large returns from additional public investment in child-care, in the form of sharp increases in female workforce participation rates.[23] The OECD finds that Australia has very low child-care subsidies compared with other OECD countries, and that Australia's female workforce participation would be highly responsive to increased child-care subsidies.[24] The OECD espe-cially supports child-care subsidies for low-income sole parents and couples with infants:

> childcare subsidies may also help low income mothers break away from welfare dependence. There is evidence that childcare subsidies are accompanied by high female participation ...This is mostly true for formal day care subsidies (i.e. for infants).[25]

This is not to suggest that policies should be developed that push mothers of infants back into the workforce when they would prefer to stay at home and look after their babies. Rather, it suggests that financial disincentives to returning to work should be reduced, allowing the mother to make a decision on whether or not to return to work without facing government-imposed financial penalties.

From 2000 the federal government removed direct subsidies to private providers of child-care and redirected the subsidies to families on a means-tested basis. This child-care benefit is highly progressive, in that it subsidises a larger proportion of the child-care costs of low-income earners than of the wealthy. Yet mothers with two or more children can be worse off from working full-time than from working part-time.[26]

During the 2004 election campaign the government announced a new 30 per cent rebate on out-of-pocket child-care costs. Although the child-care benefit introduced in 2000 is progressive, the child-care rebate is regressive: it is of greater benefit to high-income earners.[27] The reason is that out-of-pocket child-care expenses remaining after receipt of the child-care benefit are greater for high-income earners, and the rebate is directed at these expenses. Since child-care costs are more likely to be a deterrent to workforce participation by low-income mothers, the child-care rebate is not only inequitable but is also highly inefficient in increasing workforce participation by mothers.

The child-care rebate should at least be modified and the savings used to increase the child-care benefit, improving both the equity and efficiency of the Commonwealth's system of child-care subsidies.

CHAPTER 10

POPULATING AUSTRALIA'S REGIONS

AUSTRALIA'S SETTLEMENT PATTERN

Only about 27 per cent of governments around the world are satisfied with the geographic distribution of population in their countries.[1] Successive Australian governments have been unhappy with the distribution of the country's population, but not since the Whitlam government have they systematically sought to influence it.

Australia is one of the most sparsely populated countries in the world, yet it has one of the world's most spatially concentrated populations.

Between the mid-1950s and the early 1970s Australia experienced a decline in the proportion of its population living in rural areas, and a corresponding increase in the proportion living in major urban areas. But since then the drift to the major cities has slowed. More recently, there has been an increase in the proportion of the population living not only in the towns and cities on the coast, but also in a number of inland regional centres.

This changing settlement pattern can be explained by the decline in large-scale manufacturing in the major cities, the expansion of knowledge-based industries made more footloose by a revolution in transport and communications technologies, shifts in lifestyle preferences, and expansions in government income-support payments where eligibility is not tied to living in a specific locality.[2]

Population is drifting from rural areas and small country towns to larger regional centres and coastal areas rather than to the major capitals. In the post-war era population growth in Sydney and Melbourne was driven by both overseas immigration and natural increase. Net overseas migration has contributed half of the post-war population growth of Sydney and Melbourne – closer to two-thirds if the children of migrants are counted.[3]

A popular misconception is that, while Sydney and Melbourne have large ethnic communities, very few overseas migrants settle in rural and regional areas. In fact, around 20 per cent of Australia's overseas-born population lives outside the major urban areas, and in the early post-war years this was as high as 40 per cent.[4]

A POPULATION POLICY?

No developed country has a population policy expressed as a target population or a target population growth rate. Governments have an array of policies that affect population size and growth, including health policies to increase life expectancy and reduce infant mortality; education, child-care and family payment policies that affect fertility; and immigration policies. But it is hard to conceive of a uniquely optimal population for any country. Confronted with the challenge of an ageing population, Australia would benefit from a bigger population with an age profile revitalised by a bigger immigration intake directed at working-age migrants and their children. But is this feasible?

IMMIGRATION

Current immigration policy emphasises skilled migration, so that net migration mainly adds to the working-age population.[5] But working-age migrants get older, too; so the question becomes whether the rate of future migration can be large enough to moderate population ageing.

Official ABS population projections assume constant *levels* of net migration, the mid-range assumption being 100 000 a year. But as total population increases over time, a fixed *level* of migration equates to a declining *rate* of migration expressed as a proportion of the population. Arguments can be made for using either migration rates or migration levels in future population projections.[6]

One way of approaching the issue is to consider the upper range of net migration used by the ABS of 125 000 per annum. This is high by recent historical standards. From 1950 to the middle of the 2000s net overseas migration has fluctuated around an average of about 85 000, the same average as for 1995–2002. However, net overseas migration was 117 600 in 2003–04.

Compared with the mid-range case of 100 000 per annum, net migration of 125 000 per annum would reduce the projected proportion of the population aged 65 and over in forty years' time from 26.1 per cent to 25.6 per cent.[7] This is hardly a significant difference, leading to the conclusion that:

> net overseas migration cannot realistically be engineered to avoid
> or even substantially moderate Australia's demographic transition
> to an older population.[8]

These projections also demonstrate the absurdity of the polar positions on a desirable population for Australia – six to twelve million advocated by prominent biologist Tim Flannery in 1994, and fifty million advocated by former prime minister Malcolm Fraser in 1997. If Australia were able to raise its net overseas migration to 125 000 over a sustained period and to stabilise its fertility rate at 1.8, the effect would be to raise our population in 2051 from 26.4 million to 31.4 million, an addition of just 5 million people.

Increased levels of overseas migration will be needed just to cushion the impacts of population ageing and to prevent Australia's population from declining from the mid-2030s. To gain some perspective on the potential role of immigration in augmenting the future workforce, consider an alternative policy of raising workforce participation rates for men to where they were in Australia 30 years ago, and for women to the highest current international level (in Denmark). Doubling net overseas migration to 220 000 from 2005 would achieve an increase in the Australian workforce by 2030 very similar to what would be produced by these high participation rates.[9]

Raising net overseas migration to 220 000 would severely stretch the tolerance of the Australian people. But net overseas migration of at least 125 000 a year would seem highly desirable, so long as the additional migrants were mainly young, skilled and settled outside the Sydney basin. Attracting young, skilled migrants to Australia would increase our pool of knowledge workers. Almost half of Australian workers in the top 10 per cent of occupations by skill level are in the 25 to 39 age bracket.[10]

At present, almost 60 per cent of migrants seek to settle in Sydney and Melbourne.[11] While Melbourne seems to be willing and able to absorb these migrants and the Victorian government continues to welcome more of them, the Sydney basin is suffering from congestion and population sprawl, and its state government has been less receptive to more overseas migration.

SETTLING IN AUSTRALIA'S DYNAMIC REGIONS

During the 1990s the population in a number of regional centres declined, but other centres gained population. Substantial gainers were Maitland and Queanbeyan (New South Wales), Geelong, Bendigo and Ballarat (Victoria), Cairns (Queensland), Port Lincoln (South Australia) and Albany (Western Australia).[12]

Separate population analysis for the state of Victoria for a twenty-year period ending in 2002 reveals four geographical patterns: strong growth in most regional centres, in areas of natural amenity (along the coast and the Murray River) and in the urban fringe; and a population decline in more remote rural areas and towns.[13] Similar patterns are evident elsewhere in Australia.

Can Australia's regions become a location for increased overseas migration, boosting the Australian skilled workforce while easing the pressure on the Sydney basin? An analysis of official population projections to 2019 for non-capital cities with populations of more than 15 000 people reveals a trend of inland Australia declining in population as the capital cities and coastal cities continue to grow.[14] But population growth in a number of regional centres is expected to be strong, pointing to opportunities for regional development in more dynamic areas, and possibly also arresting the decline of some regions. The analysis finds that of the 61 regional centres with a population exceeding 15 000, a total of 15 are expected to have population growth of more than 20 per cent. Another 21 regional centres are expected to have positive population growth of up to 20 per cent. Around half of these are inland centres.

These trends can be volatile; so not too much emphasis should be placed on the projections for a particular regional city. But separate research undertaken for the Property Council of Australia identifies regional centres likely to grow over the next twenty years as including Albury-Wodonga, Wagga Wagga, Tamworth, Orange, Dubbo, Shepparton, Cairns, Rockhampton, Bundaberg, Hervey Bay, Gladstone, Mandurah and Darwin.[15] Most of the expanding inland regional centres have gained jobs through manufacturing and service industries, with employment growth linked to population changes, migration, local amenity value and rising incomes.[16]

A tremendous opportunity exists to enhance the attractiveness of Australia's dynamic regions, and of some of the declining regions, so that larger numbers of skilled people, including skilled migrants, would settle in them. The circumstances of today and the coming decades are very different from those of the early 1970s when the Whitlam government experimented with regional growth centres:

> In an era where development of communication systems has greatly reduced the need for business and people to be located in major urban areas, and decentralisation is occurring in other

Euro-American societies, this issue needs revisiting ... structural change in the economy has seen the focus of employment shift away from manufacturing ... growing industries like tourism and information technology are frequently locatable outside of large cities, or relatively footloose ... Moreover, in some large cities, especially Sydney, the diseconomies of large city locations in terms of high costs of operation, congestion and pollution are being felt. Accordingly, the current era is quite different from that prevailing in the 1970s when the Australian government made a major attempt to foster regional development.[17]

The Victorian state government is a strong supporter of population growth in regional areas, and understands that advances in ICT are allowing workers to telecommute. It advocates the establishment of a *national regional infrastructure development fund* for investing in regional infrastructure.[18]

ATTRACTING MIGRANTS TO REGIONAL CENTRES

Before 2004, Australia had only a very weak set of incentives designed to attract prospective migrants to regional Australia. Labor called for a strengthening of regional migration incentives,[19] and commissioned a report to develop recommendations for ways of bringing this about.[20]

In 2004 the Howard government strengthened regional migration incentives along the lines recommended in the report.[21] The most significant of the changes was a new visa category for skilled migrants prepared to settle in regional Australia. This is a two-stage visa, involving a three-year temporary stage during which applicants are required to live and work in regional Australia, with pathways to permanent residence if they comply with the requirements of the temporary visa and live in some part of regional Australia for the three-year period. The visa is available to applicants who fall short of the general skilled pass mark.

Time will tell whether these new regional migration incentives are successful in attracting skilled migrants to regional Australia and retaining them there. In April 2005 the federal government announced a further strengthening of regional migration incentives, granting more points to skilled applicants for settlement in regional areas.

A further incentive for migrants to remain in regional Australia could be provided through the vehicle of family reunion. Most migrants value family reunion opportunities highly. Skilled migrants who obtain permanent residence through regional migration incentive schemes could be encouraged to remain in regional Australia beyond the three-year qualifying period through the offer of family reunion opportunities in subsequent periods. Family reunion opportunities already exist, but only for family members who also possess the requisite skills. Family reunion could be extended to family members who do not achieve the skill pass mark but are sponsored by established skilled migrants living in regional Australia. Like their sponsors, those family members would need to live in a regional area for a minimum of three years before being eligible for permanent residence.

Foreign students paying full fees to study at Australia's universities mostly come from wealthy families. Their families should be encouraged to join the students attending regional universities during the course of their studies and, like the students, be allowed to apply for permanent residency while in Australia.

At present, migrants entering Australia under regional migration schemes are counted in the Commonwealth's annual migration planning numbers. Local communities and their representatives are best placed to determine their regional migration requirements. The size of the regional migration component of Australia's total immigration program should not be determined solely from the top down by the Commonwealth, but should be based on input from the bottom up by local councils, local communities and state governments. And for the purposes of regional migration incentives, regional Australia should be defined by local and state governments and not by the Commonwealth.

Some states are very active in encouraging migration to regional areas. South Australia[22] and Victoria[23] are strong advocates of regional migration incentives, both are interested in locating applicants under the humanitarian program (including refugees) in regional areas, and they are intent on making it easier for foreign students attending their universities to obtain permanent residency. These states, in particular, are demonstrating the wisdom and foresight of engaging migrants in the task of strengthening their regions.

Box 10.1 describes a resettlement program in the Victorian city of Warrnambool for refugees from the Sudan.

BOX 10.1 SUDANESE REFUGEES IN WARRNAMBOOL

From 2004, refugees from civil-war-torn Sudan began arriving in Warrnambool in Victoria's western district. In all, 78 refugees had settled in Warrnambool by mid-2005. Twelve families had relocated from Melbourne, and three families directly from refugee camps along with 11 individuals.

Almost all the men are employed in the local meatworks. As they improve their English and continue their studies they will diversify into jobs in other local businesses.

The predominantly Christian settlers have been welcomed into the local community. Three Sudanese babies had been born in Warrnambool by mid-2005, and are likely to grow into very dark-skinned, very tall adults. Though Sudanese children love playing soccer, it will only be a matter of time before a 200-centimetre Sudanese teenager is playing in the forward line in the local Australian Rules competition.

The Sudanese refugee resettlement project is being funded by John Singleton through his commitment to refugee resettlement in Australia. The project is being supported by the Victorian government and the Warrnambool City Council in cooperation with the Commonwealth.

ATTRACTING AUSTRALIANS TO
REGIONAL CENTRES

If it makes sense to attract skilled migrants to regional Australia, it would make even more sense to seek to attract Australians from the big cities to regional centres. After all, Australians are already familiar with the local language, culture and laws, so barriers to entry for them are lower than those facing migrants coming from overseas.

Who should regional centres seek to attract? Pioneering work has been done by Richard Florida[24] on the formula for successful regions. Traditionally, local and state governments have sought to attract companies to regions, sometimes through large public subsidies and tax breaks. But Florida's analysis of patterns of movement reveals that companies follow people, not the other way around. And to be attractive and successful it is insufficient to be world-class in just one or two dimensions. Instead, synergies are needed across Florida's '3Ts' of talent, technology and tolerance.

Regional development strategies therefore need to be directed at attracting smart people – or, as Florida calls them, the creative class. The core of the creative class is people in science and engineering, architecture and design, education, arts, music and entertainment. Around the core are creative professionals in business, finance, law and health care: 'regional economic growth is powered by creative people, who prefer places that are diverse, tolerant and open to new ideas.'[25]

The creative class seeks music, art, technology and outdoor recreation. Places rich in social and cultural capital are powerful magnets for them. There is often an active gay community in places the creative class finds attractive. This does not mean the creative class is necessarily attracted to gays; what it does mean is that the open existence of a gay community is a leading indicator of tolerance.

The creative class seeks amenity not in the form of big sporting stadiums but of opportunities for outdoor recreation (to keep fit and recharge the batteries), a vibrant street life and, ideally, a cutting-edge music scene.

Though Florida's theories have been developed out of empirical observation of the pattern of regional development in the United States, they have relevance for Australia. But, disturbingly, applying Florida's Creative Index to Australia reveals no high-ranking regional areas outside the major capitals and coastal areas. These areas – including Sydney, Melbourne, Brisbane, Adelaide, Perth, the Gold Coast, the Sunshine Coast, the north and central coasts of NSW and the Illawarra – are already magnets for the creative class.

State governments are becoming conscious of the need to attract creative people. Queensland launched a creative policy in 2004, and NSW and Victoria have been working on policies to generate creative capital. But the nation's inland regional centres have more work ahead of them in attracting the creative class. They need world-class ICT through broadband rollout, excellent education and medical facilities, and a reputation for tolerance and welcoming strangers, including overseas migrants.

America's economic success appears to be founded on openness to new ideas and energetic people from around the world. The largest immigration wave in America's history occurred in the decade of the 1990s. Immigration in the 1990s has fuelled the resurgence of both older places like New York and Chicago and newer places like Phoenix. In Silicon Valley almost a quarter of the population, and one-third of high tech scientists and engineers, are overseas-born. And it has been suggested that one reason for the decline of Japan has been its racial homogeneity.[26]

Three observations should be taken on board by decision-makers in regional Australia. First, those who choose to leave their countries are predisposed to risk and can be thought of as 'innovation outsiders'. Second, openness to immigration is particularly important for smaller cities and regions. And third, young people are especially valuable, since they are able to work longer and harder and are more prone to taking risks precisely because they are young and childless.[27]

Australia's regional centres need a people climate more than they need a business climate. They need to be creative, diverse communities rather than close-knit, closed communities. But our regional centres should not seek to create huge science parks based on Silicon Valley, a place that has become very congested. Seeking to re-create such a place is essentially betting the future on an economic development model from the past.[28]

In summary, we need to develop a program for boosting the global competitiveness and population of Australia's more dynamic inland regions. World-class telecommunications, transport and energy facilities are needed. Efficient energy transmission systems will need to be established for those regions specialising in energy-intensive production. And to appeal to managers and other creative people from the big cities, the liveability of regional centres will need to be enhanced, through such amenities as golf courses and jogging vistas, cafes, restaurants and music. Attracting the creative class to regional Australia will require excellent schools and medical facilities. A good university campus would be a big advantage.

A national infrastructure plan will be needed to coordinate these efforts. Chapter 11 discusses a national infrastructure plan for Australia.

SLOWING EMIGRATION

At least three-quarters of a million Australians are living overseas on a long-term or permanent basis.[29] Over the five-year period to 2003, Australia appears to have lost about 5 per cent of its total stock of employed professionals as of 2001.[30] Australia continues to lose around 50 000 people a year to overseas countries:

> Indeed, with emigration of many of our best and brightest running at 50 000 or more a year, some substantial immigration is needed to fend off even earlier decline and loss of skills.[31]

While it is true that Australia has a net brain gain in numerical terms, with annual inflows of skilled migrants exceeding outflows of skilled Australians moving overseas by around 36 000,[32] this is not an argument against attracting expatriates home and encouraging them not to leave in the first place. It is true that Australia can benefit substantially from its best and brightest gaining experience overseas. But in the coming decades there will be fierce international competition for the world's pool of creative talent, and it will not be good enough for Australia to accept up to 50 000 permanent or long-term departures a year so long as overall there is a net numerical brain gain:

> If those people are the brightest and best – if they are that really top group of achievers; if they are people who, if they stayed here, could really make the difference in making the social and economic breakthroughs which improve the country – then one person does not equal one person ...[33]

Australia needs a better understanding of the reasons why such large numbers of the creative class are lost to overseas countries before we can develop appropriate policy responses. The need for that better understanding is urgent if Australia is to maximise its share of the pool of creative talent that will be so fundamental to determining the prosperity of nations in the coming decades.

CHAPTER 11

MODERN INFRASTRUCTURE FOR AUSTRALIA'S REGIONS

IS AUSTRALIA'S INFRASTRUCTURE FAILING?

A general impression has been formed that Australia's infrastructure has declined since the 1980s. Proving the proposition is more difficult. There are no statistics on national investment in infrastructure. Information is available on public gross fixed (non-defence) capital formation – a proxy for public infrastructure investment. By this measure public infrastructure investment has declined as a share of GDP from around 7 per cent in the mid-1980s to about 3.6 per cent in the early 2000s.

But drawing conclusions from these figures is complicated by two trends: the privatisation of government corporations, and a shift from the public sector to the private sector in financing infrastructure investment. Privatised former government-owned corporations continue to invest in infrastructure, but this no longer shows up in the public infrastructure investment figures. And the increasing use of public–private partnerships (PPPs) to undertake infrastructure investment also takes much investment activity outside the official figures.

In the absence of reliable figures, a better way of assessing whether Australia's infrastructure is deteriorating is to assess the state of different types of infrastructure. Various report cards have been prepared by infrastructure groups. Generally, they show that some classes of infrastructure are adequate and others not. They also show great variability across the nation, and over time, in the state of different types of infrastructure. It is therefore wrong to assert that all Australia's infrastructure is in decline, or that it is all adequate.

But there is plenty of evidence of different types of infrastructure at full capacity, or nearing the end of its useful life. Australia's stormwater infrastructure is generally old and dilapidated, a number of major ports need deepening, rail freight infrastructure – especially the north–south track – is badly run down, and broadband rollout is poor by international standards.[1] A major study on Australia's infrastructure prepared for the Business Council of Australia by Port Jackson Partners reports that Australia's energy system requires extra investment of up to $35 billion by 2020, public roads and rail will require almost $10 billion more than has been budgeted, and urban water storage capacity will need substantial upgrading.

Funding is but one issue in modernising Australia's infrastructure. Coordination and regulatory reform are essential to any overall strategy for upgrading the nation's infrastructure. Problems in these areas have created infrastructure constraints that threaten the sustainability of Australia's future economic growth.

INFRASTRUCTURE FUNDING

Australia's governments have become averse to debt as they continue a process of fiscal consolidation:

> Governments in Australia appear to have squeezed infrastructure spending to achieve essential fiscal consolidation ... A significant part of the fiscal adjustment burden may have been applied to infrastructure because deferring or cancelling large and expensive projects provides less backlash than other programs and services that impact directly on many vocal members of the community.[2]

But even this observation should be qualified: once the effects of privatisation and the increased usage of PPPs are taken into account, aggregate levels of infrastructure investment might not have declined.[3] And major new infrastructure investment programs have been announced by the Queensland, NSW and Victorian state governments. But at the Commonwealth level there appears to be a reluctance to undertake major new investment in infrastructure. The Coalition government's Future Fund is being established to meet unfunded Commonwealth superannuation liabilities. Returns on wise investment in infrastructure are likely to be much greater than returns generated by the Future Fund. Part of the proceeds of asset sales and budget surpluses that are being directed into the Future Fund should instead be directed into a national infrastructure fund.

A rigorous analysis of alternative infrastructure financing vehicles concludes that government debt is the most economically beneficial, followed by special-purpose funding vehicles, including PPPs,[4] leading to the conclusion that:

> By restricting infrastructure development in the name of fiscal conservatism, the approach of Australian governments has undermined our future economic potential.[5]

Early PPPs suffered from an imbalance of negotiating and commercial skills between private-sector proponents and state governments. Private proponents successfully sought risk-adjusted returns, and then succeeded in shifting most of the risk onto governments. But governments mostly have since become more sophisticated and experienced in negotiating PPPs, to the extent that an international ratings agency has concluded that this method of financing is probably more advanced and more successful in Australia than in any other country.[6]

REGULATION OF INFRASTRUCTURE

Following the implementation of National Competition Policy from the mid-1990s, a system of regulating access to infrastructure and the prices charged to consumers has emerged. The Australian Competition and Consumer Commission (ACCC) and state competition commissions have been empowered to set access charges by competitors to infrastructure facilities, and to regulate prices to end-users.

Competition commissions have rightly sought to facilitate competition so as to maximise consumer benefits. But, on occasion, they might not have made enough allowance in access charges for the cost of replacing assets. Electricity price-caps in NSW have been set at levels that do not cover the full cost of supply; access pricing for rail freight has been kept low to help rail compete with road transport, but too low to sustain the rail system; and the Queensland Competition Authority for a long time contemplated setting a cost of capital for the Dalrymple Bay coal-loading facility that was insufficient to warrant expansion of the facility by the private owner.[7] Telstra considers the regulated access charges for competitors to the telephone network to be too low to justify new investment in the network.

If regulation is preventing crucial infrastructure investment, the regulatory system needs to be reviewed. Telecommunications is experiencing rapid technological change, which is rendering the fixed-line network increasingly obsolete. This needs to be taken into account in setting the regulatory framework for telecommunications.

A NATIONAL INFRASTRUCTURE PLAN

The absence of any coherent baseline information about the state of Australia's infrastructure and future infrastructure needs is a symptom of a lack of national infrastructure planning and coordination.[8] Australia needs a national infrastructure plan.

The plan should be developed by a National Infrastructure Council, comprising the three levels of government. The council should operate under the auspices of the Council of Australian Governments, and be advised by an independent Infrastructure Commission (as proposed by Tanner),[9] or by a well-resourced Productivity Commission. But in addition to assessing individual proposals, the commission should have the job of developing a draft rolling plan for consideration by the Infrastructure Council.

The draft plan would be prepared on the basis of initial guidance from the council. It should not only react to existing infrastructure constraints, but also anticipate future infrastructure needs. And it should not simply react to population pressures, but should support a better dispersal of population by boosting infrastructure in Australia's expanding regions and any other regions that are considered to have future growth potential. In other words, the plan should seek to influence the future pattern of economic and population development in Australia.

The national infrastructure plan should encompass not only transport, communications, energy and water infrastructure, but also schools, universities and medical facilities needed to attract skilled and talented people to designated areas. And it should take into account regional migration goals and incentives for attracting skilled overseas migrants.

Projects eligible for government support under the national infrastructure plan would need to pass several tests to ensure that they were of genuine national worth, not just a sop to particular political constituencies. They would need to offer substantial spillover benefits for the nation that could not be captured by a private investor in the infrastructure project. One positive spillover that should be taken into account in project evaluations is the benefit of regional infrastructure in attracting and retaining population to relieve the spillover costs of congestion and poor air quality in major metropolitan areas. A further spillover benefit would be environmental improvements or lower environmental costs through, for example, the use of more greenhouse-friendly energy sources.

A second type of benefit that would not be picked up in purely commercial evaluations of infrastructure proposals arises where the actual national cost of an alternative is greater than the price charged for that alternative. For example, from the discussion on freight that follows, it is clear that road-freight user-charges are well below the true costs to the nation, which include the costs of road damage and accidents involving trucks. Where it is impractical to lift road user-charges to reflect the full costs to society of road transport, evaluations of rail freight proposals should include the benefit of avoiding these extra costs.

A third consideration is the role of the public sector in sharing risks with the private sector. The North-West Shelf gas fields would not have been developed when they were if the Western Australian government had not entered into a take-or-pay contract for the supply of gas to the south of the state. This is not to argue that the contract was good policy (in fact, it almost bankrupted the Western Australian state government). But it does illustrate that the connection of large energy sources to regional Australia, desirable as it is on broader national grounds, might on occasion require some risk-sharing by the public sector. A pipeline will not be built without the identification and securing of foundation customers. And foundation customers will be reluctant to commit themselves until the supply of gas is secured. Government equity in projects of this sort would improve their bankability. At a later date, when the project achieves profitability, the commercial entity could repay the equity funds for return to the national infrastructure fund.

The application of these tests would not assure a particular infrastructure project of support from the national infrastructure fund, but proposals would need to possess these features to qualify for evaluation. The government of the day would need to be satisfied, on the basis of rigorous independent evaluations, that a proposal was likely to generate large benefits for the nation beyond those captured in purely private commercial cost–benefit analyses.

FREIGHT

ROAD VERSUS RAIL

The Commonwealth's AusLink program is supposed to integrate road and rail freight infrastructure and boost spending on them. But it does not commit the Commonwealth to funding any part of the freight network. Nor does it commit the government to funding projects on the basis of rigorous economic assessments, which creates ample scope for funding decisions motivated by electoral considerations.[10] Yet the freight reform task is both pressing and enormous.

Even after AusLink, the estimated level of under-investment in public roads and rail is $9.6 billion.[11] Inter-capital freight is projected to grow 20 per cent faster than the economy to 2020, causing it to double between 2000 and 2020.[12] A dramatic shift is occurring in the proportion of freight carried by road and rail. Whereas in the early 1970s rail carried 70 per cent of inter-capital freight, the position had reversed by 2005; and it is projected that by 2020, road will have an 80 per cent share.[13] At these rates the number of trucks on our inter-capital roads will have increased by 65 per cent, and in metropolitan areas by 90 per cent, by 2020.[14] Congestion costs are projected to increase to almost $30 billion per annum by 2015.[15]

The north–south rail system is losing market share because it is in a poor state of repair, and because road freight is underpriced. Compared with road freight, rail offers much inferior transit times, reliability and timeliness of services. Yet when all costs are taken into account, rail transport is more efficient than road. The heaviest trucks are undercharged for the true cost of their road use, and rail charges are set to recover more of the total cost of the infrastructure than road charges.

Confronted with road freight continuing to take market share, rail freight charges are being set at rates that are insufficient to cover the costs of rail track investment. This is causing a downward spiral in rail infrastructure. It has been suggested that reform of road and rail pricing could increase rail's share of the north–south freight task to 60 per cent.[16] But a natural bottleneck would appear on the north–south rail route at a market share of around 30 to 40 per cent, necessitating a new rail route.

THE INLAND RAIL PROPOSAL

Proposed by Australian Transport and Energy Corridor Limited (ATEC), the inland rail freight proposal is for a standard gauge railway from Melbourne passing west of the Great Dividing Range through NSW and Queensland and ultimately to Darwin. The core component is the Melbourne to Brisbane section. The corridor for the rail line would be designed to also accommodate road, gas, electricity, water and fibre optic infrastructure.

An early Bureau of Transport Economics study estimated very large national returns from the project, though the estimates were based on the proponent's freight estimates, considered overly optimistic. But sensitivity analysis, using much more pessimistic estimates of capital costs and freight flows, still showed economically desirable returns.[17]

The federal government has funded four studies on the proposal, including a study on a Melbourne–Brisbane corridor announced in April 2005. In announcing this latest study the government acknowledged that rail has less than 20 per cent of the market on the north–south corridor, compared with 80 per cent on the east–west corridor to Perth.[18]

The government plans to spend $2 billion over the next five years to improve the current east coast rail links, but expects that to allow rail to carry, at most, 35 per cent of the freight task. At this point the case for the inland rail route is expected to become strong.

ENERGY

If many of Australia's regional centres are to fulfil their potential, they need inexpensive energy supplies. The national electricity market is still in its early stages of development, but will mature over the course of the next decade or so. Eastern Australia is blessed with abundant coal reserves, capable of providing the energy for base-load electricity generation at globally competitive tariffs. Though the greenhouse challenge must be met, it would be folly for Australia to abandon coal as an energy source.

But gas will have an increasing role in complementing coal. Gas is more greenhouse-friendly than coal, and is better suited to the generation of electricity for peaking and intermediate uses. Gas, too, is a direct input for a number of mineral processing and other manufacturing activities.

Yet commercial gas sources in eastern Australia are inadequate to meet the demands of thriving regional centres and the big capital cities. A supply shortfall is expected to occur as early as 2007.[19] Supply from existing gas sources is expected to level out at around 11 000 petajoules per annum (PJ/a) from early in the next decade, and a gap between supply and potential demand will continue to widen.[20] That is why a proposal has been developed to supply gas to eastern Australia from the highlands of Papua New Guinea (PNG). The PNG gas project will have access to reserves estimated at 10 000 PJ, dwarfing the remaining higher cost reserves in the Cooper Basin, estimated at 2500 PJ. In the southern part of Australia, PNG gas will exert competitive price pressure on supplies from the reserves in Bass Strait (7800 PJ) and the Otway Basin (2100 PJ). Coal-seam methane from Queensland and NSW will also form part of the overall gas supply for eastern Australia.

The PNG gas pipeline would go a long way towards completing an eastern Australian gas grid. It is likely to connect into a hub at Moomba in the Cooper Basin in far north South Australia that could then supply NSW and South Australia.

From around 2015, as gas demand continues to rise for major mineral processing and electricity generation projects, the PNG gas project and existing gas sources in eastern Australia will not be fully capable of meeting potential demand. A gap between supply and potential demand is expected to re-emerge, and to continue widening.[21] In the longer term there will be the possibility of connecting gas reserves in the Browse Basin off north-western Australia (28 000 PJ) to the Moomba gas hub. Another possibility is gas from the Northern Territory. Australia would literally be cooking with gas, and processing its abundant supplies of minerals for the massive Chinese and wider Asian markets in environmentally friendly processing facilities.

WHAT ABOUT WATER?

Though Australia is the driest continent on earth it receives huge amounts of rainfall at particular times of the year, mostly in sparsely populated areas. It is widely believed that eastern Australia has too little available water to sustain a much larger population. But the real problem is that the available water is under-priced and over-allocated. In rural areas of the Murray–Darling Basin, water is usually priced to cover only operating expenditure and capital maintenance (depreciation).

If water were priced at its true value and a system of permanent trading in water rights were introduced, lower value users would be able to sell out to higher value users, making both the seller and the buyer better off. Higher uses would include the buying back of water allocations – improving river flows and restoring the rivers to health.

The value of water for human consumption is many times greater than its value for agricultural production. But even in agricultural production the variations are enormous. Value added per thousand kilolitres ($/kL) is around $1.80 for vegetables, $1.40 for fruit, $1.00 for grapes, 60 cents for cotton and only 20 cents for rice. Cotton uses 15 per cent of irrigation water but produces only 13 per cent of the gross value of irrigated production; rice uses 11 per cent of the water but produces a tiny 4 per cent of value. In contrast, vegetable production uses 3 per cent of irri-

gation water while producing 19 per cent of the total value of irrigated production, while grapes use 5 per cent of the water to
produce 14 per cent of the value.[22] The higher price for water in a
system of water trading would also provide strong incentives to
avoid wastage, which is very important – it is estimated that one-
third of irrigation water is wasted.[23]

In short, there is adequate water for a bigger population
settled in Australia's dynamic regional hubs. But a system of permanent trading in water is essential for allocating water to its
highest uses, and for restoring the rivers of the Murray–Darling
system to health. A move to permanent trading in water rights
will require the establishment of secure rights and the overcoming
of rigidities in the present water allocation system,[24] which should
be done without further delay.

Some bold thinking has started on moving water from places
that receive abundant rainfall to areas that face acute water
shortages. The Western Australian government has commissioned preliminary work on transporting water from the
Kimberley region to Perth. Flood flows in the major Kimberley
rivers – the Ord, Drysdale, Prince Regent, Isdell and Fitzroy
Rivers – are the largest of anywhere in the world. Around 90 per
cent of the Kimberley flow occurs in the four-month period from
December to April. Possibilities include a 1750 kilometre
pipeline from the Fitzroy River to Kalgoorlie, where it would
connect to the existing pipeline between Kalgoorlie and Perth,
and solar-powered super-tankers to carry the water directly to
Perth.

Bold proposals such as these, and even the possibility of transporting water from the north to south-eastern Australia, should
not be ruled out. Private proponents should be encouraged to
develop competing proposals, incorporating any propositions for
government financial and risk-sharing support. They should then
be evaluated independently, and advice provided to government
as a basis for decision-making.

CHAPTER 12

KEEPING AUSTRALIA
OPEN FOR BUSINESS

THE TYRANNY OF PROXIMITY – TOO CLOSE FOR COMFORT?

Since European settlement, Australia has been dogged by its distance from the European and American centres of global economic activity. For most of that period, until the middle of the twentieth century, Australia suffered the competitive disadvantage of having to move its exports over vast distances to the main markets in the northern hemisphere.

More recently, as knowledge has become a much stronger influence on the competitive advantage of nations, Australia has again suffered, this time from remoteness from the intellectual, creative centres of the globe. True, we have been highly adept at absorbing mainly American technological breakthroughs in the information age. But Australia's capacity to create its own new ideas has been limited by the size of its own pool of creative talent and its isolation from much bigger pools in the United States and Europe.

Though Australia's remoteness from the world's economic powerhouses during the nineteenth and twentieth centuries hampered our export competitiveness, it provided a natural protective shield for industries producing for the domestic market. But in the twenty-first century the situation is set to be reversed, providing new export opportunities for Australia but intensifying competition in the Australian domestic market.

Australia's resource industries will continue to benefit from supplying raw materials to China as the factory of the world, but our manufacturing industries are coming under intense competitive pressure from China. The survival of Australian manufacturing beyond energy-intensive mineral processing will depend on its capacity to embody skills and new ideas in high-value products. And these industries will need to make use of inexpensive components imported from Asia.

Similarly, Australian service industries will increasingly need to outsource parts of their service operations to India and other south Asian countries where English is spoken. And Australia's education exports, a big source of export growth, will come under intense competitive pressure as the rapidly developing countries of the region expand and upgrade their own educational institutions.

Australia's trade and investment policy has failed to grasp these new imperatives. It is doubtful whether policy-makers in the federal government are fully aware of them.

THE FOLLY OF PREFERENTIAL TRADE DEALS

Trade policy since the change of government in 1996 has been dominated by the negotiation of preferential trade deals. These deals discriminate in favour of the parties to an agreement and against countries excluded from it.

Yet Australia's export expansion during the 1990s, following the recession of the early 1990s, was its strongest ever. That expansion was, in turn, made possible by the Labor government's trade liberalisation beginning in the mid-1980s.

Labor in government built its trade policy on three pillars. The first was reductions in domestic protection to secure national gains from a more efficient and productive economy. The second was priority for multilateral negotiations as a means of securing better access to foreign markets. The third pillar was a non-discriminatory approach in pursuing bilateral and regional trade liberalisation.

The Hawke and Keating governments reduced Australia's trade barriers without first requiring other countries to do so, on the basis that it was in the national interest to lower our protective barriers. They opened up the Australian economy to competition from abroad, rejecting the mercantilist view that imports are intrinsically bad. They recognised the absurdity of the proposition that 'we'll stop wrecking our economy by restricting trade only if and when you stop wrecking yours'. This approach has been endorsed by the OECD:

> much of Australia's trade liberalisation policies have been unilateral, undertaken regardless of other countries' action. Such an approach reflects the recognition that the benefits of trade come more from opening up the economy to cheaper imports, than waiting for other countries to open their markets. As a result, domestic productivity and resource allocation improves, paving the way for higher living standards, as well as making exports more competitive. Of course, there should be additional gains if foreign barriers decline as well, but the focus on getting 'concessions' from trading partners during trade talks misses the point.[1]

The Hawke and Keating governments put enormous effort into the Uruguay Round of Multilateral Trade Negotiations. Trade Minister John Dawkins established the Cairns Group of Fair Trading Nations as a powerful third force in the multilateral negotiations, succeeding in getting agriculture on the negotiating table for the first time.

The Hawke and Keating governments established the Asia-Pacific Economic Cooperation forum (APEC) as a regional forum for giving impetus to the Uruguay Round. APEC members signed the Bogor Declaration in 1994, committing members to free and open trade and investment in the Asia–Pacific region by 2020. Trade liberalisation would be pursued in a manner that encouraged and strengthened trade and investment liberalisation in the world as a whole, reducing barriers among APEC economies but also between APEC and non-APEC economies.

In successfully opening up markets in East Asia, Labor in government did not seek preferred access to these markets at the expense of other countries, only an opportunity to compete. This non-discriminatory approach to trade liberalisation was a defining feature of Labor's trade policy, and was a lesson of the very unfortunate history of discriminatory international trade policies.

The beggar-thy-neighbour policies that contributed so heavily to the global Depression of the 1930s should have taught us the folly of discriminatory trading blocs being pursued so enthusiastically by the present Australian government. Though it was the post-war champion of an open, multilateral trading system, the United States was actively involved in the breakdown of the multilateral system before the war. In 1930 the United States imposed a tariff that triggered retaliation by many of its European trading partners. Among them, Great Britain abandoned its hundred-year commitment to free trade and established preferential regimes with other Commonwealth countries, to rival other discriminatory trading blocs dominated by the United States, Japan, France, the Netherlands and Germany.

Australia, under the Scullin Labor government, joined the rush to protectionism. It applied heavy import restrictions in 1930, and used them as negotiating coin in entering the highly discriminatory Commonwealth preferential system. Under this, the Ottawa Agreement of 1932, Australia gained preferential access to the British market for its agricultural products, while Britain secured preferential access to the Australian market for its manufactured goods. And so was entrenched Australia's heavy trade dependence on selling agricultural products to Great Britain and relying on the Mother Country for manufactured goods.

These discriminatory practices were followed a few years later by the Lyons government's 'trade diversion policy', when tariffs were raised against Japan and lowered on some items within the British Empire in a deliberate attempt to divert imports from Japan in favour of imports from Britain and the Empire.

The establishment of the General Agreement on Tariffs and Trade (GATT) after World War II marked a return to a global trading system conducted under a set of agreed rules. It was never free trade, but it was much freer than the discriminatory arrangements that had been in place before the war. Successive rounds of multilateral trade negotiations made greater or lesser progress in reducing global trade barriers. The last concluded round was the Uruguay Round, which was completed in 1994 and in which Australia played a constructive role through the Cairns Group. A new round, the Doha Round (named after Doha in Qatar where the first ministerial meeting was held), was launched in 2001 and is ongoing.

Since the early 1990s, discriminatory trade deals have proliferated at an astonishing rate. More than half of the 300 preferential trade deals notified to the World Trade Organization (WTO) by late 2004 had been notified since the beginning of 1995.[2]

Preferential trade deals violate the central organising principle of the world trading rules, the so-called 'most favoured nation' clause as set out in Article 1 of the GATT. This clause requires that the best tariff or non-tariff treatment given by a country to any other member of the world trading system must be automatically and unconditionally extended to every other member country. The trouble is that so many exceptions to and exemptions from the most-favoured-nation rule have been inserted into the world trading rules that it is no longer the rule; it is almost the exception.[3]

Advocates of discriminatory trade deals, including the Australian government, argue that they are building blocks, not stumbling blocks, to global trade liberalisation. Yet progress in the Doha Round of multilateral trade negotiations has been slow, as negotiators concentrate on concluding discriminatory deals. According to the WTO, many developing countries, having secured favoured access to rich country markets through preferential trade deals, are proving reluctant to give up this favoured access in the global negotiations towards genuine free trade.[4]

The OECD has warned against the Australian government's liking for preferential trade deals:

> bilateral and regional trade agreements can have a trade distorting as well as a trade creating component. There is furthermore a danger that the coherence and predictability offered by multilateralism will be weakened if governments increasingly turn to regional agreements to manage their trade interests. A maze of conflicting regional regulations, standards and rules of origin risk becoming the new 'walls' between blocks. Against this background, the recently negotiated FTAs with Singapore, Thailand and the US merit close scrutiny as they run counter to Australia's general unilateral/multilateral approach.[5]

By excluding other countries, preferential deals not only can incite retaliation but can divert trade from more efficient suppliers. If trade diversion exceeds trade creation, a preferential trade deal can make the parties to the deal worse off. A Productivity Commission study finds that twelve out of eighteen preferential trade deals it examined had diverted more trade than they created.[6]

THE RULES OF ORIGIN

In determining whether an import qualifies for favoured treatment in a preferential trade deal, *rules of origin* must be established. They are designed to favour imports produced in a country that is party to the agreement and to discriminate against imports produced in other countries. But since not all of a product's inputs are necessarily produced in the same country, rules need to be established to determine an acceptable level of imported content.

Restrictive rules of origin can be used to defeat the stated purpose of so-called free trade agreements. The more restrictive they are the smaller will be the range of goods and services that are eligible for favoured treatment. A proper analysis of the benefits and costs of a preferential trade deal cannot be conducted without knowledge of its rules of origin. Yet the Australian government announced the completion of the Thai–Australia Free Trade Agreement and sought Opposition support for it before finalising negotiations on the rules of origin that would apply.

Two main types of tests are applied in setting rules of origin: change in tariff classification, and proportion of local value added. A change in tariff classification occurs when a product is transformed through production processes; for example, when yarn is fabricated into clothing. The local value added to a product is the value of the product less the value of imported products used to make it; for example, the value of a car less the value of imported components.

A value-adding process is needed to bring about a change in tariff classification, so the two types of rules of origin are related. Indeed, in many preferential trade deals a hybrid of the two is used for selected products.

Where rules of origin are based on domestic or regional value added, they are more trade restricting the greater the proportion of local value added that is required to satisfy the rule. Before hailing a preferential trade deal as a huge trade-creating opportunity, it is advisable to assess the restrictiveness of the rules of origin.

An analysis of the relative restrictiveness of the rules of origin contained in various preferential trade deals[7] indicates that the rules applying in the North American Free Trade Agreement (NAFTA) are the most restrictive. Next most restrictive is a group of agreements that includes the US–Australia Free Trade Agreement and the Thai–Australia Free Trade Agreement. They are much more restrictive than the rules of origin in preceding agreements made by Australia – the Closer Economic Relations (CER) agreement with New Zealand, the Singapore–Australia Free Trade Agreement (SAFTA) and the South Pacific Region Trade and Economic Cooperation Agreement (SPARTECA). These pre-existing agreements have relatively liberal rules of origin.

The restrictive NAFTA rules of origin were used as a framework for the US–Australia free trade agreement. The United States would have been very happy that the Australian government agreed to them.

In December 2004, the Australian and New Zealand governments announced their intention to change the rules of origin governing CER, rules that the Productivity Commission describes as 'relatively clean and simple'.[8] The announced shifting of the basis of the CER rules of origin to a change of tariff classification represents a departure from the approach recommended by the Productivity Commission.[9] It is to be hoped that the actual changes do not further entrench preferential trade between the two countries at the expense of third countries, though this has been the practice of the present Australian government.

The proliferation of preferential trade deals with complex, restrictive rules of origin imposes ever increasing compliance burdens on exporters. Different sets of records must be maintained, varying from country to country and even from one export product to another. A 'spaghetti bowl' effect[10] of crisscrossing rules of origin hardly seems a recipe for free trade.

OPENING UP AUSTRALIA'S PREFERENTIAL TRADE DEALS

There is an opportunity to convert bad, trade-diverting policy into good, trade-creating policy. Australia could begin extending to other countries the preferential trade deals it has already negotiated. In its purest and simplest form this would involve extending to all countries the most liberal tariff and non-tariff treatment Australia is providing to any party to a preferential trade deal.

Recognising that a political climate has been permitted to develop in Australia against unilateral trade liberalisation, a conditional approach has been mooted.[11] Under this approach Australia would allow, in each new preferential trade deal it negotiates, the most favourable terms of access it has already granted in any of its existing preferential trade deals – so long as the other party does the same for Australia.

Parties to preferential trade deals with Australia could have no valid basis for objecting to Australia liberalising these deals. Australia would simply be fulfilling its obligations as set out in Article 1 of the GATT to extend to all member countries of the WTO any favoured treatment given to a country with which it has reached a preferential trade deal. The United States, reasonably, reserves the right to extend to other countries and regions the preferential treatment it gave to Australia in the US–Australia Free Trade Agreement; no permission from Australia is required. Nor is any country with which Australia has a preferential trade deal given in that agreement any right of veto over Australia extending those preferences to other countries.

What would be the effects on Australian industry of extending to all WTO members the preferential treatment Australia has offered in its preferential trade deals? With the exception of the automotive and the textile, clothing and footwear (TCF) industries, Australian industry now receives negligible or no tariff protection. Ongoing tariff reduction programs have been legislated for the automotive and TCF industries. Automotive tariffs, at 10 per cent from 1 January 2005, are legislated to fall to 5 per cent in 2010. TCF tariffs, at various rates of up to 17.5 per cent from 1 January 2005, are legislated to fall to a maximum of 10 per cent in 2010 and then to 5 per cent in 2015.

Against this background of ongoing tariff reductions and the commercial decisions Australian businesses are making in response to these legislated reductions, the additional impacts on these industries of extending to other countries the arrangements contained in Australia's trade deals with Thailand and the United States would be small. A subsidy to compensate the automotive and TCF industries for the declining tariff protection could be calculated and added to existing adjustment assistance programs. They would be no worse off than under the generally legislated tariff reductions, and would be better off from positive assistance in repositioning them for a stronger future.

AN AUSTRALIA–CHINA TRADE DEAL?

The Australian government is contemplating a preferential trade deal with China, a Chinese precondition of which is the granting to China of full market economy status. Granting market economy status to China could make it more difficult to prove dumping against Chinese imports. Over the nine-year period from 1995 to 2004, only eighteen of Australia's 172 initiations of anti-dumping cases – that is, around one in ten – involved China.[12] Only five of the eighteen were successful. Granting full market economy status to China might not make much practical difference.

Australia's tariff regime and anti-dumping regulations will not be a big hurdle for ever cheaper Chinese manufactured imports into Australia. As China continues to increase the efficiency of its manufacturing and logistics operations, while raising the quality of its products, Australia's remaining protective wall will resemble a single brick over which a giant steps, barely noticing.

Australia can and should have a strong manufacturing sector. But its viability will not depend on a single brick of protection against China. Rather it will depend on industry's capacity to embody skills and new ideas in high-value products that can be delivered efficiently at home and abroad. Yet the Coalition government has no strategy for Australian manufacturing. A major inquiry into the future direction of Australian manufacturing is needed. Out of that inquiry industry plans should be formulated and implemented, based not on increased tariff protection but on government support for activities in which Australian manufacturing can develop a competitive advantage. Australia should be committed to a strong, growing manufacturing sector, one that can prosper in twenty-first century Asia.

AN AUSTRALIA–ASEAN–NEW ZEALAND FREE TRADE AREA?

On 30 November 2004, a joint declaration of ASEAN leaders announced the commencement of negotiations from early 2005 on an Australian–ASEAN–New Zealand free trade area. Negotiations were to be completed within two years, and would progressively remove all barriers to trade in goods and services, and to investment.

The proposed free trade area could be consistent with the Bogor Declaration of APEC member countries, and might, therefore, have merit. But Australia's trade policy is confused, with ministers and trade officials committed to numerous negotiations for bilateral and regional preferential deals. It is unclear whether and how negotiations for the proposed Australia–ASEAN–New Zealand free trade area would be conducted in tandem with negotiations for an Australia–China trade deal, an Australia–Malaysia deal and an Australia–Japan deal, all of which have been the subject of feasibility studies.

FOREIGN INVESTMENT LIBERALISATION

It is possible that preferential agreements that also liberalise investment between the parties could create trade by promoting investment. But why should investment liberalisation be restricted to the parties to the agreement? If foreign investment is good, why liberalise only for the countries with which a preferential trade deal has been negotiated?

While Australia has largely dismantled its barriers to imports, significant impediments to foreign investment remain. In negotiations for the US–Australia free trade agreement, the two countries decided to relax Australian controls on US foreign investment by raising the threshold for Foreign Investment Review Board approval of non-sensitive investment proposals from $50 million to $800 million.

A report commissioned by the federal government estimates that this liberalisation will increase Australian living standards by more than $30 billion in net present value terms.[13] No one seriously believes this estimate; but, if it were anywhere near the mark, the policy implications would be clear – extend this liberalisation to all countries, and more than treble the benefits!

The Australian government should immediately raise the threshold for Foreign Investment Review Board approval of non-sensitive investment proposals from $50 million to $800 million for all countries, not just the United States.

CHAPTER 13

TAX REFORM

WHY WE NEED TAX REFORM

Our tax system is holding Australia back. It is holding back
Australians wanting to move from welfare to work. And it is
holding back Australians who are already in work but want to get
ahead.

Australia's incentive-crushing tax and welfare system is giving
the unemployed little financial reason to move from welfare to
work. A person on the dole with an unemployed partner and two
young children who is offered a 20-hour-a-week part-time job
paying $15 000 a year would end up keeping just $5 an hour after
losing part of the dole and paying tax. An analysis of the government's welfare reforms announced in 2005 confirms that single
mothers will lose up to 75 cents in each extra dollar they earn
from taking a part-time job – and that's not counting the cost of
travel and work clothes.[1] After taking account of these costs and
loss of rent assistance, single mothers would be expected to work
for as little as $2 an hour.[2] And this is before child-care costs are
considered.

Middle-income earners are not getting rewarded for their
efforts either. They have to pay 42 cents in tax on every extra
dollar they earn. Many are deciding that it is just not worth

working overtime or going for promotions. One million working Australians face the 42-cent rate. By 2008, almost 400 000 more Australians will be hit by an incentive-crushing 12-cent leap in tax on the extra money they earn as they move from the 30-cent rate onto the 42-cent rate. Australians facing the 42-cent rate are earning between$70 000 and $125 000 a year. They are trying to improve themselves and make a better life for their children. They are not rich – especially if they live in high-cost cities like Sydney, Melbourne and Brisbane.

All up and down the income scale, the tax system is crushing incentive. Australia needs genuine tax reform to restore incentive – to reward hard work and enterprise. That means cutting the punishing rates faced by most Australians. If 47 cents in the dollar is considered too high for top income earners, then the 75 cents in the dollar faced by many people seeking to move from welfare to work is prohibitive.

Australia's tax system provides strong incentives for debt-financed spending on property, and strong disincentives for investing in creative talent. The system not only has unnecessarily high income tax rates, the income tax base is riddled with holes, resulting in a complexity that beggars belief. Between 1996 and 2005 the Coalition government added one hundred tax breaks to the system.[3] The Business Council of Australia recognises the link between providing ever increasing tax breaks and the complexity of the *Income Tax Act*:

> Much of this complexity is due to the need to administer tax concessions targeting particular groups, or to prevent large-scale exploitation of existing 'holes' in the tax base by administrative means.[4]

The *Income Tax Act* ran to 3600 pages in 1996 when the present government came to office. By 2005 it had passed 9600 pages,[5] and continues to be amended during almost every sitting of federal parliament.

BUT WE'VE JUST HAD TAX REFORM!

In 2000, the Coalition government gave Australia what it described as a 'new tax system for a new century'.[6] The government introduced a broadly based consumption tax to replace the wholesale sales tax and a range of indirect taxes imposed by state governments. As partial compensation for the new goods and services tax (GST), the government reduced income tax and increased family payments. Later it changed the business tax system, reducing the company tax rate from 36 to 30 per cent and reducing the capital gains tax rate. The government made desirable changes to Australia's international tax regime to improve Australia's global tax competitiveness.

Yet, just five years later, the calls for comprehensive tax reform are as loud as ever. Paul Keating remarked in the early 1990s that every parrot in the pet shop was squawking microeconomic reform. Now every parrot in the pet shop is squawking tax reform. But unless the chorus of squawking is accompanied by verses about where spending should be cut, the call for tax reform will never be more than a cacophony.

TOWARDS AN EFFICIENT, FAIR TAX SYSTEM

Constant bickering about shifting the tax burden onto others will not lead to genuine tax reform. Genuine reform must start at the government spending side of the equation. Australia's welfare state is out of control. How else do we explain more than 20 per cent of working-age Australians receiving some form of income support at a time when unemployment is at its lowest level in almost thirty years? Compare that 20 per cent with only 15 per cent at the end of the 1980s, and just 4 per cent in 1969.[7]

How do we explain the fact that almost 90 per cent of families with dependent children receive taxpayer-funded family payments? And why do social security payments now contribute more than 14 per cent of gross household disposable income, compared with just 6 per cent in the last year of the Whitlam government?[8] How do we justify giving family payments to millionaire couples, so long as the mother agrees to stay at home? And why does the government provide family payments for working couples who earn up to $145 000 a year?

The family payments system was originally designed to redistribute income to those families most in need (*vertical equity*), and also to recognise the extra costs of raising children (*horizontal equity*). It has been successful in its stated objectives, redistributing income from the better off to the less well-off: three-quarters of the payments are received by the bottom 40 per cent of households.[9] But as the Coalition government has extended the family payments system right through middle Australia and on to the wealthy, the system has become less progressive. Lower income earners received a diminishing share of family payments between the mid-1990s and the early 2000s.[10] More than 38 000 families earning above $100 000 a year receive family payments for stay-at-home mothers.[11] The government has deliberately moved the family payments system away from its original redistributive role and is converting it into a giant recycling machine.

The horizontal equity argument for family payments has its limits:

> While encouraging family formation is desirable, direct assistance should be concentrated on those with lower incomes who may otherwise be deterred from raising or bringing one up.[12]

The federal government collects more than $100 billion a year in personal income tax, and immediately gives almost one-quarter of it back in payments to families with children. Over a ten-year period from the mid-1990s, when real private incomes grew by 15 per cent and unemployment fell to its lowest rate in three decades – so that welfare dependency should have been declining – real Commonwealth social security spending increased by one-half. If spending on social security as a share of GDP were to return to the level of the last year of the Hawke government, the savings would be $16 billion. Yet now, almost half the taxes paid by the top 40 per cent of households are returned to them as government benefits, and by 2008 real social security spending is budgeted to increase by 56 per cent over the levels of the mid-1990s.

A government that describes itself as a champion of private initiative and reward for effort has presided over the biggest expansion in the welfare state in the nation's history!

ABOLISHING THE TOP RATE?

Advocates of abolishing the top marginal rate of income tax need look no further for funds than the welfare the government has extended to them. Just 3 per cent of taxpayers face the top marginal rate of 47 cents, cutting in at a personal (not family) taxable income of $125 000 a year. They are not struggling, and abolishing the top marginal rate is unlikely to unleash the next round of productivity growth that Australia needs. Claims that these Australians would work harder if the top marginal rate were abolished ignore the non-monetary benefits that high-income earners derive from working. As Gittins points out:

> we should look sceptically at the incessant calls for lower tax rates to encourage people to work harder. ... higher income earners in particular have powerful non-monetary motives for working long and hard: job satisfaction and the pursuit of power and status.[13]

A more respectable argument for cutting the top marginal rate is that Australia needs to attract creative talent from overseas and avoid having so many talented Australians leave the country permanently. But as Treasurer Costello points out in defending the retention of the present top marginal rate and the income threshold at which it cuts in from mid-2006, Australia will be 'right in the centre of international practice'.[14] This tends to undermine the argument that Australia's income tax system is a major driver of emigration.

An analysis of the destinations of Australia's permanent departures raises concerns. The major destinations are New Zealand (23 per cent), Great Britain and Ireland (almost 16 per cent), Singapore (5 per cent), China (almost 6 per cent), Hong Kong (8 per cent) and the United States (10 per cent).[15] Each of these countries has a lower top marginal rate of income tax than Australia.

But an examination of the birthplaces of emigrants from Australia points to another influence. The main birthplaces of emigrants are New Zealand (12 per cent), Great Britain and Ireland (almost 8 per cent), China (more than 6 per cent), Hong Kong (more than 3 per cent) and the United States (less than 2 per cent). Many migrants are returning to their birthplaces.

However, many Australian-born emigrants are leaving for destinations that do happen to have lower top marginal tax rates. Maybe they are leaving for other reasons, such as career advancement, higher pay, lifestyle preferences and the fact that most of these countries are English-speaking. There is only one way to find out – ask them. One study does exactly that, and concludes that professional development, better job opportunities and higher pay are indeed important factors.[16] Until a comprehensive study is done on the reasons for Australia's high level of skilled emigration, the jury is out on the role of income tax rates. But even strong advocates of abolishing the top marginal rate of tax conclude that 'in all likelihood taxation is not a primary driver in emigration for most Australians'.[17]

So although the jury is still out, the evidence gathered by the prosecution is not strong.

A third argument for cutting the top marginal rate is combating tax avoidance. More closely aligning the top marginal rate of personal income tax with the company tax rate would reduce incentives for individual taxpayers to set themselves up as companies – allowing them to pay only the company tax rate on current income and to defer personal income tax until they distribute company profits to themselves and to family members as dividends. But now for a reality check. The gap between the top marginal personal income tax rate and the 30-per-cent company tax rate is 17 cents in the dollar. Incorporation in Australia costs a small amount – around $800. Removing incentives for individuals to incorporate would require dropping the top marginal rate to a level very close to the company tax rate – say 35 per cent. Cutting the top marginal rate and the second highest marginal rate of 42 per cent to 35 per cent would cost more than $6 billion a year – all to prevent a deferral of income tax payments?

The case for aligning the top personal income tax rate with the company tax rate is not strong.[18]

A GENUINE REFORM PROPOSAL

Genuine tax reform requires cuts in unnecessary spending on the wealthy, and repairs to the income tax base. The proceeds of these two exercises could be used to reduce income tax rates.

Tax reform cannot be achieved in a single budget. To be fiscally responsible, a tax reform plan should be implemented over several budgets as financial circumstances, spending cuts and base-repair work permit.

Although repairing the income tax base and using the proceeds to cut rates is advocated by economists[19] and by Coalition MPs, including Malcolm Turnbull,[20] there is little agreement on the base-broadening measures that should be adopted. Everyone who benefits likes their 50-per-cent capital gains tax discount. Everyone likes their negative gearing. Everyone likes their deductions for work-related expenses. Everyone likes their private health insurance rebate, and their child-care rebate. Company executives like their tax-favoured executive share schemes. And the Coalition government likes nothing more than Labor politicians advocating their removal.

Everyone knows there is an elephant in the Coalition party room, charging at the income tax base, urged on by frontbenchers and backbenchers alike, daring Labor to out the elephant so they can re-run scare campaigns that Labor would impose capital gains tax on wedding rings and the family home, force up housing rents and abolish the private health insurance rebate.

The onus is on the Coalition to out the elephant. They put it there; they can remove it. There is no evidence that Treasurer Costello is remotely interested in repairing the income tax base; in 2005 there were 270 special tax concessions.[21]

There are many paths to the tax reform mountain-top, and many mountain-tops of comparable grandeur. Like beauty, grandeur is in the eye of the beholder. One grand tax reform vista would feature:

- a tax-free threshold of $10 000[22] for everyone earning less than $70 000 a year
- a 15-cent rate applying over the income range $6000 to $27 000 a year
- a 30-cent rate applying over the income range $27 000 to $125 000 a year, and
- a 39-cent rate applying to incomes greater than $125 000 a year.

Increasing the tax-free threshold from $6000 to more than $10 000 for all taxpayers earning up to $70 000 a year would improve incentives to move from welfare to work. So too would increasing the upper threshold for the 15-cent rate from $21 600 to $27 000. Workers earning the minimum wage ($25 189 per annum in 2005) would enjoy a 15-cent reduction in their marginal tax rate – a big increase in work incentives.

Abolishing the 42-cent rate would leave most taxpayers on a top rate of no more than 30 cents.[23] For those taxpayers a maximum 30-cent marginal rate would restore incentive, and provide genuine reward for effort.

Lowering the top marginal rate to 39 cents should be considered only in the context of income tax base-broadening measures such as those advocated by Malcolm Turnbull.[24]

The total cost of this reform package in 2006–07 terms would be around $18 billion. It could not be afforded in a single budget. But as revenue continued to grow with the economy, as base-repairing measures were adopted and welfare for the wealthy was curtailed, and as workforce participation responded to the improved incentives, the plan could be implemented over several budgets.

A TAX REFORM DOWN PAYMENT IN 2006–07

The 2006–07 Budget presents the opportunity of making a substantial down payment on this ultimate reform package. This could consist of:

- reducing the 42-cent rate to 36 cents – half way to its complete abolition in subsequent budgets
- increasing the low-income tax offset from $235 to $625, and converting it to a weekly or fortnightly working bonus, and
- increasing the income level from which the working bonus is phased out from $21 600 to $70 000 a year.

REDUCING THE 42-CENT RATE

The one million taxpayers earning between $70 000 and $125 000 a year would enjoy a substantial reduction in their marginal tax rate on the way to the complete abolition of the 42-cent rate.

INCREASING THE INCENTIVE TO MOVE FROM WELFARE TO WORK

Increasing the low-income tax offset from $235 to $625 and converting it to a weekly or fortnightly working bonus would provide a tax-free threshold of more than $10 000 for low-income earners, substantially improving work incentives. For example, a single mother working 15 hours a week on the minimum wage would pay no tax. A full-time worker earning the minimum wage would enjoy a reduced effective marginal tax rate.

TAX RELIEF FOR THE FORGOTTEN PEOPLE

Taxpayers earning between $21 600 and $52 000 a year have been virtually forgotten in previous budgets. In fact, the only tax cuts this group will have received in the eight-year period from 2000 to 2008 are the 2004 'sandwich and milkshake' tax cut of just $4 a week and a $6 a week cut in 2005.

Parents with dependent children have received increases in family payments, but taxpayers without children who are earning less than $52 000 a year ($1000 a week) have been bearing the brunt of bracket creep. Table 13.1 reveals that these forgotten people – shop assistants, hairdressers, cleaners, hospitality workers, office clerks, farm hands, factory workers and enrolled nurses – will be paying an extra $30 to $45 a week in tax due to bracket creep by 2008 compared with 2001.

These victims of bracket creep are footing the bill for the family payments system that has now been extended to the very wealthy.

The Forgotten People would be given a tax cut of between

Occupation	2001–02	2005–06	2006–07	2007–08	2008–09
Hairdresser	4.93	14.80	19.68	24.67	29.79
Farm hand	5.14	15.86	20.94	26.14	31.48
Cleaner	5.37	16.98	22.28	27.71	33.28
Shop assistant	5.44	17.36	22.74	28.25	33.90
Receptionist	5.31	16.71	21.96	27.33	32.85
Hospitality worker	5.69	18.59	24.20	29.96	35.86
Office clerk	6.31	21.74	27.98	34.37	40.92
Labourer	6.28	21.60	27.80	34.16	40.69
Factory worker	6.24	21.36	27.52	33.83	40.31
Motor mechanic	6.16	20.99	27.08	33.32	39.71
Enrolled nurse	6.55	22.92	29.39	36.01	42.81
Machine operator	6.80	24.19	30.91	37.79	44.85
Social worker	7.16	25.98	33.05	40.29	47.72
Accounts clerk	6.86	24.47	31.24	38.18	45.30

TABLE 13.1 EXTRA TAX PAYABLE THROUGH BRACKET CREEP IN DOLLARS PER WEEK, 2001–02 TO 2008–09

$7.50 and $12.00 a week by increasing the low-income tax offset from $235 to $625 a year, and phasing it out from $70 000 a year.

REDUCTIONS IN MARGINAL TAX RATES

The proposed tax reform down payment to be delivered in the 2006–07 Budget would reduce effective marginal tax rates for people seeking to move from welfare to work, and for taxpayers earning between $70 000 and $125 000 a year.

TAX CUTS

Every taxpayer receives a tax cut under the proposed reform down payment (see table 13.2). The tax cut is $7.50 a week for

Taxable income ($pa)	Tax cut ($pw)
10 000	7.00
15 000	7.50
20 000	7.50
25 000	10.00
30 000	12.00
35 000	12.00
40 000	12.00
45 000	12.00
50 000	12.00
55 000	12.00
60 000	12.00
65 000	12.00
70 000	12.00
75 000	14.00
80 000	15.80
85 000	17.75
90 000	23.00
95 000	28.75
100 000	34.50
110 000	46.00
120 000	57.50
125 000 +	63.30

TABLE 13.2 TAX CUTS PROPOSED FOR THE 2006–07 BUDGET

taxpayers earning between $10 500 and $21 600 a year. A wage earner on the minimum wage of $25 188 a year would receive a tax cut of more than $10 a week.

Taxpayers earning between $27 500 and $70 000 a year would get a tax cut of $12 a week. Those earning between $75 000 and $120 000 a year would receive tax cuts ranging from $14 a week to $57 a week. A taxpayer earning $100 000 a year would receive a tax cut of $34.50 a week. Taxpayers earning more than $125 000 a year would get a flat tax cut of $63 a week, regardless of how much extra they earned.

WHAT IT WOULD COST

The cost of the proposed tax reform down payment for the 2006–07 Budget is set out in table 13.3.

Reducing the 42-cent rate to 36 cents would cost $2.5 billion and increasing the low income tax offset to $625 would cost $5.3 billion, giving a total cost in 2006–07 of $7.8 billion.

SOURCE OF FUNDS

The 2005–06 Budget Papers forecast a continued improvement in Australia's terms of trade to their highest level in fifty years.[25] Due to a persistent under-estimation of revenue by Treasury, the revenue-forecasting methodology was changed in the 2005–06 Budget with a view to providing more reliable forecasts.[26] Yet the Budget outcome for 2004–05 was a surplus of

Tax change	Cost ($b)
Reduce the 42 cents to 36 cents	2.5
Increase low-income tax offset to $625; phase out from $70,000	5.3
Total:	7.8

TABLE 13.3 COST OF 2006–07 TAX REFORM DOWN PAYMENT

$4.4 billion above forecast, mostly owing to higher than expected company profits associated with the resources boom.

The projected surplus for 2006–07 contained in the 2005–06 Budget Papers is $7.5 billion – the same as that projected for 2005–06. If the actual surplus turned out to be around $4.4 billion above estimate, as did the 2004–05 surplus, we could be looking at a surplus of almost $12 billion in 2006–07.

After deducting the $7.8 billion cost of the tax reform proposals outlined here, the projected surplus in 2006–07 would still be more than $4 billion.

TAXING EDUCATION AND TRAINING

The Australian tax system applying to education and training is a mess. Like other OECD countries, Australia has no consistent tax treatment of investment in human capital:

> Although tax policy is in practice used in many ways to support lifelong learning, this is often done accidentally and unevenly, rather than as part of a consistent strategy.[27]

Government policy more consciously supports initial investment in human capital through the funding of schools. But because investment in lifelong learning provides benefits mainly to employers and to the individuals receiving the training, lifelong learning for adults is less of a public good than schooling.[28]

The practice of taxing income earned by profit-making training-providers, but not the income of not-for-profit providers, effectively operates as a barrier to entry for profit-making providers.[29] And the tax treatment of self-education expenses can be unduly restrictive:

> The prevailing practice has been to allow individuals to deduct expenditure from taxable earnings only when they are undertaken in connection with learning activities that are necessary for current employment. Some countries have been relaxing those restrictions

in line with the objectives of lifelong learning to allow expenditure on learning that is relevant to future employment.[30]

Some OECD countries are adding a premium to deductions for human capital investment by businesses, along the lines of R&D tax concessions:

> Some countries have used tax policy to provide an extra incentive for human capital investment in order to offer a stronger incentive for this kind of expenditure than expenditure on other business costs, such as advertising or heating and lighting ... Though the tax linked human capital investment incentives are not very widespread, they are similar in design and objective to the extra incentives that more than half of OECD countries allow for employer expenditure on R&D.[31]

Incentives and disincentives in the Australian tax system for investing in human capital formation should be systematically reviewed. As part of this review, consideration should be given to creating an entitlement for people who have dropped out of high school to complete high school at a TAFE college free of tuition charges.

BUSINESS TAX REFORM

Compliance with the tax system places a proportionately heavier burden on small businesses than on large businesses. An *option* should be offered to small businesses with an annual turnover of less than $2 million for a simplified method of completing the GST business activity statement (BAS). Based on the experience of a small business over the preceding two or three years, the tax office would calculate the average ratio of GST paid by the business to its turnover.

Usually the ratio will be between zero and 10 per cent. If the business has claimed no GST input tax credits its ratio would be 10 per cent; if it claimed credits to wipe out its GST obligations its ratio would be zero.

Suppose the ratio calculated and issued by the tax office at the request of a particular small business were 5.4 per cent. The small business would simply multiply its assessable turnover for the period by 0.054, and remit that amount. This single entry would complete the compliance task. There would be no need for an annual reconciliation as under the present system. The small business would simply have to be able to establish that all turnover had been disclosed. Nor would there be tax office audits, except in cases of suspected fraud. However, the tax office would retain the right to vary the ratio for future periods if this was justified by objective circumstances.

If the small business had incurred unusual expenses in the tax period, say the purchase of a new coffee machine, or legal expenses, it could complete a second section to claim these extra input tax credits against the amount that was determined by application of the historical ratio.

For newer businesses without a long experience in paying GST, the tax office could issue an industry ratio for the industry relevant to the business. The business would have the choice of using the industry ratio or of completing the conventional BAS for the two or three years needed to generate its own unique ratio.

Some businesses might substantially change the nature of their operations over time, so that the ratio issued by the tax office became unfavourable. They would have the right to revert to the conventional BAS process and, if they chose, to build up a new experience for a new ratio in the future.

It would be worth investigating whether the ratio method could be extended to the income tax system for small businesses. On request, the tax office would issue a business a unique ratio reflecting its income tax paid as a proportion of its turnover over the preceding two or three years. The business would then be able to apply that ratio to its turnover for the tax period, and remit the resulting amount. As for the GST, industry ratios could be developed for newer small businesses.

In 1986 the Treasury objected strongly to my proposal, as an economic adviser to Prime Minister Hawke, to streamline car-logbook-keeping requirements for fringe benefits tax purposes. Those streamlined arrangements have stood the test of time, greatly reducing compliance costs while neither over-taxing businesses nor causing significant revenue leakage. The same opportunity exists for easing the GST compliance burden.

CHAPTER 14

FINANCING THE PLAN

PUBLIC INVESTMENT IN THE FIVE I'S

It would take more than a decade to implement the plan for Australia.

Supporting the five I's of intellect, ideas, initiative, infrastructure and immigrants would yield large returns. To illustrate, attaining the average years of schooling of North America and Scandinavia, especially through supporting disadvantaged students to complete high school, would ultimately add around one-quarter of a percentage point to GDP growth.[1] And achieving a moderate increase in R&D – to the levels attained by France – would increase annual productivity growth by around 0.2 percentage points.[2] Increasing workforce participation through the policies contained in the plan would boost GDP growth. So too would the extra public investment in key infrastructure assets, and the expanded immigration program.[3]

The proceeds of growth so generated could be used to finance the ongoing implementation of the plan. In the shorter term, budget choices will need to be made: does the federal government continue to fuel consumer spending for today, or does it embark on an investment program for the future? Every component of the plan for Australia is investment, not consumption. During times of strong economic growth, such as Australia has been experiencing for more than a decade, the nation should be investing surpluses for sustaining future growth.

The following discussion sets out the main components of the plan, and identifies funding sources.

State government resources are well capable of assuring a preschool education for all four-year-old children. Most states and territories already allow for a universal preschool year. They would not ration places if more parents sought to send their children to preschool. At no extra budgetary cost the Commonwealth would apply mutual obligation through the family payments system, making payments conditional on parents sending their four-year-olds to preschool.

A needs-based funding model for government and private schools would cost an extra $2.5 billion a year. It should be phased in over time. Since education is the centrepiece of the plan for Australia, all income earned from funds placed in the Intergenerational Fund should be devoted to the needs-based funding program. The proceeds of asset sales, together with budget surpluses over the period to 2008, could be expected to be more than $40 billion.[4] Around $10 billion of this should be set aside for Commonwealth investment in infrastructure approved under the national infrastructure plan. Though the infrastructure projects would be expected to yield large benefits for the nation, they would not necessarily generate large direct financial returns for the Commonwealth in the shorter term.

That would leave an income-yielding Intergenerational Fund of around $30 billion. A market return of about 8 per cent per annum could be expected on the commercial investments of the fund, amounting to around $2.4 billion per annum. This, together with a small amount of state funding, would be enough to finance the needs-based school funding program and the modest system of scholarships for school students in disadvantaged communities.

Any extra income from the Intergenerational Fund should be used to supplement university budgets to alleviate the funding crisis that is putting pressure on universities to raise fees for HECS places and increase the number of foreign and Australian full-fee paying students.

The universal family payment for children under three can be funded by a 10-per-cent tightening of means-testing for family tax benefits for children over three. Extra child-care payments for lower income working families can be funded by modifying the child-care rebate.

A RENEWED COMMITMENT TO SUPERANNUATION

During the 1980s and early 1990s the federal Labor government understood the unsustainability of Australians in an ageing population continuing to rely on the state for their retirement incomes. Either retirement incomes would be inadequate for most working Australians, or income tax rates would become prohibitively high as baby boomers reached retirement age. In its second year of government, Labor introduced an assets test on age pensions (which was bitterly opposed by the Coalition parties).

In the late 1980s Labor introduced compulsory superannuation, aiming to divert 15 per cent of incomes into savings for retirement (which was also bitterly opposed by the Coalition). The first tranche of compulsory superannuation, called the *superannuation guarantee*, was phased in over time, and has since reached 9 per cent. The superannuation guarantee has spread superannuation to working Australians, increasing the proportion of workers covered by superannuation from around 39 per cent in 1986 to more than 90 per cent in 2003.

In 1986, only 7 per cent of casual and part-time workers were covered by superannuation. By 2003 almost 80 per cent were receiving employer superannuation contributions.[5] Australia's superannuation savings now exceed $750 billion, a massive pool for investing in income-earning assets.

A second tranche of compulsory superannuation, to achieve the 15-per-cent benchmark, was to be paid by the government and employees. It was budgeted for by Labor but, consistent with its opposition to compulsory superannuation, the incoming Coalition government cancelled it.

It is generally accepted that 9 per cent is inadequate to provide for a reasonable retirement income, especially for those Australians who started superannuation savings after 40 years of age. The Coalition government's philosophic opposition to compulsory superannuation has cost Australia dearly.

The government has introduced a voluntary scheme that provides a government co-contribution to Australians earning modest incomes. The co-contribution is up to $1.50 for each dollar saved as superannuation, to a maximum of $1500 a year.

A design fault in Australia's compulsory superannuation scheme that allows superannuation to be taken as a lump sum instead of an annuity is offering unwelcome incentives for early retirement, and reliance on the age pension following retirement. More than 75 per cent of superannuation benefits paid out are being taken as lump sums.[6] Working Australians who become eligible for large lump sums after many years of working under the superannuation guarantee will have a strong incentive to take their superannuation as a lump sum before they reach the eligibility age for the age pension. They can then use the lump sum to pay off mortgages and other debts, and make themselves eligible for the age pension. They are assisted by generous tax treatment of superannuation lump sums.

Reforms need to be made soon to encourage more superannuation savings to be accessed in the form of a pension. And further voluntary contributions to superannuation should be encouraged to improve the adequacy of retirement incomes.

Australia has one of the best retirement-income savings systems in the world, thanks to the reforms of the Hawke and Keating governments. But more needs to be done, especially to improve adequacy and to increase incentives for post-retirement income streams, where Australia's record is not nearly as good.

CHAPTER 15

LOW INFLATION, LOW UNEMPLOYMENT

ENDING THE GREAT AUSTRALIAN INFLATION – BUT AT WHAT COST?

The last two decades of the twentieth century marked the end of a long inflationary phase in the world economy. Oil price shocks in the 1970s exposed the inadequacy of macroeconomic management policies and institutions. By the early 1980s most developed countries, including Australia, were experiencing both high inflation and high unemployment, a phenomenon known as 'stagflation'.

In 1983, the incoming Hawke Labor government inherited double-digit inflation and double-digit unemployment. Labor in government embarked on a program dubbed the three R's by Prime Minister Hawke: a program of recovery, reconciliation and reconstruction. Wages growth had averaged 14 per cent per annum in the last years of the previous government. Reconciliation between the business community and the trade union movement was essential to the task of breaking the debilitating wage–price spiral. Wage moderation was gradually achieved through the Prices and Incomes Accord with the trade union movement. More than half a million jobs were created in the first three years of the new government.

Reconstruction involved the microeconomic reform program

that started with a rescue plan for the steel industry and the floating of the Australian dollar, followed by the opening up of financial, product and labour markets. Rapid growth in the newly deregulated financial market, stimulated by a loosening of monetary policy designed to cope with the 1987 stock market crash, caused a boom and a revival of inflationary pressures. Subsequent monetary tightening resulted in the recession of 1990–91.

Australia's Reserve Bank Governor, Ian Macfarlane, defended this monetary tightening in his first speech as Deputy Governor, in 1992:

> It was clear by the late eighties that policy, including monetary policy, had to be tightened to bring a substantial slowing of the economy. The economy was growing too fast, we were living beyond our means and there was an unsustainable amount of debt financed asset speculation occurring ... Some think that if only the instruments of monetary policy had been adjusted in a more skilful and timely manner, we might have avoided a recession, but I very much doubt it ... on this occasion we had to run monetary policy somewhat tighter than in earlier recessions, and to take the risk that the fall in output would be greater than forecast. To do less than this would be to throw away the once in a decade opportunity for Australia to regain an internationally respectable inflation rate ... It is true that we paid a substantial price to reduce inflation, but we had to do it at some stage ... We have paid the cost, the task now is to maintain low inflation when we return to growth.[1]

It seems that at the time the Reserve Bank believed this was the recession we had to have to break the back of inflation. Rather than rejecting the advice of the Reserve Bank and Treasury, the Labor government accepted and acted upon it.

But the advice was wrong; the tightening was too late and too severe. The government accepted responsibility, Prime Minister Hawke apologising on many occasions for this major policy mistake.

The monetary tightening, however, did succeed in ending what Professor Ross Garnaut calls the Great Australian Inflation:

The silver lining of the recession was the ending of the Great Australian Inflation. The Great Inflation had its origins during the Gorton and McMahon Prime Ministerships, had run wild in the Whitlam years, had continued above 10 per cent through the Fraser government and was falling only slowly down from 10 per cent under Hawke.[2]

By the change of government in early 1996 Australia had recorded ten successive quarters of economic growth, the economy having grown at 4.6 per cent in the final 12 months of the Labor government. But unemployment was still at an unacceptably high 8.4 per cent.

The independence of the Reserve Bank in setting monetary policy had been established under Labor, but was formalised in an exchange of letters by the incoming Howard government. These developments paralleled those occurring in the rest of the developed world:

> Economic historians will no doubt look back on the last twenty years of the 20th century as those that marked the end of a long inflationary phase in the world economy. Burnt by the experience of the 1970s, policy makers had put in place credible institutional safeguards against monetary instability. They had done so by endowing central banks with clear mandates to maintain price stability and with the necessary autonomy to pursue them.[3]

Credit must be given to the Coalition government for maintaining low inflation and ongoing reductions in unemployment. It has done so with the inflation-suppressing discipline of the open, competitive economy that Labor created, and the support of an inflation-targeting Reserve Bank. But it has done so by maintaining an imbalance that has reached worrying proportions – a current account deficit well above the benchmark of 6 per cent of GDP, a deficit that the treasurer himself has described as 'not sustainable'.[4]

It seems appropriate to recall Prime Minister Howard's harsh judgment of the Labor years:

You created a lot of jobs in the 1980s. But do you know how you created them? You created them by running an economy at an unsustainably fast rate. Any fool can create hundreds of thousands of jobs if he is prepared to go into debt with foreigners.[5]

That judgment was made when Australia's net foreign debt stood at $173 billion (37 per cent of GDP). By 2005 it had reached $450 billion (more than 50 per cent of GDP).

MAINTAINING LOW INFLATION

An independent, inflation-targeting Reserve Bank is essential to the maintenance of macroeconomic stability in Australia, as is a well-functioning prudential authority. But the use of monetary policy to stabilise the macro economy has its limitations. Time-lags between changes in interest rates and their ultimate effects on economic activity are long and variable. And raising market interest rates can be a very blunt instrument, suppressing both consumption and investment.

The length and variability of monetary policy time-lags can be better understood by examining the mechanism by which changes in interest rates affect economic activity. When the Reserve Bank raises interest rates consumers buy fewer houses, domestic appliances, cars and holidays, while businesses delay or cancel projects and hire fewer staff. Higher interest rates can cause the exchange rate to rise, which encourages imports and makes exports less competitive. Lower spending on consumption, investment and exports slows the economy down, and inflation slows.

At a rough estimate, it takes a year for monetary policy to affect spending and up to another year for inflation to slow, since it takes time for lower spending to persuade firms to moderate their price increases.[6]

The bluntness of monetary policy is illustrated the same way. Its effects are spread unevenly across the economy, impinging on people and businesses that are not necessarily in a position to bear the burden. Financial hardship, job losses and bankruptcies can follow.

Fiscal policy, too, involves variable time-lags. Discretionary budget decisions can be a long time in the making, and an even longer time in delivery. Legislation enabling the delivery of budgeted tax cuts and spending decisions has to pass through parliament. Capital spending can take not months but years, as projects are designed, tenders let and construction undertaken.

Most of the discretionary fiscal expansions in the United States since World War II have occurred after the recession they were intended to ameliorate was technically over.[7]

Compared with fiscal policy, monetary policy has the advantage of being more immediate: the independent authority meets on a monthly basis and implements decisions within days. Could the advantages of the sharper instrument of fiscal policy be combined with the advantage of the greater immediacy of monetary policy decisions to achieve more effective macroeconomic stabilisation, with fewer unintended consequences?

A body of thinking has emerged that seeks to address this question. Gruen[8] and the BCA[9] propose giving an independent authority the capacity to make limited changes to particular tax rates to improve the timeliness and reduce the unintended consequences of macroeconomic stabilisation. Possible taxes considered are personal income tax, the Medicare levy, company tax and indirect taxes.

The BCA finds attractions in giving an independent authority the capacity to vary the 1.5 per cent Medicare levy (which is not payable by very low income earners) between zero and 3 per cent, and to have discretion over a 3 percentage point range for the company tax rate.[10] This would create a discretionary fund of around $15 billion in 2005 dollars.

Gruen and the BCA canvas a range of options for the independent authority, including having two separate authorities – one monetary and one fiscal – handling macroeconomic stabilisation. But two separate authorities could develop conflicting views on the macroeconomic outlook, and apply conflicting policies. These risks could be avoided by giving the Reserve Bank the responsibility for managing this limited fiscal discretion. Though the proposal has some attractions, the case for the independent management of fiscal discretion is not a compelling one.

CAN MONETARY AUTHORITIES DEAL WITH ASSET PRICE BUBBLES?

Despite a benign inflationary environment since the mid-1990s, bubbles have developed in asset prices in Australia, most conspicuously the housing price bubble of the 2000s. The coexistence of asset price bubbles and low inflation raises the question of whether the monetary authorities should target not just general price inflation, but asset price bubbles as well.

The Bank for International Settlements (BIS) points out that if financial imbalances are allowed to build up in an otherwise benign inflationary environment, the end result can be a severe recession coupled with asset price deflation[11] – in Australia's case, a collapse in housing prices. It suggests that a monetary policy response to imbalances as they build up might be appropriate in some circumstances. Prophetically, the BIS warns that the Australian boom and bust of the 1880s–1890s possessed remarkably similar characteristics to those that had been allowed to develop in Australia in the early 2000s,[12] a warning also issued by Garnaut.[13] The Australian banking crisis of 1893 occurred after a frantic property boom in the 1880s fed by massive growth in bank credit. Property prices in Melbourne and Sydney doubled against a background of low or even negative inflation.

The BIS concludes that independent monetary authorities, rather than concentrating exclusively on keeping inflation within a target band, should respond to the occasional developments of financial imbalances that pose a threat to ongoing macroeconomic stability.[14] Economists at the Reserve Bank support these ideas:

> A large and rapid fall in the nominal price of assets that form the basis of collateral for loans from financial intermediaries can have

adverse effects on financial system stability. This ... can reduce output below potential and keep inflation below the central bank's target for extended periods ... there may be circumstances where monetary policy should be tightened in response to an emerging asset price bubble, in order to burst the bubble before it becomes too large ... [15]

Rather than adopting a second target of asset prices or financial imbalances, the appropriate response would be to adopt a flexible and forward-looking concept of inflation targets rather than concentrating purely on short-term inflation.[16] The BIS suggests there might be merit in monetary authorities explicitly setting out in advance a willingness to act against emerging financial imbalances and asset price bubbles even when the near-term prospects for inflation appear benign.[17]

THE PLAN FOR AUSTRALIA NEEDS LOW INFLATION

Rising global energy prices pose a threat to price stability. Australia would not be able to insulate itself from a new bout of global inflation, particularly if our export performance remains poor. A resurgence in Australian manufacturing and exports is essential, as is ongoing vigilance against inflation on the part of Australia's monetary authorities.

The plan for Australia can be effectively implemented only in an environment of sustained economic growth and low inflation. Our bright future depends on it.

NOTES

CHAPTER 1

1   See Eslake (2005b), p.2.

CHAPTER 2

1   The comparisons with earlier decades are cited in Eslake (2003, p. 8).
2   See also Banks (2004, table 2).
3   Productivity Commission (2005b, pp. xii, 140).
4   Productivity Commission (2005b, pp. 9, 22).
5   Access Economics (2005, p. 5).
6   Commonwealth Treasury (2002, Chart 15).
7   OECD (2004b, p. 83).
8   See, for example, *Hansard*, 6 March 2001, and Emerson (2002).
9   Parkinson (2004, p. 10).
10 Pitchford (1989).
11 Attributed to British Chancellor, Nigel Lawson, commenting on the current account deficit in the late 1980s.
12 IMF (2004a, p.23), Standard & Poor's (2004) and Garnaut (2004c).
13 Goldman Sachs (2005).
14 Garnaut (2004c, pp. 10–15).
15 In 1999–2000, the year preceding the introduction of the GST, income taxes accounted for 58.3 per cent of taxes collected at all levels in Australia. By 2003–04 the share was 55.3 per cent (ABS, 2005b).

CHAPTER 3

1   See Eslake (2005c, p. 7).
2   Hyde (2002).
3   EPAC (1996).
4   Porter (1991, p. 6).

5   Krugman (1994, p. 13).
6   OECD (2004b, p. 88); OECD (2005b, pp. 46, 128).
7   EPAC (1996).
8   Productivity Commission (2004b, p. 40). Separate estimates are that productivity improvements have made every Australian on average at least $3000 better off. See BCA (2005b, pp. 3, 15). This is consistent with $7000 per household.
9   Productivity Commission (2003b, p. 3).
10 Parham (2004, p. 253).
11 See, for example, Productivity Commission (2003b, p. 6); Productivity Commission (2004b, pp. 35, 41); OECD (2003a, p. 90); OECD (2004b, p. 82); IMF (2003, p. 14); Henry (2004, pp. 2–3).

CHAPTER 4

1   Henry (2004, pp. 6–11).
2   ABS (2003, p. 35). These are the mid-range projections; Series B in the official projections.
3   ABS (2003, p. 83).
4   Withers (2004, p. 14).
5   Redding & Schott (2003).
6   Florida (2003).
7   See Corden (2003, p. 13).
8   Calculations based on Eslake (2005a, table 1).
9   Port Jackson Partners (2005, p. 65).
10 Estimates range from just over 60 per cent (Port Jackson Partners 2005, p. 65) to three quarters (OECD 2004b, p. 38).
11 Productivity Commission (2005b, p. 9).
12 Henry (2004, p. 11).
13 Peter McDonald, personal communication. Fertility is rising in the UK, a country comparable to Australia for these purposes.
14 The *Intergenerational Report* projects that the fertility rate will fall to 1.6 by 2042, whereas the mid-range ABS projections are for fertility to fall to 1.6 by 2011 and remain constant thereafter. The Productivity Commission's report on population ageing assumes that total fertility will stabilise at 1.8 from 2005.
15 See Productivity Commission (2005a, p. 32).
16 Productivity Commission (2005b, p. 32).
17 ABS (2003, p. 4).
18 Productivity Commission (2005b, pp. 23–4).
19 OECD (2004b, p. 164). The participation rate for Australia of 73 per cent is based on OECD definitions. Using ABS definitions it is around 64 per cent.
20 There is a striking correlation for Australian women between level of educational attainment and fertility; see Carmichael & McDonald (2004, p. 56).
21 Commonwealth Treasury (2002, p. 28).
22 Productivity Commission (2005b, p. xxi).
23 Gruen & Garbutt (2003); Productivity Commission (2005b, pp. 81–2).
24 Productivity Commission (2005b, pp. 139–40).

25 Productivity Commission (2004b, p. 151).
26 Rahman (2005, pp. 33, 41).
27 Battersby (2005).
28 Keller (2002).
29 See Eslake (2005a, p. 2).
30 See Headley, Muffels & Wooden (2004) cited in Gittins (2005, p. 123)
31 See references cited in Gittins (2005, p. 123).
32 See references cited in Gittins (2005, p. 123).
33 Gittins (2005, pp. 123–4).
34 Headley & Wooden (2004, p. S28).
35 Cummins et al (2004, p. x).
36 Cummins et al (2005, p. 2).
37 Available at <http://www.wellbeingmanifesto.net/>.

CHAPTER 5

1 OECD (2003b).
2 IMF (2004b, p. 26).
3 Productivity Commission (2005a).
4 For example, Treasurer Peter Costello, *Hansard*, 1 December 2004; 8 February 2005.
5 Treasurer Peter Costello, *Hansard*, 27 May 2004.
6 OECD (2003a, p.100; 2005b, p. 44).
7 OECD (2004a, p. 63).
8 OECD (2004a, p. 99).
9 Wooden (2005, p. 16).
10 Eslake (2005d, p. 4).
11 Gittins (2005, p. 124).
12 Robson (2005).
13 Brown (2005, p. 10).
14 OECD (2003b).
15 Romer (1990).
16 See Dowrick & Day (2003) for a fuller discussion.
17 Greenspan (2004, pp. 2, 4).
18 Day & Dowrick (2004, p. 5).
19 Deutsche Bank (2005, p. 1).
20 Florida (2003).
21 Bassanini & Scarpetta (2002).
22 Day & Dowrick (2004, p. 9). This is consistent with the findings of the OECD Growth Project that a 10 per cent increase in the average number of years of education of the working age population would increase per capita GDP by between 4 and 7 per cent. See OECD (2004b, p. 170).
23 Day & Dowrick (2004, p. 10).
24 See Dowrick (2003, pp. 11–13).
25 Guellec & van Pottelsberghe de la Potterie (2003).
26 See Dowrick (2003, pp. 9–10).
27 Dowrick (2003, p. 17).
28 Allen Consulting Group (2003).

29 Dowrick & Lau (1998, p. 61).
30 Dowrick & Lau (1998, p. 61).

CHAPTER 6

1 Productivity Commission (2005b, pp. 143, 175).
2 Productivity Commission (2005b, p. 184).
3 Statistics are from Private Health Insurance Administration Council, Membership Statistics, as at the end of 2004.
4 Keating (2004, p. 85)
5 Keating (2004, pp. 87–8).
6 John Howard, *A Current Affair*, Nine Network, 22 September 2003.
7 See Productivity Commission (2005d, p. xxxiii).
8 Richardson & Robertson (1999).
9 Productivity Commission (2005b, p. 164).
10 See Duckett (2002, p. 130).
11 Tony Abbott, address to CEDA Conference, Sydney, 25 February 2005.
12 Tony Abbott, *Hansard*, 22 and 23 June 2004.
13 Allen Consulting Group (2004, pp. 138–9).
14 'Bracks pushes funding reform', *Australian Financial Review*, 12 November 2004, p. 3.
15 See O'Loughlin (2005).
16 Richardson (2003).
17 Keating (2004, p. 110).
18 Dawkins et al. (2004, p. 47).
19 Dawkins et al (2004, pp. i, iii).
20 Dawkins et al (2004, p. ii).
21 Butler (2002); Segal (2004, p. 10).
22 Segal (2004, p. 10).
23 Dawkins et al. (2004, p. ii).
24 Walker et al. (2003).
25 Dawkins et al. (2004, p. ii).
26 Walker et al. (2005, p. 67).
27 A relative must have been living in the house for at least two years, must have been providing care and must be eligible for a Commonwealth social security benefit. A carer must have been providing care for at least five years, and be eligible for a social security benefit.
28 Bishop (2005, p. 25).
29 Hogan (2005, p. 35).
30 Allen Consulting Group (2005a).
31 Delaat (2005).
32 Fitzgerald (1999).

CHAPTER 7

1 Productivity Commission (2005b, p. 9).
2 Access Economics (2005, pp. 8–9).
3 OECD (2005d, p. 38).

4   Access Economics (2005, p. 11).
5   OECD (2003b, pp. 17, 78–9).
6   Thurow (1996, p. 68).
7   Access Economics (2005, p. 8).
8   Cited in Parham (2004, p. 251).
9   Banks (2003, p. 5).
10 OECD (2003b, pp. 37–38).
11 Eslake (2003, p. 6).
12 OECD (2005a, p. 278).
13 Dowrick (2002, p. 17).
14 Deutsche Bank (2005, p. 16).
15 Day & Dowrick (2004, p. 15).
16 Day & Dowrick (2004, p. 17).
17 Dowrick & Day (2003, p. 16).
18 Day & Dowrick (2004, p. 5). See also Dowrick & McDonald (2002); Dowrick (2002); and Dowrick & Day (2003).
19 Productivity Commission (2004c).
20 ABS, *Australian social trends*, cat. no. 5204.0 (tables 8, 44, 51, 64, 65).
21 OECD (2005a, p. 238).
22 Commonwealth Treasury (2002, p. 47).
23 Eslake (2003, p. 7).
24 OECD (2004b, p. 171; 2005a, p. 101).
25 Allen Consulting Group (2004, pp. 80–1).
26 Allen Consulting Group (2004, p. 80).
27 Leigh (2005, pp. 2–3).
28 OECD (2000).
29 Access Economics (2005, p. 6).
30 Allen Consulting Group (2004, p. 75).
31 Allen Consulting Group (2004, p. 71).
32 Allen Consulting Group (2004, p. 88).
33 Allen Consulting Group (2004, p. 88).
34 Allen Consulting Group (2004, p. 95).
35 See Anderson et al. (2005, pp. 83–5).
36 Allen Consulting Group (2004, p. 89).
37 Allen Consulting Group (2004, p. 165).
38 Access Economics (2005, p. 19).
39 See the studies cited in Watson & Teese (2004).
40 Edgar (2001, p. 174).
41 Homel (2005, pp.14, 22).
42 Brooks-Gunn, Fuligni & Berlin (2003).
43 Homel (2005, pp. 38–9).
44 Freiberg et al. (2005).
45 New Zealand Literacy Experts Group (1999).
46 Haskins & Rouse (2005) and references cited therein.
47 OECD (2005a, p. 236).
48 OECD (2005a, pp. 225, 231).
49 Walker (2004 p. 15).
50 Walker (2004, pp. 10, 26, 34)

51 Australian Education Union (2004, p. 8).

52 Kronemann (2005, p. 7).

53 Figures calculated as total state and territory spending on preschool services in 2003–04 from Productivity Commission (2005c) divided by the number of children using government-funded or government-provided preschool services.

54 Answer to DEST Question No. E131_05, Senate Employment, Workplace Relations and Education Legislation Committee, 2004–05 Budget Estimates Hearing.

55 Rowe & Rowe (2002, p. 14); Rowe (2004a) and international evidence cited therein.

56 Freebairn (2005a, p. 63).

57 Horsley & Stokes (2005).

58 OECD (2005a, pp. 384–5).

59 Rowe (2004b, pp. 5–6).

60 This includes private school principals whose salaries are paid in part by school fees. Average salaries of principals are around $85 000, and in 2004 there were 9615 schools in Australia. A 25 per cent average salary increase would cost an estimated $204 million.

61 Brendan Nelson, *Hansard*, 14 September 2005.

62 Deutsche Bank (2005, p. 1).

63 Chapman & Ryan (2003, table 1, p. 6).

64 Chapman & Ryan (2003, p. iii).

65 Australian Vice-Chancellors' Committee (2005).

66 Beer & Chapman (2004, p. 173).

67 Interview on the Jon Faine program, ABC Radio, Melbourne, 4 August 2004.

68 Educational Policy Institute (2005, p. 2).

69 OECD (2005a, p. 240).

70 Chatham House (2005, p. 8).

71 See Xinhua News Agency (2004).

72 Bracks (2005, p. 37).

73 Birrell et al. (2005, p. 63).

74 OECD (2005a, p. 299).

75 Birrell et al (2005, p. 63).

76 See comments in 'Unis to shrink in 15 years: Nelson', *The Australian*, 15 September 2005, p. 5.

77 Lleras (2004, p. 50).

CHAPTER 8

1   Dowrick (2002, p.23).

2   OECD (2003d).

3   See Commonwealth of Australia (2005), which estimates foregone revenue at $90 million in 2003–04, $90 million in 2004–05, $100 million in 2005–06, $105 million in 2006–07 and $115 million in 2007–08.

4   OECD (2002, p.12).

5   This appears to be the evidence from the US. See OECD (2002, pp.14–5).

6   OECD (2002, p. 9).
7   Business Council of Australia (2004, p. 26).
8   Banks (2000, p. 7).
9   Over a four-year budget forward estimates period.
10 Access Economics (2003, p. 1).
11 See Erskinomics Consulting (2003, p. 31).
12 Parham, Roberts & Sun (2001, figure 2).
13 Dowrick (2003, p. 17).
14 OECD (2003c).
15 Dowrick (2002, p. 23); Parham (2004, p. 253).

CHAPTER 9

1   OECD (2004b, p. 164).
2   OECD (2005c, pp. 41–42).
3   OECD (2004b, p. 164).
4   Peter Costello, Sally Loane Program, ABC radio 702, Sydney, 26 February 2004.
5   Productivity Commission (2005b, p. 81).
6   Commonwealth Treasury (2002, p. 28).
7   OECD (2004b, p. 165).
8   Productivity Commission (2004c, p. 23).
9   Productivity Commission (2005b, p. 75).
10 Productivity Commission (2004c, p. 38).
11 Harding et al (2005b, p. 205).
12 Productivity Commission (2004c, p 22).
13 Kennedy & Hedley (2003, p. 14).
14 For example RGWR (2000); OECD (2004b).
15 Toohey & Beer (2003, p. 2).
16 Beer (2003, p. S17).
17 Beer (2003, pp. S18–9).
18 Beer (2003, p. S19).
19 Toohey & Beer (2003, p. 19).
20 See McDonald 2004.
21 Garnaut (1999).
22 The Department of Family and Community Services Annual Report 2003–04 indicates that as at 25 June 2004 there were 2 155 568 families receiving Family Tax Benefit (Part A). Another 8 per cent received annual payments, taking total beneficiaries to around 2 343 000. The ABS Australian Labour Market Statistics July 2004 (cat. no. 6105.0) reveals there were 2 654 200 families with dependent children. The proportion of families with dependent children receiving Family Tax Benefit (Part A) is therefore 2 343 000 divided by 2 654 200, which equals 88 per cent. This calculation does not include recipients of Family Tax Benefit (Part B), and so is probably an underestimate.
23 Burniaux, Duval & Jaumotte (2004, p. 20).
24 OECD (2005a, p. 169).
25 OECD (2005b, pp. 167–8).
26 Toohey (2005, pp. 8, 17–8).
27 Toohey (2005, p. 18).

CHAPTER 10

1　United Nations (1998, p. 10).
2　Hugo (2003, p. 190).
3　Hugo (2003, p. 205).
4　Hugo (2003, pp. 202–3).
5　Productivity Commission (2004c, p. 2.25).
6　See the discussion in Productivity Commission (2004c, pp. 2.28–2.32).
7　Productivity Commission (2004c, p. 2.32).
8　Productivity Commission (2004c, p. 2.33).
9　McDonald (2005).
10　McDonald (2005).
11　Withers & Powall (2003, p. 3).
12　Withers & Powall (2003, p. 8).
13　Victoria (2004b, p. 30).
14　ACIL Tasman (2003).
15　Property Council of Australia (2005, p. 9).
16　Withers & Powall (2003, p. 12).
17　Hugo (2003, p. 215).
18　Victoria (2004b, p. 32).
19　Gillard (2002, p. 6); Emerson (2002).
20　Withers & Powall (2003).
21　See Withers & Powall (2003, p. 31).
22　South Australia (2004).
23　Victoria (2004a, 2004b).
24　Florida (2003).
25　Florida (2003, p. 249).
26　Pascal Zachary cited in Florida (2003, p. 252).
27　Florida (2003, pp. 253, 294, 295).
28　Florida (2003, p. 284).
29　Fullilove & Flutter (2004, p. vii).
30　Birrell et al. (2004, p. 50).
31　Withers & Powall (2003, p. 5).
32　Australian Senate (2005, p. 14).
33　Hugo (2004, p. 9).

CHAPTER 11

1　Tanner (2005, p. 3).
2　Allen Consulting Group (2003, p. viii).
3　Tanner (2005, p. 4).
4　Allen Consulting Group (2003, p. x).
5　Allen Consulting Group (2003, p. 40).
6　Tanner (2005, p. 6).
7　Port Jackson Partners (2005, pp. 12, 42, 46).
8　BCA (2005a, p. 10).
9　Tanner (2005, p. 8).
10　Tanner (2005, p. 7).
11　BCA (2005a, p. 13).

12 Port Jackson Partners (2005, p. 30).
13 Port Jackson Partners (2005, pp. 30–1).
14 Port Jackson Partners (2005, p. 31).
15 BCA (2005a, p. 12).
16 Port Jackson Partners (2005, p. 43).
17 Bureau of Transport Economics (2000, pp. 25–6).
18 Anderson (2005).
19 ABN AMRO (2003, p. 1).
20 See ACIL Tasman (2004, p. 5).
21 See ACIL Tasman (2004, p. 5).
22 Port Jackson Partners (2005, p. 65).
23 Port Jackson Partners (2005, p. 66).
24 See Krijnen (2004); Wahlquist (2004).

CHAPTER 12

1 OECD (2004b, p. 148).
2 WTO (2004, p. 21).
3 WTO (2004, p. 19).
4 WTO (2004, p. 23).
5 OECD (2004b, p. 119).
6 Productivity Commission (2003a, p. 84).
7 Productivity Commission (2004a, 2004d).
8 Productivity Commission (2004d, p. 4.15).
9 Productivity Commission (2004c, p. 4.12).
10 So named by Bhagwati (2002).
11 Garnaut (2004b, pp. 9–13).
12 Productivity Commission (2004d, p. C.4).
13 Centre for International Economics (2004).

CHAPTER 13

1 Harding et al. (2005a, p. 7).
2 Harding et al. (2005b, p. 204).
3 See the various Tax Expenditure Statements issued annually by the Commonwealth Treasury.
4 Business Council of Australia, 'Governments must target tax system for fundamental reform', media release, 11 April 2005, <http://www.bca.com.au/content.asp?newsID=97954>, cited in Allen Consulting Group (2005b, p. 35).
5 Allen Consulting Group (2005b, p. viii).
6 Treasurer Peter Costello, *Hansard*, p. 1087, 2 December 1998; p. 7760, 29 June 1999.
7 Australian Chamber of Commerce and Industry (2005, p. 15).
8 Australian Chamber of Commerce and Industry (2005, p. 15).
9 Harding, Lloyd & Warren (2004b, p. 25).
10 Harding, Lloyd & Warren (2004a), cited in Allen Consulting Group (2004, p. 40).
11 Statistics from answer to Question on Notice No 188, Senate Community Affairs Legislation Committee, 2005–06 Budget Estimates, May 2005.

12 Australian Chamber of Commerce and Industry (2005, p. 22).

13 Gittins (2005, p. 125).

14 Peter Costello, National Press Club Address, Great Hall, Parliament House, 11 May 2005, available at <http://www.treasurer.gov.au/content/speeches/2005/006.asp>.

15 DIMIA (2005).

16 Hugo et al (2003).

17 Davidson (2005, p. 9).

18 See discussion in Allen Consulting Group (2005b) pp. 25–7.

19 For example, see Freebairn (2006) and Allen Consulting Group (2005b).

20 Interview with *Inside Business*, ABC Television, 20 March 2005; Turnbull & Temple (2005).

21 See Commonwealth Treasury (2005).

22 To be precise, the plan involves a tax-free threshold of $10 166 achieved by increasing the low income tax offset from $235 to $625 per annum.

23 Taxpayers earning between $70 000 and $87 000 a year would face an effective marginal tax rate higher than 30 cents but below 42 cents from the phasing out of the tax-free threshold.

24 See Turnbull and Temple (2005).

25 2005-06 Budget Paper No 1, p. 3–4.

26 2005-06 Budget Paper No 1, p. 5–7.

27 OECD (2005d, p. 100).

28 OECD (2005d, p. 108).

29 OECD (2005d, p. 108).

30 OECD (2005d, p. 109).

31 OECD (2005d, p. 109).

CHAPTER 14

1 Professor Steve Dowrick, cited in Dawkins & Steketee (eds) (2004, p. 75).

2 Professor Steve Dowrick, cited in Dawkins & Steketee (eds) (2004, p. 75).

3 Research conducted by Access Economics for the Business Council of Australia confirms large returns from improved workforce participation, investing in education and increased immigration. See BCA (2005b, p. 28).

4 See chart in Treasurer's National Press Club address, Parliament House, Canberra, 11 May 2005, available at <http://www.treasurer.gov.au/content/speeches/2005/006.asp>. This does not appear to include proceeds from the sale of Medibank Private, which the government is likely to sell. Moreover, the actual 2004–05 Budget surplus alone was $4.4 billion more than the Budget estimate.

5 OECD (2005c, pp. 70–1).

6 Australian Prudential Regulation Authority (2004).

CHAPTER 15

1 Macfarlane (1992, pp. 4–5).

2 Garnaut (2004c, p. 6).

3 Bank for International Settlements (2002, p. 1).

4   Peter Costello told ABC's World Today radio program on 30 August 1995 that 'if you're running a current account deficit of 6 per cent of GDP it's not sustainable. It's an obvious point; it's not sustainable'.

5   Opposition Leader John Howard, *Hansard*, 30 March 1995.

6   Ball 1996, cited in BCA (1999, p. 42).

7   Keech (1995).

8   Gruen (1997; 2001).

9   BCA (1999).

10   BCA (1999, p.47).

11   Borio & Lowe (2002, p. 1).

12   BIS (2002, p. 8).

13   Garnaut (2004c)

14   BIS (2002, p.27).

15   Kent & Lowe (1997, p. i)

16   Bean (2003).

17   BIS (2004, p. 149).

REFERENCES

ABN AMRO Australia (2003) 'Oil and gas: Australia', Sydney, 12 March.

ABS see Australian Bureau of Statistics

Access Economics (2003) 'Exceptional returns: the value of investing in health R&D in Australia', prepared for the Australian Society for Medical Research, Canberra, September.

Access Economics (2005a) 'The economic benefit of increased participation in education and training', report to the Düsseldorf Skills Forum and the Business Council of Australia, Canberra, May.

Access Economics (2005b) 'The speed limit 2005–2025', a study for the Business Council of Australia, May.

ACIL Tasman (2003) 'Australia's infrastructure challenge', Melbourne, May.

ACIL Tasman (2004) 'Economic impacts of the PNG gas project', Melbourne, November.

Allen Consulting Group (2003) 'Funding urban public infrastructure: approaches compared', report for the Property Council of Australia, Canberra, August.

Allen Consulting Group (2004) 'Governments working together; a better future for all Australians', Melbourne, May.

Allen Consulting Group (2005a) 'Medical savings accounts', report to Medicines Australia, Melbourne.

Allen Consulting Group (2005b) 'Reforming income tax: broader base, lower rates, simpler system', report to the Department of Premier and Cabinet, Melbourne, June.

ALP see Australian Labor Party

Anderson, J (2005) 'North-south corridor study', media release, Canberra, 18 April.

Anderson M, Caldwell B, Dawkins P & King SC (2005) 'The structure and funding of the school system', *The Australian Economic Review*, vol. 38, no. 1, pp. 83–90.

Argyrous G & Neale M (2003) 'The "disabled" labour market', *Journal of*

Australian Political Economy, vol. 51, June, pp. 64–76.

Australian Bureau of Statistics (2003) *Population projections Australia 2002 to 2101*, cat. no. 3222.0, ABS, Canberra, 2 September.

Australian Bureau of Statistics (2004) Australian system of national accounts, cat. no. 5204.0, ABS, Canberra, 10 November.

Australian Bureau of Statistics (2005a) Research and Experimental Development, Businesses, Australia, 2003–04, cat. no. 8104.0, ABS, Canberra, 28 September.

Australian Bureau of Statistics (2005b) *Taxation Review 2003–04*, cat. no. 5506.0, ABS, Canberra, 19 April.

Australian Chamber of Commerce and Industry (2005) 'Commonwealth spending (and taxes) can be cut – and should be', a discussion paper by D Moore, Canberra, May.

Australian Education Union (2004) 'National Preschool Education Inquiry', presented at the AEU Federal Women's Conference, 2–3 October 2004.

Australian Labor Party (2004) 'Labor's tax and better family payment plan: rewarding hard work', Canberra.

Australian Prudential Regulation Authority (2004) 'Superannuation trends – December quarter 2003', APRA, Sydney.

Australian Senate (2005) 'They still call Australia home: inquiry into Australian expatiates', Legal and Constitutional Committee, Canberra, March.

Australian Vice-Chancellors' Committee (2005) 'Lack of indexation will impact on the quality of Australian universities', media release, 19 April.

Ball L (1996) 'A proposal for the next macro-economic reform', mimeo, University of Wellington Foundation, Wellington, 11 November.

Bank for International Settlements (2004) *Annual Report*, Basel, Switzerland.

Banks G (Chairman of the Productivity Commission) (2000) 'Productive R&D assistance', presentation to Melbourne Institute of Public Economics Forum, Old Parliament House, Canberra, 28 November.

Banks G (Chairman of the Productivity Commission) (2003) 'Australia's economic miracle', address to the Forum on Postgraduate Economics, National Institute of Economics and Business, The Australian National University, Canberra, 1 August.

Banks G (2004) 'An ageing Australia: small beer or big bucks?' presentation to the South Australian Centre for Economic Studies, Economic Briefing, Canberra, 29 April.

Bassanini A & Scarpetta S (2001) 'Growth, technological change and ICT diffusion: recent evidence from OECD countries', *Oxford Review of Economic Policy*, vol. 18, no. 3, pp. 324–44.

Bassanini A & Scarpetta S (2002) 'Does human capital matter for growth in OECD countries? A pooled mean-group approach', *Economics Letters*, vol. 74, pp. 399–405.

Bassanini A & Scarpetta S (2004) *Research and development investment by Australia's leading businesses*, Melbourne, December.

Bassanini A & Scarpetta S (2005) *Infrastructure action plan for future prosperity*, Melbourne, March.

Battersby B (2005) 'Does distance matter? the effect of geographic isolation on productivity levels', mimeo, Australian Treasury, Canberra.

BCA *see* Business Council of Australia

Bean C (2003) 'Asset prices, financial imbalances and monetary policy: are inflation targets enough?' paper presented to a seminar organised by the Bank for International Settlements, March.

Beer G (2003) 'Work incentives under a New Tax System: the distribution of effective marginal tax rates in 2002', *The Economic Record*, vol. 79, Special Issue, June, pp. S14–S25.

Beer G & Chapman B (2004) 'HECS system changes: impact on students', *Agenda*, vol. 11, no. 2, pp. 157–74.

Bhagwati J (2002) *Free trade today*, Princeton University Press, Princeton NJ.

Birrell B, Edwards D, Dobson I & Smith TF (2005) 'The myth of too many university students', *People and Place*, vol. 13, no. 1, pp. 63–70.

Birrell B, Rapson V, Dobson I & Smith TF (2004) *Skilled movement in the new century: outcomes for Australia*, Centre for Population and Urban Research, Monash University, Melbourne.

BIS *see* Bank for International Settlements

Bishop J (2005) 'Consumer-driven aged care', *The party room*, published by Andrew Robb & Mitch Fifield, Parliament House, Canberra, issue 2, Spring.

Borio C & Lowe P (2002) 'Asset prices, financial and monetary stability: exploring the nexus', Bank for International Settlements Working Paper No. 114, July.

Bracks S (2005) *A third wave of national reform: a new national reform initiative for COAG*, Victorian Government, Melbourne, August.

Brooks-Gunn J, Fuligni AS & Berlin LJ (2003) *Early childhood development in the 21st century: profiles of current research initiatives*, Teachers College Press, New York, London.

Brown W (2005) 'Third party labour market intervention in open economies', in JE Isaac & RD Lansbury (eds) *The deregulation of the Australian labour market: essays in honour of Keith Hancock* (forthcoming).

Burniaux JM, Duval R & Jaumotte F (2004) 'Coping with ageing: a dynamic approach to quantify the impact of alternative policy options on future labour supply in OECD countries', Economics Department Working Papers No. 371, OECD, Paris, June.

Business Council of Australia (1999) 'Avoiding boom/bust: macro-economic reform for a globalised economy', New Directions Discussion Paper 2, Melbourne.

Business Council of Australia (2005a) 'Infrastructure action plan for future prosperity', Melbourne.

Business Council of Australia (2005b) 'Locking in or losing prosperity: Australia's choice', Melbourne.

Butler J (2002) 'Policy change and private health insurance: did the cheapest policy do the trick?' *Australian Health Review*, vol. 25, no. 6, pp. 33–41.

Carmichael G & McDonald P (2004), 'Fertility trends and differentials', in SE Khoo & P McDonald (eds) *The transformation of Australia's population: 1970–2030*, UNSW Press, Sydney.

Cashin P & McDermott CJ (1996) 'Are Australia's current account deficits excessive?' IMF Working Paper 96/85, International Monetary Fund, Washington DC.

Centre for International Economics (2004) *Economic analysis of AUSTFA*, prepared for the Department of Foreign Affairs and Trade, Canberra, April.

Chapman B & Ryan C (2003) 'The access implications of income contingent charges for higher education: lessons from Australia', Centre for Economic Policy Research, Discussion Paper No. 463, The Australian National University, April.

Chatham House (2005) 'The challenges for India's education system', Asia Program, ASP BP 05/03, April at <http://www.riia.org/pdf/research/asia/BP indiaeducation.pdf>

Commonwealth Treasury (2002) *Intergenerational Report 2002–03*, Budget Paper No. 5, Canberra, 14 May.

Commonwealth Treasury (2005) *Tax expenditures statement 2005*, Canberra, December.

Corden M (2003) '40 million Aussies? The immigration debate revisited', Inaugural Richard Snape Lecture, Productivity Commission, Canberra, 30 October.

Cummins R, Davern M, Okerstrom E, Lo SK & Eckersley R (2005) 'Special report on city and country living', Australian Unity Wellbeing Index Report 12.1, Australian Centre on Quality of Life, Deakin University, Melbourne, January.

Cummins R, Eckersley R, Lo SK, Okerstrom E, Hunter B & Woerner J (2004) 'The wellbeing of Australians – job security', Australian Unity Wellbeing Index Survey 12, Australian Centre on Quality of Life, Deakin University, Melbourne, October.

Davidson S (2005) *Are there any good arguments against cutting income taxes?* CIS Policy Monograph 69, Centre for Independent Studies, Sydney, August.

Dawkins P & Steketee M (eds) (2004) *Reforming Australia: new policies for a new generation*, Melbourne University Press, Melbourne.

Dawkins P, Webster E, Hopkins S & Yong J (2004) *Recent PHI policies in Australia: health resource utilisation, distributive implications and policy options*, a report prepared for the Victorian Department of the Premier and Cabinet, Melbourne Institute of Applied Economic and Social Research, University of Melbourne.

Day C & Dowrick S (2004) 'Ageing economics: human capital, productivity and fertility', *Agenda*, vol. 11, no. 1, pp. 3–20.

Delaat W (Chairman, Medicines Australia) (2005) 'PBS reform for a healthy Australia', address to the National Press Club, Canberra, 3 August.

Department of Immigration, Multicultural and Indigenous Affairs (2005) *Immigration update July–December 2004*, Canberra.

Deutsche Bank (2005) *Global growth centres*, Deutsche Bank Research, Frankfurt, 1 August.

DIMIA *see* Department of Immigration, Multicultural and Indigenous Affairs

Dowrick S (2002) 'Investing in the knowledge economy: implications for Australian economic growth', The Australian National University, Canberra, 16 April.

Dowrick S (2003) 'A review of the evidence on science, R&D and productivity', paper prepared for the Commonwealth Department of Education, Science and Training, The Australian National University, Canberra, 11 August.

Dowrick S & Day C (2003) 'Australian economic growth: why Bill Gates and the ageing pessimists are wrong', The Australian National University, Canberra, 14 May.

Dowrick S & Lau SHP (1998) 'Rebuilding the nation's infrastructure', in R Genoff & R Green (eds) *Manufacturing prosperity: ideas for industry, technology and employment*, The Federation Press.

Dowrick S & McDonald P (2002) 'Comments on the Intergenerational Report, 2002–03', The Australian National University, Canberra, 21 June.

Duckett S (2002) 'Aged care symposium: overview', *Australian Health Review*, vol. 25, no. 5, pp. 130–1.

Economic Planning Advisory Commission (1996) *Tariff reform and economic growth*, Commission paper no. 10, Canberra, February.

Edgar D (2001) *The patchwork nation: re-thinking government – re-building community*, HarperCollins, Pymble, NSW.

Educational Policy Institute (2005) *Global higher education rankings*, Stafford, VA.

Emerson C (2002) 'Think big, Labor: it's what we do best', address to ALP Southern Regional Brisbane Conference, 7 April.

EPAC *see* Economic Planning Advisory Commission

Erskinomics Consulting (2003) 'Critical factors in successful R&D: an international comparison', discussion paper prepared for the Australian Innovation Association and the Australian Institute for Commercialisation, alex@erskinomics.com, March.

Eslake S (2003) 'Education and the economy', address to the Association of School Bursars and Administrators 2003 Annual Conference, Hobart, 15 September.

Eslake S (2005a) 'China and India in the world economy', paper presented to the International Conference of Commercial Bank Economists, Bahia, Brazil, 7 July.

Eslake S (2005b) 'Three seemingly unrelated propositions concerning Australia's identity and economic performance', address to the Royal Society of Tasmania, University of Tasmania, 6 September.

Eslake S (2005c) 'China and India – their role in the world economy and implications for Australia', luncheon address to the Australia & New Zealand Chamber of Commerce and the American Chamber of Commerce in Taiwan, Far Eastern Hotel, Taipei, 15 September.

Eslake S (2005d) 'Workplace relations reform; examining the economic data', address to a conference sponsored by *The Australian Financial Review*, Sofitel Hotel, Melbourne, 25 October.

Fitzgerald V (1999) 'Ideas for the funding of health care in the context of the ageing of the population', paper presented at the Australian International Health Institute Symposium, Allen Consulting Group, Melbourne, November.

Florida R (2003) *The rise of the creative class*, Pluto Press, Melbourne.

Freebairn J (2005a) 'Government policy and school performance: introduction and overview', *The Australian Economic Review*, vol. 38, no. 1, March, pp. 61–5.

Freebairn J (2005b) 'Income tax reform', in P Dawkins & M Stutchbury (eds) *Sustaining prosperity*, Melbourne University Press, Melbourne.

Freiberg K, Homel R, Batchelor S, Carr A, Lamb C, Hay I, Elias G & Teague R (2005) 'Pathways to participation: a community-based developmental prevention project in Australia', *Children and Society* 19, pp. 144–57.

Fullilove M & Flutter C (2004) 'Diaspora: the world wide web of Australians', Lowy Institute Paper 04, Double Bay, NSW.

Garnaut R (1999) 'Full employment in a new century', paper presented to the 'Australia Unlimited' Conference, Melbourne, 4 May, reproduced as 'Investing in full employment', in R Garnaut (2001) *Social Democracy in Australia's Asian Future*, Asia Pacific Press, The Australian National University and Institute of Southeast Asian Studies, Singapore.

Garnaut R (2004a) 'Prosperity is on the wane', *The Australian*, 29 July 2004.

Garnaut R (2004b) 'Contemporary challenges for Australia in the international economy', background notes for presentation to the Trade and Development Seminar, Division of Economics, Research School of Pacific and Asian Studies, The Australian National University, Canberra, 24 August.

Garnaut R (2004c) 'The boom of 1989 – and now', 3rd Sir Leslie Melville Lecture, National Museum of Australia, Canberra, 3 December.

GGDC *see* Groningen Growth and Development Centre

Gillard J (2002) speech to the 'Migration: Benefiting Australia' Conference, Australian Technology Park, Sydney, 7 May.

Gittins R (2005) 'An economics fit for humans', *The Australian Economic Review*, vol. 38, no. 3, pp. 121–7.

Goldman Sachs (2005) 'Do current account adjustments have to be painful?' *Global Economics Weekly*, No. 05/04, 2 February, pp. 1–7.

Greenspan A (2002) 'Education', remarks at the International Understanding Award Dinner, Institute of International Education, New York, 29 October.

Greenspan A (2004) 'Intellectual property rights', remarks at the Stanford Institute for Economic Policy Research Economic Summit, Stanford, California, 27 February.

Groningen Growth and Development Centre (2004) *GGDC Total Economy Database*, University of Groningen and the Conference Board, July <www.eco.rug.nl/ggdc>.

Gruen D & Garbutt M (2003) 'The output implications of higher labour force participation', Treasury Working Paper 2003–02, Canberra, October.

Gruen N (1997) 'Making fiscal policy flexibly independent of government', *Agenda*, vol. 4, no. 3, September, pp. 297–307.

Gruen N (2001) 'Greater independence for fiscal institutions', *OECD Journal on Budgeting*, vol 1, no 1, pp. 89–115.

Guellec D & van Pottelsberghe de la Potterie B (2003) 'The impact of public R&D expenditure on business R&D', *Economics of Innovation and New Technology*, vol. 13, no. 3, pp. 225–43.

Hakim C (2003) 'A new approach to explaining fertility patterns: preference theory', *Population and Development Review*, vol. 29 no. 3, pp. 349–74.

Harding A, Lloyd R & Warren N (2004a) 'The distributional impact of selected government benefits and taxes, 1994–95 and 2001–02', draft report to the Victorian Department of Premier and Cabinet, National Centre for Social and Economic Modelling (NATSEM), Canberra.

Harding A, Lloyd R & Warren N (2004b) *The distribution of taxes and government benefits in Australia*, NATSEM, Canberra, October.

Harding A, Vu QN, Percival R & Beer G (2004a) *The distributional impact of the proposed welfare-to-work reforms upon sole parents*, report to the

National Foundation for Australian Women, NATSEM, Canberra, 25 August.

Harding A, Vu QN, Percival R & Beer G (2005b) 'Welfare-to-work reforms: impact on sole parents', *Agenda*, vol. 12, no. 3, pp. 195–210.

Haskins R & Rouse C (2005) 'Closing achievement gaps', The Future of Children, Princeton-Brookings, Spring, at <http://www.futureofchildren.org>

Headley B, Muffels R & Wooden M (2004) 'Money doesn't buy happiness ... or does it? A reconsideration based on the combined effects of wealth, income and consumption', Working Paper No. 15/04, Melbourne Institute of Applied Economic and Social Research, Melbourne, July.

Headley B & Wooden M (2004) 'The effects of wealth and income on subjective well-being and ill-being', *The Economic Record*, vol. 80, Special Issue, September, pp. S24–S33.

Henry K (Secretary to the Treasury) (2004) address to the Australian Industry Group's National Industry Forum, Canberra, 9 August.

Hogan W (2004) *Review of pricing arrangements in residential aged care*, Commonwealth Government, Canberra, April.

Hogan W (2005) 'Policy issues in aged care', paper presented at the 34th Conference of Economists, University of Melbourne, 26–28 September.

Homel R (2005) 'Development crime prevention', in Nick Tilley (ed.) *Handbook on crime prevention and community safety*, Willan Publishing, Devon, UK (forthcoming).

Horsley M & Stokes A (2005) 'Teacher salary relativities: a benchmarking approach', *Journal of Australian Political Economy*, vol. 55, pp. 94–122.

Hugo G (2003) 'Changing patterns of population distribution', in SE Khoo & P McDonald (eds) *The transformation of Australia's population: 1970–2030*, UNSW Press, Sydney.

Hugo G (2004) Hansard transcript of oral evidence to *They still call Australia home: inquiry into Australian expatriates*, Senate Legal and Constitutional Committee, Canberra, 28 July.

Hyde J (2002) 'The big dry ... our saviour', *The Australian*, 10 December.

IMF *see* International Monetary Fund

International Monetary Fund (2003) *Australia: 2003 Article IV Consultation*, IMF Country Report No. 03/337, Washington, October.

International Monetary Fund (2004a) *Australia: 2004 Article IV Consultation*, IMF Country Report No. 04/353, Washington, November.

International Monetary Fund (2004b) *Australia: selected issues*, IMF Country Report No. 04/354, Washington, November.

Keating M (2004) *Who rules? How government retains control in a privatised economy*, The Federation Press, Leichhardt.

Keech W (1995) *Economic politics: the costs of democracy*, Cambridge University Press, Cambridge.

Keller W (2002) 'Geographic location of international technology diffusion', *American Economic Review*, vol. 92, no. 1, pp. 120–42.

Kennedy S & Hedley D (2003) 'A note on educational attainment and labour force participation in Australia', Treasury Working Paper 2003–03, Canberra, November.

Kennedy S & Hedley D (2003) 'A note on educational attainment and labour force participation in Australia', Treasury Working Paper 2003–03, Canberra, November.

Kent C & Lowe P (1997) 'Asset price bubbles and monetary policy', research discussion paper 9709, Economic Research Department, Reserve Bank of Australia, December.

Khoo SE & McDonald P (eds) (2003) *The transformation of Australia's population: 1970–2030*, UNSW Press, Sydney.

Krijnen T (2004) 'Tradeable water entitlements in the Murray–Darling Basin', *Natural Resource Management*, vol. 7, no. 1, March, pp. 2–7.

Kronemann, M (2005) *Early childhood education 2005 update*, Australian Education Union, 19 July.

Krugman P (1994) *The age of diminished expectations*, MIT Press, Cambridge, MA.

Leigh A (2005) 'The progressive case for reforming Australia's schools', Progressive Essays, Canberra, 7 July, available at www.craigemersonmp.com

Lleras MP (2004) *Investing in human capital: a capital markets approach to student financing*, Cambridge University Press, Cambridge.

Macfarlane I (1992) 'The structural adjustment to low inflation', talk by the Deputy Governor to the Sydney Institute, 21 May, at <http://www.rba.gov.au/PublicationsAndResearch/Bulletin/bu_jun92/bu_0692_2.pdf>.

McDonald P (2000) 'Gender equity, social institutions and the future of fertility', *Journal of Population Research*, vol. 17, no. 1, May, pp. 1–16.

McDonald P (2003) 'Australia's future population: population policy in a low-fertility society', in Khoo & McDonald (2003).

McDonald P (2004) 'Reform of family support policy in Australia', the Australian National University, Canberra.

McDonald P (2005) 'Labour supply futures for Australia: policy options', presentation to the Labor Caucus Economic Committee, Parliament House, Canberra, March.

Madden G & Savage S (1998) 'Sources of Australian labour productivity change 1950–94', *Economic Record*, vol. 74, pp. 362–72.

National Office for the Information Economy (2004) 'Productivity growth in Australian manufacturing', NOIE Occasional Economic Paper, Canberra.

New Zealand Literacy Experts Group, (1999) *Literacy experts group report to the Secretary for Education*, Ministry of Education, Wellington.

OECD *see* Organisation for Economic Co-operation and Development

O'Loughlin, MA (2005) 'Making hospital the last resort', *The Australian*, 21 February.

Organisation for Economic Co-operation and Development (2000) *Literacy in the information age: final report of the international adult literacy survey*, <http://www1.oecd.org/publications/e-book/8100051e.pdf>, Paris.

Organisation for Economic Co-operation and Development (2002) *Tax incentives for research and development: trends and issues*, Paris, June.

Organisation for Economic Co-operation and Development (2003a) *OECD economic surveys 2002–2003: Australia*, March.

Organisation for Economic Co-operation and Development (2003b) *The sources of economic growth in OECD countries*, OECD, Paris.

Organisation for Economic Co-operation and Development (2003c) *ICT and economic growth: evidence from OECD countries, industries and firms*, OECD, Paris.

Organisation for Economic Co-operation and Development (2003d) *OECD science, technology and industry scoreboard*, Paris.

Organisation for Economic Co-operation and Development (2004a) *OECD employment outlook 2004*, Paris.

Organisation for Economic Co-operation and Development (2004b) *OECD economic surveys: Australia*, Paris, December.

Organisation for Economic Co-operation and Development (2005a) *Education at a glance: OECD indicators 2004*, Paris.

Organisation for Economic Co-operation and Development (2005b) *Economic policy reforms: going for growth*, Paris.

Organisation for Economic Co-operation and Development (2005c) *Ageing and employment policies: Australia*, Paris.

Organisation for Economic Co-operation and Development (2005d) *Education policy analysis*, Paris.

Organisation for Economic Co-operation and Development (2005e) *Main science and technology indicators*, Paris.

Otto G & Voss G (1994) 'Public capital and private sector productivity', *Economic Record*, vol. 70, pp. 121–32.

Otto G & Voss G (1996) 'Public capital and private production in Australia', *Southern Economic Journal*, vol. 62, pp. 723–38.

Parham D (2004) 'Sources of Australia's productivity revival', *The Economic Record*, vol. 80, no. 249, pp. 239–57.

Parham D, Roberts P & Sun H (2001) 'Information technology and Australia's productivity surge', Productivity Commission staff research paper, Canberra, October.

Parkinson M (2004) 'Australia's medium term challenges', address to the ABE Forecasting Conference, Commonwealth Treasury, 14 December.

Pitchford J (1989) 'A sceptical view of Australia's current account & debt problem', *Australian Economic Review*, vol. 86, pp. 5–14.

Port Jackson Partners (2005) *Reforming and restoring Australia's infrastructure*, report prepared for the Business Council of Australia, Sydney, March.

Productivity Commission (2001) *Review of the national access regime*, Melbourne.

Productivity Commission (2003a) 'The trade and investment effects of preferential trading arrangements – old and new evidence', staff working paper, Canberra, May.

Productivity Commission (2003b) *Annual Report 2002–03*, Canberra.

Productivity Commission (2004a) 'Rules of origin under the Australia–New Zealand Closer Economic Relations Trade Agreement: restrictiveness index for preferential rules of origin', Canberra, June.

Productivity Commission (2004b) *Review of national competition policy reforms*, discussion draft, Canberra, 27 October.

Productivity Commission (2004c) *Economic implications of an ageing Australia*, draft research report, Canberra, November.

Productivity Commission (2004d) *Trade and assistance review 2003–04*, Canberra, December.

Productivity Commission (2005a) *Review of national competition policy reforms*, final report, Canberra, February.

Productivity Commission (2005b) *Economic implications of an ageing Australia,* final report, Canberra, March.
Productivity Commission (2005c) *Report on government services 2005,* Canberra.
Productivity Commission (2005d) *Impact of advances in medical technology in Australia,* Canberra, September.
Property Council of Australia (2005) *Australia on the move: population growth and dwelling demand 2001–2031,* Sydney.
Rahman J (2005) 'Comparing Australian and United States productivity', *Economic Roundup,* Australian Treasury, Canberra, Autumn.
Redding S & Schott PK (2003) 'Distance, skill deepening and development: will peripheral countries ever get rich?', NBER working paper No. 9447.
Reference Group on Welfare Reform (2000) *Participation support for a more equitable society: final report on welfare reform,* Department of Family and Community Services, Canberra.
Reserve Bank of Australia (2005) *Statement on monetary policy,* Sydney, 7 February.
RGWR *see* Reference Group on Welfare Reform
Richardson J (2003) 'Financing health care: short run problems, long run options', working paper No. 138, CHPE, Monash University, Melbourne.
Richardson J & Robertson I (1999) 'Ageing and the cost of health services', in *Policy implications of the ageing of Australia's population,* Productivity Commission and Melbourne Institute, Canberra, March.
Robson A (2005) *The costs of taxation,* Centre for Independent Studies Policy Monograph 68, Sydney, May.
Romer P (1990) 'Endogenous technological change', *Journal of Political Economy,* vol. 98, no. 5, part 2, p. S71.
Rowe K (2004a) 'The importance of teaching: ensuring better schooling by building teacher capacities that maximize the quality of teaching and learning provision – implications of findings from the international and Australian-based research', paper presented at the 'Making Schools Better' Conference sponsored by the Melbourne Institute of Applied Economic and Social Research in association with *The Australian,* Faculty of Education, University of Melbourne, 26–27 August.
Rowe K (2004b) invited submission to Inquiry into the Sex Discrimination Amendment (Teaching Profession) Bill 2004, by the Australian Senate Legal and Constitutional Legislation Committee, available at <http://www.acer.edu.au/research/programs/learningprocess.html>.
Rowe KJ & Rowe KS (2002) 'What matters most: evidence-based findings of key factors affecting the educational experiences and outcomes for girls and boys throughout their primary and secondary schooling', supplementary submission to the House of Representatives Standing Committee on Education and Training: Inquiry into the Education of Boys, May.
South Australia (2004) *Prosperity through people: a population policy for South Australia,* Government of South Australia, March.
Standard & Poor's (2004) 'Australia's "AAA" rating affirmed as government finances remain strong', Melbourne, 8 June.
Tanner L (2005) 'Renewing Australia's infrastructure', speech to Australian Council for Infrastructure Investment, Sydney, 21 March.

Thurow L (1996) *The future of capitalism: how today's economic forces shape tomorrow's world*, William Morrow, New York.

Toohey M (2005) 'The effectiveness of child care benefit at improving returns to work for women', NATSEM, Canberra, February.

Toohey M & Beer G (2003) 'Is it worth working now? The financial impact of increased hours of work for mothers under Australia's new tax system', NATSEM, Canberra, December.

Turnbull M & Temple J (2005) *Taxation reform in Australia: some alternatives and indicative costings*, available at <http://www.malcolmturnbull.com.au>, August.

United Nations (1998) *National population policies*, UN, New York.

Victoria (2004a) *Commonwealth–Victoria Working Party on Migration: final report*, Department of the Premier and Cabinet, Melbourne.

Victoria (2004b) *Beyond five million: the Victorian government's population policy*, Department of the Premier and Cabinet, December.

Walker A, Percival R, Thurecht L & Pearse J (2003) 'Public policy and private health insurance: distributional impact on public and private hospital usage in New South Wales', paper presented at the International Microsimulation Conference on Population Ageing and Health, Canberra, available at <www.natsem.canberra.edu.au>

Walker A, Percival R, Thurecht L & Pearse J (2005) 'Distributional impact of recent changes in private health insurance policies', *Australian Health Review*, vol.29, no.2, pp. 167–76.

Walker K (2004) *For all our children*, National preschool education inquiry report, Australian Education Union, Southbank, Victoria.

Watson L & Teese R (2004) *Goals and purposes of education and training*, a report to the Victorian Department of Premier and Cabinet, University of Melbourne Centre for Post-compulsory Education and Lifelong Learning.

Whalquist A (2004) 'Farms tap into water trading', *The Australian*, 25 March.

Withers G (2002) 'Population issues for Australia', in P Duncan & R Maddock (eds) *Aspire Australia*, Business Council of Australia, Melbourne.

Withers G (2004) *Australia's population future: a position paper*, Business Council of Australia, Melbourne, April.

Withers G & Powall M (2003) *Immigration and the regions: taking regional Australia seriously*, report prepared for the Chifley Research Centre, Canberra, October.

Wooden M (2005) 'Australia's industrial relations reform agenda', paper presented at the 34th Conference of Economists, University of Melbourne, 26–28 September.

WTO *see* World Trade Organization

World Trade Organization (2004) *The future of the WTO: addressing institutional challenges in the new millennium*, report by the Consultative Board to the Director-General Supachai Panitchpakdi, Geneva.

Xinhua News Agency (2004) 'Job market to improve for 2004 university grads: official', 7 January 2004 at <http://www.zju.edu.cn/english/news/2004 (1–3)/news040107.htm>.

INDEX

Abbott, Tony 82, 208
Adelaide 9–10, 30, 152
aged care 8, 10–12, 64, 75–84, 86,
   90–95
   accommodation deposits 11–12,
   77–78, 90–91, 93–94
ageing of the population 2, 5, 7,
   10–11, 20, 32–35, 41, 49, 52–56,
   61, 75, 80–81, 85, 90–91, 94, 97,
   99–100, 118, 135–37, 144–45, 196,
   206
Albany 146
Albury-Wodonga 9–10, 147
Allen Consulting Group 83, 207–09,
   212–14
Apple, Nixon xiv
apprenticeships 18, 114, 126
Armidale 9–10
Asian century 3, 6, 8, 15, 51, 118
Asia-Pacific Economic Cooperation
   forum (APEC) 168–69, 176
AusLink 161
Australian Competition and
   Consumer Commission (ACCC)
   158
Australian Industrial Relations
   Commission 64
Australian innovation fund 19, 130
Australian student equities 17,
   121–23, 125–26

Australian Transport and Energy
   Corridor Limited (ATEC) 162
Australian workplace agreements
   (AWAs) 65–67
Austria 51, 57, 65, 128

baby boom 49, 52–54, 80, 123, 196
Ballarat 9–10, 146
Barry, Rosemary xv
Bass Strait 163
Belgium 57, 65, 98, 128
Belchamber, Grant xiv
Bendigo 9–10, 146
Bracks, Steve xiv, 83, 208, 210
broadband 26, 152, 156
Browse Basin 164
bulk-billing 87
Bundaberg 147
Bureau of Transport Economics 162,
   213
business activity statement (BAS)
   191–92

Cairns 146–47
Cairns Group 168, 170
Canberra 9–10, 29–30, 214
Chapman, Bruce xiv, 210
child-care 14, 20–21, 46, 53, 112,
   137, 139, 141–42, 144, 178, 196
   child-care benefits 14, 21–22,

112, 142
child-care rebate 21, 142, 184,
    196
China 3, 15, 32, 37, 51–52, 58–59,
    63, 98, 119, 167, 175–76, 183
Closer Economic Relations (CER)
    173
coal 3, 27, 36, 163
    coal-seam methane 163
collective bargaining 65, 67
Combet, Greg xiv, 67
Commonwealth scholarship scheme
    14, 125
Connolly, John xiv
consumption 28, 37, 39–41, 52, 164,
    180, 194, 201
Cooper Basin 163
co-payments 79, 84, 86–87, 94–95
Council of Australian Governments
    159
Cowra 9–10
creative
    Australia 4, 9
    people 3, 7, 9, 27, 51, 72, 125,
        151–53
    talent 3, 6, 15, 72, 119, 154, 166,
        179, 182
current account deficit 1–2, 36,
    38–40, 62, 200, 204, 215
Czech Republic 128, 134

Dalrymple Bay 158
Davis, Glyn xiv
Darwin 9–10, 30, 147, 162
D'Alpuget, Blanche xiv–xv
Deutsche Bank 71, 98, 116, 207,
    209–10
disability support pension 136–37
Doha Round 170–71
Dowrick, Steve xiv, 207–11, 214
Dubbo 9–10, 147

early intervention 15, 56, 107–08,
    112
education
    access 46, 115
    attainment levels 55–56, 58,
        97–100, 102, 110, 206

Blair Government 114
disadvantage 101
early childhood 14, 60, 107–08,
    110–112
earnings 17, 96, 112, 190
economic performance 100
Educational Policy Institute 210
exports 167
Florida's Creative Index 152
full-service schools 14, 112–114
government spending on 53, 100,
    118, 207
higher education 6, 15–16, 18, 69,
    99, 115–23, 125, 127
Higher Education Contribution
    Scheme (HECS) 15–19, 115–22,
    124–26, 130, 196
human capital 71
international comparisons 98
investment 4, 16, 20, 32, 60, 97,
    100–01, 106–07, 110, 116, 118,
    123, 132, 190, 214
Marsden High School 14, 112–13
Nelson, Brendan 210
outcomes 101, 114
policy 64, 102, 114, 144
preschool 14, 107–12, 195, 210
productivity 8, 97
quality 4, 8, 56, 96–97, 101–02,
    107, 152
regional 151
retention 138
secondary 53, 98
Senate Employment, Workplace
    Relations and Education
    Legislation Committee 210
vocational 18, 96, 112, 125–26
ecologically sustainable development
    2, 28, 57
Emerald 9–10
environment 1, 4–5, 9, 28–29,
    43–44, 50–51, 57, 59–61, 109, 159,
    164, 203–04
Eslake, Saul xiv, 67, 98, 205–07, 209
exports 1, 3, 27–28, 30–32, 36–37,
    41–42, 44–46, 50, 62–64, 120,
    166–68, 173, 201, 204

family payments 14, 20–22, 46, 112,
138–41, 144 180–181, 187, 195–96
  Family Tax Benefit (Part A)
  139–40, 211
  Family Tax Benefit (Part B) 139,
  211
family reunion 29, 149
fertility 52–55, 99, 141, 144–45, 206
Finland 48, 57, 65, 128
Fitzgerald, Vince xiv, 208
Flannery, Tim 145
Florida, Richard 71, 151–52,
206–07, 212
Forbes 9–10
foreign debt 1–2, 36, 39, 201
foreign investment 32, 64, 176–77
Foreign Investment Review Board
177
Fraser, Malcolm 43, 46, 80, 145, 200
freight 26, 156, 158, 160–62
Fry, Chris xiv

Garnaut, Ross xiii–xiv, 39, 140, 199,
203, 205, 211, 213–15
gas 13, 27, 160, 162–64
Gates, Bill 132
Geelong 146
General Agreement on Tariffs and
Trade (GATT) 170, 174
Gillard, Julia 212
Gittins, Ross 182, 207, 214
Gladstone 9–10, 147
greenhouse gas emissions 27, 159,
163
Greenspan, Alan 71, 207
Griffith 9–10
goods and services tax (GST) 25, 41,
139, 180, 191–93, 205
gross domestic product (GDP) 47,
71–72, 75, 99–101, 110, 127–28,
155, 181, 194, 200–01, 207, 215
Gruen, Nicholas xiv, 202, 206, 215

Harding, Ann xiv, 211, 213
Hawke, Bob xiv, 5, 22, 25, 43,
45–46, 62, 67, 115, 168, 182, 193,
197–200
health

accounts 95
and aged care 8, 64, 75–76,
  78–82, 84, 86, 95
community health 84–85
co-payments 79, 84, 86–87,
  94–95
cost efficiencies 83
GP corporate service 11, 85–87
indigenous 56
integrated 11, 84, 86–87
Lifetime Health Cover 88–89
mental health 85
preventative health 87–88
Private Health Insurance
  Administration Council 208
private health insurance 41, 76,
  79, 86, 88–90, 95, 208
private health insurance rebate 76,
  88–89, 184–85
public 11, 76, 79
public health insurance 75–76
quality 7–8, 10–11, 56, 75–76,
  80–81, 83, 86–88
research and development 130
reform 80, 82, 84, 206
regional 80, 84, 151
spending 75–76, 81
sustainability 75, 82, 85, 90, 93
rationing 78–79
universal insurance 80
Hervey Bay 147
Higher Education Contribution
  Scheme (HECS) 15–19, 115–22,
  124–26, 130, 196
Hobart 9–10, 30
Hogan, Warren 93, 208
Homel, Ross xiv, 209
horizontal equity 181
housing bubble 37
Hyde, John 43, 205

immigration 5, 7, 28–29, 49, 52,
  125, 144–45, 149, 152–53, 194,
  214
  family reunion 29, 149
  permanent residency 29, 148–50
  regional incentives 7, 29–30,
  148–150

imports 2, 32, 36, 39, 45, 62, 168, 170–71, 175, 177, 201
India 3, 15, 51, 58–59, 98, 119, 167
indigenous children 4, 56, 110–11
infrastructure 4–5, 7, 10, 26–29, 32, 62, 64, 73–74, 122, 155–62, 194–95
  National Infrastructure Advisory Council 27, 158–59
  national infrastructure plan 7, 27, 29, 153, 158–59, 195
  public-private partnerships (PPP) 155, 157
  regional 27, 148, 159
inland rail project 27, 162
innovation 7, 18–19, 48, 51, 64, 78, 124, 130–32, 152
intellectual property 64, 72, 131–32
Intergenerational Report 34–36, 54, 56, 81, 99–100, 135–36, 206
International Monetary Fund (IMF) 39, 205–07
investment
  and trade 169, 176
  for tomorrow 2, 37
  infrastructure 7, 26, 73–74, 155–58, 161, 195
  ethical 17, 123
  education 4, 16, 20, 32, 60, 97, 100–01, 106–07, 110, 116, 118, 123, 132, 190, 214
  property 20
  foreign 32, 64, 176–77
  human capital 20, 190–91
  mining 38
  manufacturing 38, 45
  new ideas 71–72
  OECD 45, 72, 118
  research and development (R&D) 32, 72–73, 127, 129 130–33
Ireland 48, 57, 128–29, 183
irrigation 164–65

Kalb, Guyonne xiv
Keating, Michael xiv, 208
Keating, Paul xiv, 1, 5, 22, 41, 45–46, 62, 67, 115, 168, 180, 197
Krugman, Paul 44, 206

labour market regulation 41
Lawson doctrine 39, 205
life expectancy 35, 54, 100, 144

Macfarlane, Ian 199, 214
Mackay 9–10
Maitland 146
Mandurah 9, 147
Mann, Jennilyn xv
manufacturing 6, 32, 38, 42, 46, 143, 147–48, 163, 167, 175–76, 204
Marsden High School 14, 112–13
McDonald, Peter xiv, 206, 209, 211–12
Medicare 8, 11, 46, 76, 79, 83, 85–86, 88, 202
microeconomic reform 22, 180, 198
multilateral trading system 169
Murray-Darling system 164–65

National Competition Policy 158
National Infrastructure Council 158
Nelson, Brendan 210
new growth theory 70
New South Wales 33, 82, 111, 146, 152, 157–58, 162–63
Newton, Isaac 70–71
Northern Territory 52, 111, 147

OECD 18, 21, 35, 43, 45, 53, 55, 57–58, 61, 65–67, 69, 72–73, 98, 100–01, 110, 114, 118, 120, 127–29, 133–35, 141, 168, 171, 190–91, 205–11, 213–14
open, competitive economy 5, 10, 26, 42, 45–46, 48, 133, 200
Orange 9–10, 147
Otway Basin 163

Parham, Dean xiv, 206, 209, 211
Papua New Guinea 27, 163
Parkes 9–10
permanent residency 29, 148–50
Perth 9–10, 30, 152, 162, 165
pharmaceutical benefits scheme 88, 94

Pitchford thesis 39, 205
pooled funding 82–85, 87
Port Lincoln 146
Port Jackson Partners 156, 206, 212–13
population
    ageing 2, 5, 7, 10–11, 20, 32–35, 41, 49, 52–56, 61, 75, 80–81, 85, 90–91, 94, 97, 99–100, 118, 135–37, 144–45, 196, 206
    bigger 4, 10, 26, 28–29, 35, 50–52, 144–45, 147–48, 164–65
    decline 28, 49, 145–47
    density 52, 83, 147
    distribution 143
    drift 26, 144
    educated 115, 119
    English speaking 3
    health-care 75–76, 81, 84, 87, 89
    infrastructure 159
    migrant 28, 144–45
    policy 29, 52, 144
    post-war 144
    projections 34–35, 49, 54, 76, 99–100, 145, 147, 206
    skilled 50
    stagnant 49–50
    student 100–01, 103, 113
    target 29
    regions 9, 27, 143, 146–47, 153
    workforce participation 8, 35, 54–55, 134, 139, 14
preschool 14, 107–12, 195, 210
private health insurance 41, 76, 79, 86, 88–90, 95, 208
    rebate 76, 88–89, 184, 185
private versus public 8, 75, 88, 92, 96, 101
Productivity Commission 28, 56–57, 81, 97–99, 130, 136, 159, 171, 173, 205–213
productivity growth 2, 8, 10, 12–13, 33–36, 43–44, 48, 56–58, 61–62, 64–65, 67, 69, 71, 73, 97–99, 133, 135, 138, 182, 194
public–private partnerships (PPP) 155, 157

Queanbeyan 146
Queensland 9, 33, 146, 152, 157–58, 162–63

ratio method 25, 192
reading recovery 109
reform
    aged care 90, 94
    competition policy 41
    education 13, 102–03
    goods and services markets 64
    health 80, 82, 84, 206
    infrastructure 156, 161–62
    labour market 33, 67
    microeconomic reform 22, 180, 198
    productivity 2, 61
    program 2–3, 41–42, 44–46
    research and development (R&D) 129
    tax 19, 22, 24, 40, 178–80, 184–86, 188–91
    welfare 19–20, 140, 178
regional
    education 151
    health 80, 84, 151
    hubs 9, 26, 165
    infrastructure 27, 148, 159
    migration incentives 7, 29–30, 148–150
research and development (R&D) 4, 18, 19, 32, 48, 69, 72–73, 127–133, 191, 194
Reserve Bank 34, 40, 199–201, 203
Rockhampton 9–10, 147
Rowe, Ken xiv, 210
rules of origin 171–73

Scandinavian countries 55, 134
Scotton, Richard 83
Shepparton 9–10, 147
skills 6, 12–14, 32, 40, 50, 65, 68–71, 74, 97–100, 105, 109, 125, 137–38, 149, 153, 157, 167, 175
Simes, Ric xiv
Singapore 31–32, 183
    Singapore–Australia Free Trade Agreement 171, 173

Singleton, John 150
small business 25, 40, 65–66, 129,
    134, 191–92
sole parents 20, 137, 139, 141
spaghetti bowl effect 173
spillover benefits 58, 73–74, 124,
    159
Standard and Poors 39, 205
Sudan 150
superannuation 16–17, 33, 40, 46,
    95, 122–23, 157, 196–97
Sweden 51, 57, 65, 98, 128
Sydney basin 9, 51, 146–47

Tamworth 147
Tanner, Lindsay 159, 212
tax
    education and training 190
    Family Tax Benefit (Part A)
        139–40, 211
    Family Tax Benefit (Part B) 139,
        211
    goods and services tax (GST) 25,
        41, 139, 180, 191–93, 205
    income tax 20–25, 32–33, 41, 69,
        76, 130, 138–39, 179–86,
        188–89, 192, 196, 202, 205, 214
    low income tax offset 186,
        188–89, 214
    reform 19, 22, 24, 40, 178–80,
        184–86, 188–91
    tax-free threshold 24, 185–86,
        214
    tax concession 18–19, 127–31,
        179, 185, 191
    the Forgotten People 187
    top marginal rate of income tax
        182–85
Telstra 27, 158
Thailand 31–32, 175
    Thai–Australia Free Trade
        Agreement 171–72
Toowoomba 9–10
Townsville 9–10
trade
    APEC 168–69, 176
    Cairns Group 168, 170
    Closer Economic Relations (CER)
        173
    Doha Round 170–71
    deficit 36–39
    GATT 170, 174
    multilateral trading system 169
    preferential trade deals 31–32,
        167, 170–74
    rules of origin 171–73
    Singapore–Australia Free Trade
        Agreement 171, 173
    spaghetti bowl effect 173
    terms of trade 36–37, 189
    Thai–Australia Free Trade
        Agreement 171–72
    Uruguay Round 168, 170
    US–Australia Free Trade
        Agreement 32, 172–74, 177
    WTO 170–71, 174, 213
trade union movement 45–47, 65,
    198
treasury 25, 34, 37, 189, 193, 199,
    205–06, 209, 211, 213–14
Turnbull, Malcolm 24, 184–85, 214
tyranny of distance 3, 51, 58, 166

unfair dismissal laws 64–66
United States 3, 31–32, 48, 58–59,
    98, 107, 122, 128–29, 131–33, 152,
    166, 169, 202
    US–Australia Free Trade
        Agreement 32, 172–74, 177
Uruguay Round 168, 170

vertical equity 181
Victoria 9, 27, 30, 33, 83, 111, 146,
    148, 150, 152, 157, 212
vocational education 18, 96, 112,
    125–26

Wagga Wagga 9–10, 147
Walsh, Geoff xiv
Warrnambool 9, 150
water 9, 28, 52, 74, 156, 159, 162,
    164–65
welfare state 22–23, 69, 134, 180,
    182
welfare to work 6, 20, 24, 135, 138,
    178–79, 182, 185–86

wellbeing 1, 4–5, 8, 33, 59–60, 68, 105, 207
  wellbeing manifesto 60
Whitehouse, Don 113
Whitlam, Gough 22, 115, 143, 147, 181, 200
Withers, Glenn xiv, 206, 212
workforce participation 21, 56, 76, 97, 134–38, 141–42, 146, 186, 194, 214
World Trade Organization (WTO) 170–71, 174, 213
working bonus 186

Young 9–10